FURTHER
STEPS

FURTHER STEPS

FIFTEEN
CHOREOGRAPHERS
ON MODERN DANCE

CONNIE KREEMER

1817

HARPER & ROW, PUBLISHERS, New York
Cambridge, Philadelphia, San Francisco, Washington,
London, Mexico City, São Paulo, Singapore, Sydney

Sponsoring Editor: Phillip Leininger
Project Editor: Nora Helfgott
Text and Cover Design: Robin Hessel/Brand X Studios
Cover Photo: Spiked Sonata, Dan Wagoner
and Dancers; Dennis Fleming and
Lisa Taylor Swee. Photo: Lois Greenfield.
Title Page Photo: Telegram, Mel Wong Dance Company;
Gayle Ziaks. Photo: Tom Caravaglia.
Text Art: Fine Line Illustrations, Inc.
Production Manager: Jeanie Berke
Production Assistant: Brenda DeMartini
Compositor: ComCom Division of Haddon Craftsmen, Inc.
Printer and Binder: R. R. Donnelley & Sons Company

Further Steps: Fifteen Choreographers on Modern Dance

Library of Congress Cataloging-in-Publication Data

Further steps.

  Bibliography: p.
  1. Choreographers—Biography.   2. Modern dance.
3. Choreography.   I. Kreemer, Connie.
GV1785.A1F87   1987   793.3'2'0922 [B]   86–19531
ISBN 0–06–043782–0

86 87 88 89 9 8 7 6 5 4 3 2 1

CONTENTS

ACKNOWLEDGMENTS

Most special thanks are extended to Selma Jeanne Cohen. Without her support, guidance, and insight, this book would never have been published. Wendy Shifrin is an invaluable friend who spent long hours in discussions, readings, and typing. Mel Wong deserves loving thanks for his patience and unyielding support. Katherine Power, Katy Matheson, Ellen Marshall, Barbara Hinnant, David Lauretti, Judy Dworin, Diana Greene, and Daniel Nagrin assisted with insight and constructive criticism. Most grateful thanks are also extended to Peggy Jarrell Kaplan for generously contributing 13 of the choreographers' portraits. Always with patience and a smile, Nora Helfgott, Editorial Production Manager, uncompromisingly spent many tedious hours keeping the format of the text consistent and attending to a myriad of details. And finally, my greatest appreciation also goes to the choreographers, whose creativity, cooperation, and patience made this book possible.

Connie Kreemer

FURTHER STEPS

INTRODUCTION

Since the earliest barefoot steps of Isadora Duncan and Loie Fuller, a distinguishing characteristic of modern dance has been that it allows for a choreographer's individuality of form and style. From its inception it has been an art of image makers who reflect, stretch, twist, push to the extreme, and rebel against existing forms and ideas by breaking barriers to introduce new incarnations of dance. Above all, modern dance has been made by individuals following their own paths. This is what keeps the art vital and fresh.

Each generation of choreographers has had its own ideas about the reasons for making dance. Like an apprentice to a great chef, a new choreographer learns from the older masters but takes the same ingredients (the body in time and space) and alters them to his or her own specifications. By adding a pinch of something (spins, shoes, video, artwork), by mixing the ingredients in a slightly different way (altering the use of time and space), or by using a different shape (changing the performance space), the choreographer produces a new creation.

Modern dance has gone through many phases since its beginning around the turn of the century. The focus seems to flicker between dramatic, expressive dance and dance that emphasizes movement itself, its structure, theory, rhythm, or virtuosity. These phases are given labels: modern, interpretive, experimental, avant-garde, minimal, contemporary, new wave, next wave, postmodern, or neo-expressionist.

Certainly in the early 1900s, when Loie Fuller and Isadora Duncan threw away shoes and began dancing barefoot, when their disdain for the *ballet blanc* costume led them to loose, more fluid material, modern dance meant, in the most fundamental sense, rebellion. Theirs was a time to break away from the confines of the classical ballet tradition, the five positions, turnout, and the fairy tale stories of nymphs, sylphs, and princes. For Fuller, dance was about motion without emotion—voluminous material and brightly colored lights. For Duncan, movement emanated from the inner being, from the soul. Using nature as a source of inspiration, she expressed deep emotions with simple movements.

While Fuller and Duncan achieved their fame in Europe, Ruth St. Denis and Ted Shawn were home creating a sensation throughout the United States. Their spiritual, mystical, and theatrical exoticism combined into a high art form—modern dance. But what modern dance meant to them around the turn of the century was very different from what it meant in the late 1920s to two young Denishawn dancers, Martha Graham and Doris Humphrey.

Graham presented her first solo concert at the Forty-eighth Street Theater in New York City in 1926. Not wanting to display the decorative technique of her mentors, she pared down the movement and costumes to the extreme. Over the years she danced about war, sorrow, rejoicing, passion, sin, sensuality, spirituality, and about the many states of being a woman. Along the way she developed her own vocabulary of movement to aid in self-expression: contraction-release, parallel positions, flexed feet, angularity, and percussive rhythms.

Doris Humphrey and Charles Weidman presented a concert under the aegis of Denishawn on March 24, 1928, at the Brooklyn Theatre, also in New York. The ten dances—including *Air for the G String, Concerto in A Minor,* and *Color Harmony,* to name a few—clearly indicated that Humphrey was setting out on her own personal choreographic path. While communicating human emotions in a nonrepresentational manner, her dances displayed a strong sense of design and musicality.

Literature, a musical form, American themes, and psychological states were some of the inspirations for the early pioneers (Mary Wigman, Martha Graham, Doris Humphrey,

Helen Tamiris, Charles Weidman, Hanya Holm) as well as many others (José Limón, Anna Sokolow) who came a little later. Each choreographer developed his or her own personal movement style, which often grew into an institution in itself.

Growing out of this tradition came choreographers such as Merce Cunningham, Erick Hawkins, Alwin Nikolais, and Paul Taylor. Their choreography reacted against the expressive-interpretive dance of their predecessors. Each one developed an individual approach to dance, but the common theme was the belief that dancing need not have emotional overtones; movement itself was reason enough for dance and could be interesting in its own right. Whether it was about dancing for its own sake (Cunningham), a ritual-like spiritual awakening of "our animal heritage"[1] (Hawkins), or an integration of movement, sound, lights, costumes, props, and sets, combined into total theater (Nikolais), the primary force behind modern dance in the 1950s was a reaction to what had gone before.

Another generation evolved as an offshoot of the abstract dance of the 1950s. The Happenings of the 1960s introduced the element of surprise. Their appeal lay in their unpredictability, since they were partially planned and partially spontaneous events. Feeding on these ideas in San Francisco, Anna Halprin mixed lifelike situations with dance. She wanted the audience to be able to identify with the experience, so she introduced everyday movements outside of a technical idiom—crawling, climbing, stamping, punching, hugging, laughing, yelling, disrobing. Most often her experiments took place out of the theater in environmental spaces.

On the East Coast Merce Cunningham was investigating chance dance, indeterminacy, movement isolation of body parts and the idea that any movement may follow another. He pronounced dance, music, and set design as equal but independent art forms that could exist in the same time and space. These concepts later spurred other choreographers to explore, in-depth, the ramifications of each element.

---

[1]Jamake Highwater, *Dance: Rituals of Experience* (New York: A & W Publishers, 1978), p. 197.

Halprin and Cunningham, along with the ideas of musician John Cage, and the composition classes of Robert Dunn, planted the seeds that grew into the Judson Dance Theater. Formed in 1962, the Judson Dance Theatre evolved into a democratic group committed to breaking the rules of conventional theatrical dance. Rehearsing and performing in the Judson Memorial Church in New York City, dancers, visual artists, poets, and musicians concerned themselves with movement from everyday life; there was often no emphasis on technique. Structure could come from a children's game, from play or sports, or from any movement, gesture, or posture, and it could use total energy exertion (Carol Schneemann's *Lateral Splay,* 1963) or little at all (Steve Paxton's *Transit,* 1962, or David Gordon's *Mannequin Dance,* 1962). The dancers could perform in street clothes or in the nude (*Word Words,* 1963, by Steve Paxton and Yvonne Rainer); they could be barefoot or wear sneakers. They performed in parks, churches, museums, outdoors, or in any available space. By incorporating ordinary gestures and mundane events, such as putting on plastic curlers or moving furniture, by bringing what was previously thought of as nondance onto the performance space (whatever the surface), the choreographers turned conventional reality into unconventional dance.

Out of these ideas spring the postmodern dancers of the late 1960s and early 1970s. As in the Judson days, dance did not have to make logical sense. Any object, movement, or gesture could follow another for no apparent reason; movements could be ordinary, uninflected, repetitive, or reductive. It was no longer essential to use metered time; as in life, a gesture, a task, or a movement phrase could take the time and effort it needed to take.

A dance could be about formal choreographic elements, a mathematical system, or improvisation (see Sally Banes's *Terpsichore in Sneakers, Post-Modern Dance,* Houghton Mifflin, 1980). Virtuosic or pedestrian, movement for movement's sake, devoid of emotive references, either representational or expressive, dominated postmodern dance. No implied meaning was beyond the visual image itself—what you saw was what you got.

In the mid-1970s, Steve Paxton created contact improvisation. An extension of postmodern dance concepts, contact improvisation involves a democratic partnership (usually a duet) incorporating the same kind of everyday activities as postmodern dance. It uses gravity and the give and take of body weight between partners, who maintain corporeal contact.

This history brings us to the 1970s, to the height of postmodern dance. Where does that leave us today? I wondered whether today's choreographers think of themselves in the context of a postmodern movement. What exactly *is* the difference between modern dance and postmodern dance? These are just some of the questions I set out to answer when I began conducting interviews with 15 choreographers.

As a dancer, teacher, and spectator of modern dance, I had immensely enjoyed Selma Jeanne Cohen's *The Modern Dance: Seven Statements of Belief,* published in 1965. The book helped me, as a dancer and student, gain a better understanding of the latest thinking and current trends in modern dance. As a teacher, I found it a valuable primary source for comparing the methods, goals, and beliefs of artists; finally, it enlarged the scope of my appreciation for and enjoyment of modern dance.

Two decades after *Seven Statements* was published, a whole new generation of artists has emerged. I wanted to find out from the artists themselves what they were doing and thinking about—how they differed from earlier generations and whether there were any commonalities in modern dance of the 1970s and 1980s. What I found was that their dances are as varied and complex as today's society.

The nature of the times and people is altogether different from the 1960s. Today's artist registers that change, whether consciously or not. Whereas for Graham life was "nervous, sharp and zigzag," life in the 1980s is high speed, high-tech, and complex.

For example, the restoration of relations with China has produced a renewed interest in the East. An Egyptian poster or Indian dance that once inspired mystical and exotic ideas in an enamoured Ruth St. Denis is commonplace to today's choreographer. Merce Cunningham and Erick Hawkins may have let Eastern philosophies filter into their approaches, but today's generation is more of a true product of cross-culturalization. Its members have grown up with *I Ching,* books by Alan Watts, yin and yang, martial arts, Zen, Hare Krishna, and the Beatles' mysticism, to name a few. Today's choreographers, in many cases (Takei, Meehan, Wong, Fenley) have a first-hand knowledge of Eastern dance and have absorbed elements from cultures around the world. Their dances reflect both Eastern and Western thoughts.

Laura Dean's mystical use of spinning, and her use of repetitive movement, along with that of Lucinda Childs's, can be linked, beyond the minimal music of Steve Reich and Philip Glass, back through centuries to the Sufis or to the Temples of a Thousand Buddhas. Minimalism is not new—what is new is the way the dances are put together.

Kei Takei, a Japanese, and Mel Wong, a Chinese American, are true products of the fusion of cultures. Takei's use of uncomplicated, nonballetic movement reflects a Zen-like philosophy. On the other hand, Wong's complexity may find its roots in the ornate intricacies of Chinese art, while the movement remains Western-based. Nancy Meehan creates unadorned natural movement, in keeping with the aesthetic simplicity of a Japanese garden, to suggest metaphors of the mind. Molissa Fenley tries to create dance that comes from a fusion of the world's cultures, not just from that of the United States.

Space shuttles, videos, telecommunication satellites, and computers have made the world a faster and smaller place. This is reflected in choreography through the use of high technology. Kenneth King and Mel Wong are long-time experimenters in video art. Lucinda Childs and Wong have collaborated with other artists to produce computerized art in their dances. The technology of laser beams is readily becoming more accessible to artists.

Film has also influenced artists. Meredith Monk, Bill T. Jones and Arnie Zane, Louis Falco, and Gail Conrad often think of their dances as images from a movie. Some, like Monk, make the film an integral part of the piece. In fact, Monk's work reveals a multidimensionality that defies categorization.

There are dancers who manifest today's speed and high-tech through movement. Intricate rhythms, patterning, and the use of space reflect contemporary complexity, while quick changes of rhythm, fast, jerky robotlike movements, or non-stop aerobic dance reveal its speed. Others, like Meehan and Takei, take the opposite extreme by rebelling against high-tech dehumanization. They go back to basics and pare down the movement in order to regain awareness of nature and universal concerns.

Choices of music also demonstrate life in the 1980s. With John Cage's innovations as a springboard, these 15 artists run the gamut from creating their own music to using natural sound of homemade instruments, classical music, jazz, rock, gamelan, ethnic, or explosive new wave.

The equal rights movement has had an impact as well. No longer are there just romantic lifts where the men effortlessly elevate the women. Senta Driver has turned the tables so that women hoist men and show the required effort. Still others reveal an influence from contact improvisation—the lifts are asexual. Today's dance roles are often androgynous, since they need not be about sexuality or human emotion.

These thoughts are not intended as conclusive analogies, but as keys to introduce ideas of how life has changed and as examples to develop other ways to look at the diversity of the artists. At least for the time being, it appears that Lucinda Childs, Douglas Dunn, Gus Solomons, Jr., and even Dan Wagoner are primarily concerned with the movement itself, without the embellishment of emotional overtones (though Wagoner seems more humanistically oriented than the others). At the opposite extreme are Gail Conrad and Louis Falco, who are creating dramatic dances based on their own personal views of life. Rosalind Newman "colors movement with dramatic or emotional quality," and Bill T. Jones and Arnie Zane try to include everything—technical dancing, architecturally structured, that simultaneously entertains and comments on society.

Molissa Fenley and Nancy Meehan are involved with abstract movement that creates spacial metaphors or landscapes of the mind, while Kenneth King and Meredith Monk emphasize movement using symbolism or subtle suggestions of social concerns or metaphysical energies. At another point along this road are Kei Takei and Mel Wong, who express spirituality about the beauty, pathos, and mystery of this life and beyond.

Many of the artists' explorations spill over into other areas—pure dance, theater, music, visual arts, politics, or high-tech media. Each person is busy pursuing his or her own path, and though the intent of one artist may be similar to that of another, the results can look very different. Besides, there is no guarantee that a choreographer will keep working in the vein he or she is currently exploring. Above all, choreographers feel the freedom to follow whatever direction their creativity takes.

The choreographers included in this book were selected because they emerged into prominence in the late 1960s and during the 1970s. Most formed companies in the 1970s. Initially I had wanted to trace a direct lineage from those choreographers who appeared in Cohen's *Seven Statements.* Choreographers such as Falco, Meehan, Solomons, and Wagoner are direct descendants from the first book. But Merce Cunningham had not been in Cohen's book, and he is perhaps the single most important influence on today's generation. Then there were people who had not danced with either the choreographers from *Seven Statements* or with Cunningham. They had had no single important mentor, but had sprung up from a myriad of different backgrounds, also gaining recognition in the late 1960s or 1970s. The remaining choreographers were selected, not out of a personal aesthetic preference, but because they are recognized as significant innovators.

Certainly there are many other choreographers who could have been interviewed. Twyla Tharp, Laura Dean, David Gordon, Lar Lubovitch, and Pilobolus were all asked but declined. Karole Armitage, Johanna Boyce, Trisha Brown, Tim Buckley, Blondell Cummings, Eiko and Komo, Hanna Kahn, Bebe Miller, Tim Miller, Mark Morris, Charles Moulton, Jennifer Mueller, Dana Reitz, Kenneth Rinker, and Jim Self are just a few of the people working today who deserve to be mentioned and could have been included in a limitless book.

Moreover, since my first interview, in 1979, the dance scene has changed and continues to change tremendously. It is becoming increasingly decentralized from New York to an international dance world, with important new blood such as Pina Bausch, Sankai Juku, and Robert Derosiers.

Each of the 15 choreographers, with the exception of Dan Wagoner and Gus Solomons, who wrote their own statements, spoke in a two-hour taped interview that I transcribed and edited. Using only their words, I tried to make a cohesive statement into a readable format. If thoughts or words needed to be clarified for sentence structure or meaning, I notated it so that the artist would know that the input was mine. In this way, each statement evolved. As will be evident, Douglas Dunn rewrote his statement. Lucinda Childs and Kenneth King also revised theirs considerably. The titles at the beginning of each chapter, for the most part, were my creation based on my perceptions of their statements. The chronologies were given to me by each artist; thus, they vary in detail.

I wanted to know something about the artists' creative process. I wanted to know what they thought about when they were making dances, how they approached the movement, what their influences were. Were they trying to communicate a fascination with form, structure, a thought, a message, or spirituality? What were the challenges in this process?

Each choreographer responded to the same questions, which were asked in no particular order and followed the flow of the interview. The questions fall into two categories. The first concerns labels, backgrounds, and choreographic ideas; the second focuses on the application of these ideas into the end product—a particular dance.

The first set of questions asks: With whom did you study and what do you think you have retained from that/those person(s)? What are you trying to do with your choreography? Why is it important to you to choreograph? What is the greatest challenge of choreographing? What are you trying to get across to the audience? How has your work evolved since you started to choreograph and where do you feel you have diverged from your first ideas? What kind of choreographer do you consider yourself—modern, postmodern, avant-garde, minimalist, or other?

The last question was of particular interest to me, bewildered by today's obtuse terminology, so I thought, "Why not let the artists label themselves, let them tell me what kind of choreographers they are?" As I suspected, most of them are unconcerned, even mildly annoyed at these words, or too busy creating to worry about it. Basically they think of themselves as artists who don't want their work defined or restricted by labels.

If postmodern dance no longer indicates movement for its own sake, devoid of emotional overtones, if it embodies a conceptual approach to dance, then perhaps these choreographers are postmodern. Perhaps the label has changed along with the artists' creativity—and has become a catch-all phrase to indicate a period in history.

The second category addresses a dance in terms of how and why it works. How is it a reflection of the state of our culture? I asked the last question not because I thought this generation was necessarily a message-oriented group, but rather because I hoped their answers would better reveal where their interests lay. I wanted to learn from them whether they fit into the postmodern "what you see is what you get" idea, or whether there are other, deeper layers of meaning beyond the movement. I was also curious to learn how much each person is concerned about our society and whether or not there is a conscious intent to comment on it.

Is there anything that remains true or constant from one generation to the next? Yes—like Isadora Duncan, today's choreographers participate in the art of modern dance. As she searched for her own way, so each artist is seeking a personal path and must be honest to the self in order to find it. As the world changes, that need is fulfilled in very different approaches. Each generation has new things to tell us in ways that have never been done before. Honesty, exploration, change, and creativity are important criteria for making dances. This holds true throughout history.

Having emerged as the next generation, whether called postmodern, new wave, next wave, or the next new wave, the people expressing themselves in this book are making their mark on the dance world. The journey that started with bare feet has worn shoes, taken them off, put them on again, and changed styles many times. As the shoes change from sneakers to jazz shoes, slippers to taps, high heels to pointe shoes and back to bare feet, whether it happens in Bangkok, Berlin, or Boston, further steps continue to explore new creative paths.

Kei Takei

Photo: Peggy Jarrell Kaplan.

KEI TAKEI

Kei Takei is a native of Tokyo, where she spent her childhood studying dance and drama and exploring the surrounding countryside. It was while she was serving a "traditional" apprenticeship with creative dance master Kenji Hinoki that she began to choreograph seriously.

A Fulbright scholarship and encouragement from Anna Sokolow brought Takei to the United States in 1967 to study at the Juilliard School. She also studied at the Martha Graham School, the Merce Cunningham Studio, the American Ballet Theater, and with Anna Halprin and Alwin Nikolais. In 1969 she assembled a company, Moving Earth, to perform her works. That same year she embarked on her major choreographic project, *Light,* composed of some two dozen solos and large-group pieces; though part of an interconnected whole, each section can stand alone.

Moving Earth has appeared in numerous cities throughout the United States and around the world. Takei has been on the faculty of the American Dance Festival, Sarah Lawrence College, Radcliffe College, Wesleyan University, and other schools; she regularly teaches workshops in New York City. Groups that have commissioned Takei's works include the Netherlands Dance Theater; Improvisations Unlimited, of Washington, D.C.; the Kibbutz Dance Company and the Inbal Dance Theatre, both of Israel; and the Modern Dance Company of Hong Kong.

The recipient of many choreographic honors, Takei has been awarded grants from the National Endowment for the Arts and was named a Guggenheim Fellow in Choreography in 1978. She has also served on the selection committee for the New York Foundation for the Arts's individual fellowship award.

KEI TAKEI

Sensitivity Fields

I feel very lucky to have been born into this world. Choreographing and performing are the most beautiful ways for me to use all of my possibilities to live as a human being. In order for me to survive in this world I cannot think about any other work except creating and performing. That is when I feel alive. Any other work would be incomplete.

As a child in Japan I became interested in many arts—modern dance, drama, drawing, poetry, etc. Later, I studied with Kengi Hinoki, who taught creative dance. His method of teaching was different from American dance in that he did not move if he did not have a feeling for the movement. His dancers were like poetry, and I learned a lot from him.

Hinoki's wife, Kiyue, was a Japanese classical dancer and choreographer. Before I saw her I thought classical dancing was too slow and boring, but she was able to open my eyes, to move my soul. I studied with both husband and wife for three years.

In 1967 Anna Sokolow came to Japan along with Lavina Hoving. I studied technique and choreography with them and auditioned and was given a Fulbright scholarship to go to America in September of that year.

I continued studying with Anna Sokolow at Juilliard. She was a very strong figure to me because she made me realize that many people dance without actually feeling the movement. She once told a student who was dancing about loneliness to stay under a table until she felt lonely. It is important to have one's own feelings about the movement so that that awareness can be translated to an audience.

Ann Halprin came to New York in 1971 and saw my concert, *Light, Part 5,* at Dance Theater Workshop. She told me to come to San Francisco to study with her for three months, and it was an excellent opportunity for me. I was influenced by her body training and use of outside space as well as by just watching her as a human being. Since then I have not studied formally with anyone, but learn more from the street and friends.

I started choreographing to folk songs at a very early age. I remember when I was 12 I got a prize for a choreographic school program. I still remember some of that movement and I view that time as very pure and creative.

When I came to America I lost that purity by becoming intellectual and too serious about modern dance. Limitations were created by the structure of costumes of leotards and tights and stylistic movement.

For the first few years I had a terrible time in the States because I could not speak English. I felt restricted by American modern dance, unfree, and unable to move. I could not jump, leap, or walk unless it conformed to a certain style, and that made me angry. As a result I refused to learn English because of the difficulty of relating to people and was forced to learn everything by feeling. I used to make faces so that people would not talk to me. Then I started thinking about what I was doing here and why I could not do what I wanted to do. *Light, Part 1* in May of 1969, at Dance Theater Workshop, was the result.

Light, Part 1 involved dancers carrying a sack with dry leaves. They performed only walking, as if transfixed in a dreamlike world, and I was on the floor doing rocking or somersaulting movement and continually watching them.

They carried a sack because, to me, a person is more than just a head and body with arms and legs. Symbolically a human being carries something, maybe hope, all of the time.

Each part of *Light* is very much different from the other parts. *Part 7* was a breakthrough piece for me where I arrived at a different place. It was a long piece called the *Diary of the Field.* The dancers came into the field like farmers and proceeded to plant and work. Growing a vegetable is similar to growing or creating art to me. I was master of that field, commanding the others to work hard, but at the same time I was choreographing in that field. I was also a cripple, who was in my mind similar to a weak rabbit. Although the farmers were very dumb, in the end they caught me.

It was a breakthrough piece for me because creation was actually happening during the piece. It was not as set choreographically as previous dances. As the master I would call out to the dancers, "Talk to me by your hip," etc. There was an order with flexibility, and many changes could happen within it. The dancers could explore their own creativity, and they had much more freedom than in a set choreographed piece. It required time to be more alive and to feel their dancing in relationship to the other dancers. For me, it created

Light, Part 16 (Vegetable Fields). Kei Takei's Moving Earth. Laz Brezer, Kei Takei. Photo: Richard Beckman.

a different dimension. As I watched the piece, the intensity to the present, along with my own awareness, was different.

Light, Part 8 brought another change because it was all solo pieces. Up until that time I had not choreographed solos in the States. Then *Part 9* was a very large group piece. It was a way of ending that period of time—*Parts 1* through *8*. In *Part 9* we moved from one field and started a new journey to somewhere else.

In *Part 9* each dancer carried a sack filled with bird seeds. The sacks had holes in them so that the seeds trickled out, tracing a line as we walked from one world to another. *Part 9* was a finishing period which brought us to the stone field.

Light, Part 10, Part 12, Part 13, and *Part 11* was one stone field piece in four parts. *Part 10* was a solo for me, where I had a series of movements that I also used in *Part 12*, except *Part 12* was a group piece and a circle dance. There was a stone fight in *Part 11; Part 12* was more primitive, almost warlike. The movement in both came from hitting the stones together as well as from not stepping on them. I had to use my feet in a special way to avoid stepping on them.

I think I grew to love stones a long time ago when I saw my father hitting stones together to make fire for his Buddhist prayer. I was very affected by the sound of the stones and have always loved them. They move me.

One day I was walking down the street and felt a connection with a big huge stone in my path. I could not leave it there, it was somehow relating to me. So I asked it, "Do you want to come with me or stay there in the way?" And I took it with me and then I found another stone, and now I dance with the same two stones in my hands, even today.

My choreography has evolved over the years from being very simple to being more complex. In *Light, Part 1*, I limited myself to

Light, Part 12 (The Stone Field). Kei Takei's Moving Earth. Cydney Wilkes, Brian Laurier, Michael Kasper, Elsi Miranda, Luis Gonzalez, Laz Brezer, Kei Takei, Carol McDowell, John Wilson, David Dorfman, Lori Boulanger. Photo: Richard J. Lane.

just walking because I felt that in order to be honest with myself I could only do one thing. Now my choreography has broadened. Now, to be honest, I need to use more.

I have sometimes been labeled a postmodern choreographer, sometimes modern, and sometimes avant-garde. Somehow I like the avant-garde world because of the craziness. Within that world there can be changing. It does not have a fixed position.

The greatest challenge of choreographing for me is to be honest to my creative need. After a piece is finished, I must face the public with my work. I owe it to myself not to be disturbed by the public but to believe in my work, to continue, and to be strong. I try to enter every new piece with the spirit of a new choreographer. I should not be safe in my creativity.

When I am choreographing, I do not think about the audience. If I go my way and am honest with myself, that is the best thing I can do for the audience. I must be myself and be honest and that will come across.

Light, Part 16 (Vegetable Fields). Kei Takei. Photo: Richard Beckman.

Light, Part 10 is a solo for me with two men. At first I am by myself on stage, hitting the two rocks together. There is a big black X mark on my face which covers my eyes so that I cannot open them. The costume is of muslin, a small white panty and a small apron over my chest. It is similar to what little children use in my country to keep their bellies warm, so there is no implication of gender.

I am barefoot, and depending on the performance day, I imagine myself in a desert, on a primitive beach, or sometimes in a wood. Using my imagination helps to produce a movement quality that is necessary to the piece. I usually imagine myself as a primitive animal, or a human, or a creature, but I could not describe that creature any further because it would never exist in America.

As I perform a series of choreographed movements, alternately creating a rhythm by hitting the rocks together, two men appear. On their shoulders they each carry a big black sack filled with small pebbles which they throw at my/the creature's feet during the piece.

I keep dancing and communicating but in the meantime the stones become disturbing to the things I want to do. There are two opposing forces represented: they could be weak and strong, or yin and yang.

The men begin throwing more and more rocks at my feet. My movement comes from trying to avoid the rocks, from relating to the situation. I do not just do movement on stage but I have to do movement because of the situation created. The mysterious thing is that, blinded by the X mark, most of the time I do not step on the rocks. If I peek, or if it becomes too intellectual, then I step on them.

During the dance I accidentally drop the stone. The movement stops and everything freezes. I must decide where the stone went and then it becomes "find my stone." Then I move more. Two or three times I drop the stone. Finally I lose both stones and as soon as that happens the two men become more aggressive and pile the stones at my feet so that I do not kick up anymore but stay in one spot. The movement becomes very different: I use my head, torso, and arms and create a more frightening quality of anger. Finally with the pile so huge I see/feel one way out. Although I do not have my stones anymore, I can still survive. The men give up or give me a chance. It is similar to two hunters and an animal trying to survive—symbolic of death and survival.

I think the dance is effective because of the rhythm of the stones, similar to a heartbeat. When the rhythm breaks, it is like a danger point for an animal. If I did not have the stones, or if the two men were not there, then my movement would be pretentious. The audience can see the relationship between the stones and my feet and the resulting movement. Otherwise, without the stones, there would be no reason for it. Only this kind of dance is honest.

Light, Part 10 is a reflection of both the Japanese and American cultures. If the animal lived somewhere, it would live in Japan. I do not feel age in America, and this animal would not live in a young land. But violence, or war, or survival is very much in America, in my New York life.

All around I see weak or small, passive things being destroyed. When I see a butterfly or a plant die, or a flower smashed on the floor, I am very upset. Or when I see a bee trapped in a bus or a car, I cannot rest until the bee is freed.

In *Part 10* I made that animal survive because the soul should survive. I do not want the hunters of this world to survive. I am on the side of the weak.

I am afraid of something moving that suddenly does not move. Maybe it is death or the message of death. Unconsciously these things come to the work and reach out through the creation to another kind of dimension. Once when I was walking on the street, it was raining, and I saw a rainpool and felt something very deeply. It was the start of *Light, Part 3*. It was a shock, but somehow these things come out.

Beautiful things can be found in this world only if you are very sensitive. How you live and how you feel about things affects your life.

September 24, 1979

All dances are choreographed by Kei Takei and performed by Moving Earth (unless another company is listed). Costumes are also designed by Kei Takei, unless otherwise listed.

Date	*Title of Work*	*Place and Details*
April 1969	*Light, Part 1*	Dance Theater Workshop, New York City.
January 1970	*Lunch*	Cubiculo, New York City.
August 1970	*Light, Part 2*	Cubiculo, New York City. Music by Geki Koyama.
November 1970	*Light, Part 3*	Dance Theater Workshop, New York City.
December 1970	*Light, Part 4*	Cubiculo, New York City. Music by Lloyd Ritter. Set by Maxine W. Klein.
July 1971	*Light, Part 5*	Dance Theater Workshop, New York City. Music by Marcus Parsons III.
December 1971	*Light, Part 6*	The Kitchen, New York City. Music by Jacques Coursil and Marcus Parsons III.
April 1973	*Light, Part 7 (Diary of the Field)*	International House, New York City. Music by Maldwyn Pate and Lloyd Ritter, with traditional Spanish folk song. Sets by Richmond Johnstone and Maxine W. Klein.
January 1974	*Light, Part 8*	Clark Center, New York City. Traditional Buddhist pilgrimage chant.
March 1975	*Light, Part 9*	Brooklyn Academy of Music, New York City. Set by Maxine W. Klein.
June 1975	*After Lunch*	School of Fine Arts, New York University, New York City.
May 1976	*Light, Part 10 (The Stone Field)*	Cathedral of St. John the Divine, New York City.
October 1976	*Light, Part 11*	Commissioned and first performed by the Nederlands Dans Theater at the HOT Theater, The Hague, Netherlands.
October 1976	*Light, Part 12*	Schauspielhaus, Graz, Austria. Traditional Japanese folk song.
October 1977	*Light, Part 13*	Scott Theater, Fort Worth, Texas.
June 1978	*Windfield*	Circus Theater, The Hague, Netherlands. Commissioned by the Nederlands Dans Theater.
July 1979	*Light, Part 14 (Pinecone Field)*	Dibden Auditorium, Johnson, Vermont. Music sung by Julie Balliett and Maldwyn Pate; adapted from a traditional Welsh folk song.

Date	*Title of Work*	*Place and Details*
June 1980	*Light, Part 15* *(The Second Windfield)*	American Dance Festival, Durham, North Carolina. Music adapted from a traditional Japanese folk song. Props by Richmond Johnstone and the Company.
August 1982	*Light, Part 16* *(Vegetable Fields)*	Performing Garage, New York City.
August 1982	*Daikon Field Solo I*	Performing Garage, New York City. Performed by Kei Takei. Buddhist chanting by Lazuro Brezer. Costumes and props designed by Tetsuhiko Maeda; executed by Hirotoshi Shirato. Stick carving by Bruce Elledge.
June 1982	*Light, Part 17* *(Dreamcatcher's Diary I)*	American Dance Festival, Durham, North Carolina. Music by Norma Reynolds Dalby.
April 1983	*Light, Part 18* *(Wheat Fields)*	Performing Garage, New York City. Music by David Moss. Set design by Bruce Edelstein. Stick carving by Bruce Elledge. Costumes by Takoko Takase, Erika Tsukamoto, and Bruce Edelstein. Set special effects by Masaatsu Takahashi.
July 1983	*Daikon Field Solo II*	Performed by Kei Takei and Lazuro Brezer. Costumes and props designed by Tetsuhiko Maeda; executed by Hirotoshi Shirato.
March 1984	*Light, Part 19* *(Dreamcatcher's Diary II)*	La Mama E.T.C., New York City. Koto and voice by Fusako Yoshida. Piano/synthesizer music composed and recorded by Suzane Northrop. Sets and costumes designed by Tetsuhiko Maeda; executed by Hirotoshi Shirato, assisted by Takako Takase, Mayumi Isshiki, and Mor Eden.
June 1985	*Light, Part 20* *(Dreamcatcher's Diary III)*	La Mama E.T.C., New York City. Music by David Moss. Sets and costume design by Bruce Edelstein.

Light, Part 10 (Stone Field). Kei Takei. Photo: Martin S. Selway.

Dan Wagoner

Photo: Peggy Jarrell Kaplan.

DAN WAGONER

Dan Wagoner was born and raised in Springfield, West Virginia, the youngest of ten children in a farmer's family. He began dance training in the mid-1950s with Ethel Butler. After graduation from West Virginia University with a bachelor's degree in pharmacy, Wagoner served two years in the Army and continued his dance training wherever he could. Upon release from the service in 1956, he was granted a scholarship to Connecticut College's Summer School of the Dance and worked with Doris Humphrey's repertory group there. This workshop resulted in a scholarship to Martha Graham's school and eventually an invitation to join her company, where he remained for five years. As a principal dancer, he created roles in *Samson Agonistes* and *Acrobats of God.* In 1962, he joined the Paul Taylor Company, where again as a principal dancer, he created roles in Mr. Taylor's *Duet* and *Aureole.* He also performed with the Merce Cunningham Dance Company before forming Dan Wagoner and Dancers in 1969. Wagoner has since created more than 35 dances that are in the repertory of his own company and other American, Canadian, and British companies. A section from Mr. Wagoner's outdoors choreography, "George's House," produced by WGBH-TV and recorded at the eighteenth-century New Hampshire farmhouse of poet George Montgomery, appeared in August 1985 on the public television series "Alive from Off-Center." Dan Wagoner and Dancers has toured widely in North and South America, Europe, and Asia. In 1984 the company was selected by the South Carolina Arts Commission to establish a second home in that state, marking the first such partnership in the nation.

DAN WAGONER

The Frontier Within

1. What kind of choreographer do you consider yourself, modern, postmodern, avant-garde, minimalist, or other?

I don't think about what kind of choreographer I am. I concentrate on *being* a choreographer.

I find this at times absolutely thrilling, and at other times so frightening and depressing that it's only a fine thread by which I hold on to the idea that I am a choreographer. So many of the elements of dance are impermanent; it's hard to get a hold on ideas to examine them thoroughly. Each run-through, each performance of a dance, no matter how exactly set, is slightly different because the dance instruments are living creatures who are constantly changing. This vulnerable element of dance making is beautiful and fascinating, capable of producing memorable moments of enormous passion and immediacy, but it can also be elusive and often exasperating. It is like the wild beauty and honor of placing one's hand on the throat of a sparrow and feeling its pulse. But just get a sparrow to stand still and let you touch it!

Of course, the overwhelming task of choosing an aesthetic problem, then gathering up enough courage to jump off into unknown territory, is a big enough job in itself. And not only must this be accomplished through the beautiful but elusive and impermanent medium of the human creature—you've got economic and marketplace problems of hiring dancers, finding space, costumes, accompaniment, etc., and it all adds up to an almost insurmountable task. It is easy to understand why one's time is totally taken with *being* a choreographer. I find the question "What kind of choreographer is he?" much like "How many angels can dance on the head of a pin?"

2. What are you trying to do with your choreography?

I'm not trying to do something *with* my choreography. I'm trying to *do* it.

I believe very much that dance is doing. But of course it is a special way of doing, of existing, that requires nurturing and protecting. The human creature is magnificent, born with wonderful internal gyroscopes and a strong urge to listen to and follow these instincts. But much of our education, and other social and cultural pressures, go against our listening to these delicate longings. And at times the world absolutely demands that we *not* listen. Rediscovering these urges, listening to them, and, most important, acting on them—that is what a dancer tries to do, that is his life.

Many young dancers may not even know at first that this is what's happening. I didn't. But dancing felt good, so I danced. And fortunately, I come from a family that encourages such behavior. (I believe such behavior—doing what feels right, and good—marks the threshold of all insight.)

At first look, you would never think that such an enlightened attitude could exist in my family. But I was left alone to find my own way, and that was, perhaps, enough. (With the exception of frequent requests to pick up or to stay out of the way of nine older brothers and sisters, there were few real demands made on me.) But in addition there was the simply accepted concept that if you loved to do something and it felt good, you did it. And much of this was brought about by my father—a hard-working farmer and sawyer who in school had gone only as far as *McGuffey's Fifth Reader.* He chewed tobacco, spat a lot, and could curse with great fluency. A friend once described him this way: "He was the most natural and most graceful 'cusser' I ever knew. He could make a 'goddamn' sound almost theological, and 'son-of-a bitch' a compliment. I never heard him cuss in anger or malice. His cursing was colorful, appropriate, and more eloquently descriptive than Oxford diction."

He read a lot, planted crops according to the signs of the moon, provided for a large family, and operated very much on his feelings and instincts, teaching himself everything he needed to know. He had more insight and wisdom than anyone I have ever known. His life was one tremendously energetic, pioneering dance, at the same time vulnerable and strong. The frontiers he explored are gone now, so I turned to the frontier within.

Actually, I'm simply trying to do—to listen to myself, to follow my instincts with commitment and delight. I'm trying to demonstrate my life.

3. And why is it important to you to choreograph?

   So I can continue my life.

4. What is the greatest challenge of choreographing?

I can always find a million reasons for not going to the studio alone to start a new dance. I know there is a good chance it will take me to new and exciting places, but at the same time there is great dread. I know the new dance will be totally revealing of my weaknesses and strengths, to myself and also to my dancers. (And in the back of my mind is always the knowledge that this dance may very well expose me to a group of total strangers—the audience.) At the beginning I usually can feel only weakness. As many times as I've started a new dance, this initial struggle never goes away. If some part of a past dance pleases me, I look at it and think, "There, that's not bad, and now next time I'll know exactly how to get started." But I never do.

This is the same problem I talked about in trying to describe what kind of choreographer I am. Aside from the physical problems of making a dance—finding space, dancers, costumes—there is the metaphysical problem of aesthetically jumping off a cliff—or at least spinning dangerously along the rim. It's this adventure that terrifies and at the same time exhilarates. (And turning yourself over to such an adventure can make you go mad.)

5. What are you trying to get across to the audience?

I'm really trying to get something across to myself. Choosing a problem that's to be solved by movement, exploring the problem as deeply as I can, and from this making movement choices that are finally put together as a dance, gives me a structure within which to dance and live. Repeating this dance, remaining as true to its structure as I can, and living as completely as I can within the movement structure, generates an activity through which I have my strongest moments of insight—only then do I think anything can happen for an observer.

It doesn't mean, of course, that you aren't aware in constructing movement that certain moves can be seen better if done at a certain angle to the audience. Specific movement information can be made obvious or somewhat concealed depending on space, juxtaposition of bodies, and other tricks of the trade. But brilliant craftsmanship, virtuoso technique, and glossy facades can never make up for or conceal the absence of insight, the touching beauty of the courage to make a choice.

6. With whom did you study, and what do you think you have retained from that person?

I feel that primarily I have studied with myself and· taught myself most of the important things I need to know. (Perhaps my father's influence is stronger than I first realized.)

Spiked Sonata. Dan Wagoner and Dancers. Dennis Fleming. Photo: Lois Greenfield.

This process of self-teaching was helped along, of course, by the work I did with Martha Graham and Paul Taylor. When I first came to New York City, I was fortunate enough to dance in a piece of Doris Humphrey's, and she directed the rehearsals herself. I danced one season with Merce Cunningham, four with Martha Graham, and spent the greatest number of years with Paul Taylor touring and performing extensively. Each of these people has a strong sense of self, passionate commitment to an individual artistic point of view, and extraordinary energy. I was caught up in an exhilarating and exciting work, a world I had been looking for. And this world brought me tremendous delight and pleasure. In addition to their strengths, I was touched by the vulnerability of these choreographers, their self-doubts, indecisions, and even depressions. Although my responsibilities were not yet those of a choreographer, I could see what I was in for.

It was taken for granted that you would work with total commitment, wear your costume well, warm up, and enter the stage at the proper time with accuracy and awareness.

I studied with these people by observing how their dances went together and how it felt to perform them. More than actual steps or subject matter or a specific point of view, I learned what to me were interesting values and a way of working that could lead me where I wanted to go.

Surprisingly enough, I feel I have learned the most about dance technique from a classical ballet teacher. Ballet's reflection of eighteenth- and nineteenth-century European court manners has never interested me. But when I studied with Maggie Black, I became aware that ballet movement could give a strong centered alignment which in turn allowed good muscle quality, balance, and speed. This aware use of the body has given me a clear, unmannered center from which to move in any direction I choose—both physically and aesthetically. More than any teacher I've ever observed, Maggie Black seems to have both a knowledge of technical correctness (dealing primarily with getting centered) and a rare intuitive gift for teaching.

But what is most interesting to me is her generous, creative, and apparently tireless use of her gifts. Her work is always objective and her corrections are always specific. Yet many subtle, important things are at work underneath. She seems to sense the limitations, assets, and needs of each individual anatomy; she knows when a person is working at his or her full capacity (and this varies tremendously with each anatomy), and the speed with which the student can handle new material. Her end product is a dance instrument and not a dance composition, yet she works with the same energy, commitment, and creativity as the choreographers I worked with. Although her technical help has been invaluable, it is from this spirit of creativeness that I've learned the most. And all of her help has been given with a feeling of great positiveness—that everything is possible if you'll just stand straight, get your weight on both feet, and "lift your pelvis."

There is no way to translate into words the influence George Montgomery has had on my life. He is a poet. He is a long-time friend and accomplice. He has pointed out wild columbine, a hawk's nest in the crotch of a huge pine tree on his property, and the fact that sandpipers never get their feet wet.

7. Where do you feel you have diverged from your first ideas?

The idea for the various dances I've made have come from many different sources. Some were fairly simple, others quite elaborate and complex. Each dance idea or problem was dealt with at the time with all the craft, invention, delight, energy, and courage I could muster.

Over the years some of the basic tools of my craft have been honed. Control of phrasing, ability to achieve the desired rhythmic structure, and overall command of the space have gotten a little easier. And the solving of one dance idea has often suggested a new idea or problem which then becomes the next dance. For instance, after I had made *Stop Stars* (1981), I realized that there was a process of evolution followed by dissolution at work in this dance. I later consciously used this idea as the structuring element of *Amara* (1984).

As this chain of activity fills the years, it becomes a history or record of a life. And through it runs a thread of a metaphysical journey bringing many hoped-for moments of insight. And this in turn brings me to the basic dance values which I have tried to apply to all of my dances. I am absolutely absorbed with movement. I love movement. And I trust movement. So all of my dances begin with movement, and the basic problem or idea is always a movement problem. As I make movement choices, I dance them over and over, turn them around, add on—explore in as many directions as possible and then trust the movement will lead me somewhere interesting. The use of instincts and intuitive feeling comes very much into play. As well as I can understand my process of working, this is basically how all of my dances have been made. Although my craft may have become keener, and although experience has brought enlightenment and growth, these basic values seem to remain the same.

8. How has your work evolved since you started to choreograph?

As answered in the previous question, my basic idea for making a dance is movement and trust of movement—this was my first way of choreographing and remains so today. The evolution that there is has mostly to do with keener craft, emotional growth, and the energy to persevere. And this evolution has come only through an extraordinary expenditure of energy, both physical and emotional. Sustaining a career in dancing has meant living outside the economic and cultural systems. So you have to be inventive, imaginative, and creative, and willing to work hard. It means a real commitment, or the work will never get done.

Perhaps the answer to this question is that the work must have evolved, since I've survived as a dancer and choreographer for 23 years.

9. Choose a dance you have choreographed and discuss it in terms of why it worked.

Any dance works, literally, because I am working. That is, I go to the studio and between a busy schedule of regular repertory rehearsals and out of town touring, I set aside time for myself and with the dancers to work on the new piece. *Spiked Sonata* (1981), for example, is accompanied by popular music from the 1940s arranged in what might loosely be called a sonata form. George Montgomery suggested the music, found the old records, and put it on tape for me. It includes music by Clyde McCoy, Wayne King, Spike Jones, and others. James Welty designed the costumes.

The simple statement "I go to the studio and work" implies much more and of course is not so simple a statement. The studio rent has been paid for 15 years and there is an accumulation of energy that comes from sustaining a dance company and a repertory for that long. The dancers have been with me an average of five years. There is a coming together of effort, energy, and a common understanding that cannot exist without tremendous effort, sacrifice, and dedication.

Out of this energy I choose certain structural conceits, make movement choices, and launch myself into the midst of a new place —a new dance. This energy is rocked and bombarded by pain, fatigue, doubt, and fear. But the energy endures.

This is the only way I can judge if a dance works. If it becomes a strong part of my life, then I feel it works. The reactions of people who eventually see it interest me. But if someone suggests I change it—well, I can no more do that than change the color of my eyes.

I compose all the movement, perform in the dance myself, and teach the movement to the other dancers. For the sections I'm not in I observe and direct. When I'm in the dance, my observation is from a different angle. I try to shape and point up the "dance information" as clearly as I can, and then dance the "information" as generously as possible.

To return to *Spiked Sonata,* the music for that dance has rather obvious construction which invited going against it. Much of it has a beat that's beautifully seductive—strong, sassy, and syncopated. There are references to my own (probably mistaken) idea of what the

*Spiked Sonata. Dan Wagoner and Dancers. JoAnn Freglaette-Jansen,
Kristin Draudt, Edward Henry, Dennis Fleming. Photo: © Johan Elbers
1986.*

social dances of the 1940s were. The dance starts in silence with
movement references to forties social dances and to a rather complex
and constant changing relationship of the dancers to each other. This
changing of partners, so far, continues through the dance. I found
movement shapes and phrases, rhythmic structures, and dancer relationships that pulled me further into this particular dance.

Sometimes as I make a dance, moments are evoked which I feel
I've experienced somewhere before. So each dance begins to find its
own way, and I keep nudging it along. I am working.

10. How is this a reflection of our culture?

First of all, the struggle to bring any dance about reflects many
aspects of our culture. Dance as I know it is not a marketplace
industry. So to provide the basic essentials—space and dancers—
takes a tremendous amount of effort and planning. Nonchoreo-
graphic activities such as teaching and fundraising must be engaged
in so as to "buy" choreographic time. Dancers and choreographers
often live at poverty level in order to do their work. They cannot

*Spiked Sonata. Dan Wagoner and Dancers. Diann Sichel, Lisa Taylor
Swee, Dan Wagoner, JoAnn Freglaette-Jansen. Photo: Lois Greenfield.*

expect the usual rewards, but can have the satisfaction that comes
from hard work. The work has an integrity that is often missing from
the marketplace.

When I first came to New York City about 25 years ago, modern
dance was totally outside the regular economy. Dancers worked at
nondance jobs all year long, rehearsed at night, and did one or two
performances a year. Gradually dance interest grew, and statistics
finally proved that it was big business. Professional administrators
and business people began to move in and manage companies. It was
necessary for companies to show growth—not necessarily artistic

growth, but most certainly material growth. Many of the aesthetic ideas which first attracted me to dance can hardly survive in this atmosphere. Just as small businesses and even farms have been mostly swallowed up by corporations, so is it difficult for a small dance company to stay alive. The fragile yet beautiful values of dance seem imperiled. I often think about the disappearance of the Native American culture, the destruction of mountains, pollution of streams and air, and diminished creature population.

A gentle playfulness, dignified stance, and element of risk are qualities I've worked for in a recent dance to the music of Gottschalk. I've tried to respond to this silken, romantic, and robust music and hope the dance will have an optimism, energy, strength, and celebration of the individual. These are things I'd like our culture to have, and of course it will have them as long as there are dancers who bring wisdom, insight, and commitment to their work.

March 1982

Year	Title of Work	Place and Details
1968	*Dan' Run Penny Supper*	Judson Memorial Church, New York City. Danced by Wagoner and 11 women.
1969	*Brambles*	Cubiculo, New York City. Danced by Wagoner, with spoken text by George Montgomery.
1969	*Duet*	Massachusetts Institute of Technology, Cambridge. Music by Henry Purcell.
1969	*Le Jardin au Monsieur Macgregor*	Judson Memorial Church, New York City. Danced by Wagoner, George Montgomery, and 3 women.
1970	*Westwork*	Judson Memorial Church, New York City. Hammering and sawing sounds. Costume design by Remy Charlip.
1970	*Night Duet*	Judson Memorial Church, New York City. Performed by 2 dancers in silence.
1970	*Iron Mountain*	Merce Cunningham Studio, New York City. Violin Sonata by Hindemith. Performed by 5 dancers.
1971	*July Thirteenth*	Loeb Student Center, New York University, New York City. Music by John Herbert MacDowell. Performed by 5 dancers.
1971	*Cows and Ruins*	New York City. Country western hits. Performed by 5 dancers.
1972	*Numbers*	Loeb Student Center, New York University, New York City. Spoken sentences. Group work.
1972	*Changing Your Mind*	Dance Umbrella, Roundabout Theater, New York City. Spoken words, text, and night sounds. Group work.
1973	*Meets and Bounds*	Hunter Playhouse, Hunter College, New York City. Performed by 4 women in silence.
1973	*Broken Hearted Rag Dance*	Hunter Playhouse, Hunter College, New York City. Solo for Wagoner to Scott Joplin's "Maple Leaf Rag."
1974	*Taxi Dances*	University of Maryland, Baltimore. Popular music; piano played by Michael Sahl. Performed by 7 dancers.

Year	Title of Work	Place and Details
1975	A Sad Pavanne for These Distracted Times	Essex County YMHA, East Orange, New Jersey. Solo for Wagoner to Thomas Tompkins on harpsichord.
1975	Summer Rambo	Schimmel Center, Pace University, New York City. Music by J. S. Bach. Costume design by Kae Yoshida. Performed by 6 dancers.
1976	A Dance for Grace and Elwood	Dance Umbrella, Roundabout Theater, New York City. Composed score by Robert Salier and Carol Webber. Performed by 7 dancers.
1976	Songs	Stephen Foster Theater, Pittsburgh. Music by Mendelssohn, Grieg, Brahms, and Dvořák. Costume design by Santo Loquasto. Performed by 7 dancers.
1977	Allegheny Connection	Dance Umbrella/Roundabout Theater, New York City. Tibetan religious horns and bell. Costumes by Kae Yoshida. Performed by George Montgomery and 3 other men.
1978	Yonker Dingle Variations	Dance Umbrella, Entermedia Theater, New York City. Costume design by Remy Charlip. Variations on "Yankee Doodle Dandy" composed by Michael Sahl. Performed by 7 dancers.
1978	Green Leaves and Gentle Differences	Dance Umbrella, Entermedia Theater, New York City. Composed score by Robert Salier and Carol Webber. Performed by 4 dancers.
1978	Lila's Garden Ox	Judson Memorial Church, New York City. Solo for Wagoner to Bach's Violin and Oboe Sonata. Revised and expanded in 1980 for 7 dancers; premiered at Charleston, West Virginia, Cultural Center.
1979	Seven Tears	Judson Memorial Church, New York City. Music by John Dowland. Costume design by Patty Varney. Performed by 7 dancers.
1979	A Play, with Images and Walls	Judson Memorial Church, New York City. Composed score by Natalie Gilbert. Costume design by Patty Varney. Performed by 7 dancers and George Montgomery speaking poetry.

Year	Title of Work	Place and Details
1981	*Spiked Sonata*	Schimmel Center, Pace University, New York City. Radio theme music of the 1930s. Costumes by James Welty. Performed by 7 dancers.
1981	*Stop Stars*	Royal Court Theatre, Edinburgh Festival, Scotland. Recorded natural sounds. Performed by 6 dancers.
1982	*Otjibwa Ango, Parts I & II*	Schimmel Center, Pace University, New York City. Traditional Native American music/Charles Tomlinson Griffes. Set and costume design by James Welty. Renamed *AMARA I & II* in 1984; performed at Northrup Auditorium, Minneapolis. Set and costume redesigned by Karen Schulz.
1983	*'Round This World, Baby Mine*	Swarthmore College, Swarthmore, Pennsylvania. Traditional and country western music. Costume design by Liz Garden. Costumes redesigned by Jess Goldstein for New York premiere, Joyce Theater, 1984.
1984	*Magnolia*	Joyce Theater, New York City. Music, "A Night in the Tropics," by Louis Moreau Gottschalk. Costumes by Jess Goldstein. Performed by 5 dancers.
1985	*Episode*	Cottingham Theater, Columbia, South Carolina. Taped collage of natural sounds and Tibetan horns and bells. Performed by 4 dancers.

Commissioned Choreography

Year	*Title of Work*	*Place and Details*
1981	*Dolly Sods*	Commissioned by Mantis Dance Company, London. Traditional American folk music. Performed by 6 dancers.
1985	*An Occasion for Some Revolutionary Gestures*	Manchester Theatre, Manchester, England. Commissioned by Ballet Rambert, London. "Piano Variations on Yankee Doodle Dandy" composed by Michael Sahl. Set and costume design by John Macfarlane. Performed by 8 women and 6 men.
1985	*Flee as a Bird*	Commissioned by Janet Smith and Dancers, London. "Flee as a Bird" by Art Hodes and other American blues songs. Performed by Janet Smith and Dancers, 5 women and 2 men.

All of Dan Wagoner's dances have been lit by Jennifer Tipton.

Louis Falco

Photo: Peggy Jarrell Kaplan.

LOUIS FALCO

Louis Falco began dancing professionally with the Charles Weidman Dance Company before he had graduated from the High School of Performing Arts in New York City. Joining the José Limón Dance Company in 1960, he appeared as a featured member of that company until 1970. During that decade, Limón created many ballets specifically for Falco, in some of which he performed opposite Limón. He formed the Louis Falco Dance Company in 1967. Since then the company has performed throughout the world and in all major festivals in the United States and Europe.

As a choreographer, Falco has created over three dozen works for the Louis Falco Dance Company, as well as ballets for many other companies around the world, among them La Scala Opera Ballet, Alvin Ailey American Dance Theater, Australian Ballet, Netherlands Dance Theater, Boston Ballet, Ballet Théâtre Contemporain de Nancy, and Ballet Rambert. Falco's numerous appearances as a dancer include guest-starring at La Scala and with Rudolph Nureyev on Broadway in *The Moor's Pavane.* He has received grants from the National Endowment for the Arts, the New York State Council on the Arts, the Guggenheim Memorial Foundation, and the 1979 Harkness award as Outstanding Male Modern Dancer.

Falco has always been interested in photography, and his photos have appeared in many New York galleries. This interest has spurred him to explore new directions with dance and the camera. In addition to video work in Holland and the United States, he choreographed the MGM feature film *Fame.* In 1981 he created six programs for RAI-TV, Channel 1, the Italian national network, which were performed by the Louis Falco Dance Company, culminating in a 11/2-hour special *Superfalco.*

LOUIS FALCO

Freedom

What I try to get across to an audience depends on the specifics of a particular work. Sometimes the thrust of a piece is political, sometimes physical, sometimes emotional. Then, apart from that basic thrust, on a practical level, a lot of other elements come into play. That's why I believe categories like modern, ballet, or minimalism are less important than content. I think the creative process, the making of the piece, is really the most interesting part. When it comes to a performance, the process is already history. And then when you think of repertoire, when you think of works from ten years ago, to me that always boggles me, because it feels like holding back, like never being able to let go. The frustration comes from trying to keep the past present, to keep the energy and conviction it took to instill the life into the dancers, and to get it where it was when you first made it.

Each work is different. A lot of the pieces I have made are dramatic by nature, but not in terms of particular plot and story line. *Kate's Rag*, 1980, based on the *Taming of the Shrew*, was a little of each. It was set in 1906 and Kate was a suffragette.

In the *Taming of the Shrew* I was interested in the idea that both people become victimized at the end. There is no master, there is no slave, and the roles are dependent on each other. Power is given, power doesn't exist on its own. In the end, even though Kate is victimized, groveling on the floor when she sets Petruchio up on a table, he is victimized on the pedestal. Both of them are stuck in their roles and neither has freedom. He has to be the master, she has to be the slave, and they're both victims.

What kept motivating each section in *Kate's Rag* was the dramatic plot. I treated it like a play. Each time I'd make a section, I would look at it along with my collaborator, Rocco Bufano, who also did the costumes and sets. Even though there was a great deal of invention choreographically (in terms of new themes or wonderful combinations), if it didn't tell us anything new about the characters, it didn't belong in the piece.

So things were edited out. There was one section I choreographed four times and still it wasn't communicating where the action had to go at that moment. The script ended up dictating what had to be dealt with at each point. What happened ultimately was that I sat out front during the dress rehearsal and looked at it and cut it out completely because the section didn't belong. So that was the nature of the work process particular to developing *Kate's Rag.*

A piece like *Escargot,* 1978, was basically an exploration of movement, of the circle and the line, and of the couples working within that circle and that line. Its form came out of that exploration, which, in this case, was what dictated the development of the work. It was abstract but dramatic. All movement has emotional content. I don't think movement exists without emotional content, even if those emotions are not what you're focusing on in a particular piece.

For me, the greatest challenge of choreography is trying to get as close as possible to the idea that's in my mind. How close I get to my intention is the most difficult thing to achieve, whether or not the work itself meets with success. For me, that success is based on how clearly I realize my intentions. The success of a work to the public is based on something only they know. Sometimes when I'm making a work, I know what the finished idea looks like in my mind's eye. There are times when the end results are known to me, but always it is an exploration.

There are so many obstacles in the making of a piece: the clarity of ideas, the people collaborating, how organized I am or how inspired. I think inspiration is a luxury. It's a matter of how well you know your craft, and how close you feel to what you're dealing with.

Choreography is one of the things I like doing most and it's one of the things I do best. It's something I would want to do even if I was unable to earn a living at it.

I studied with everybody: Graham, Limón, Cunningham, Joffrey, American Ballet Theater—everybody from that period of time 20 years ago. I danced with Charles Weidman's company while I was still in the High School of Performing Arts. I would take off from school and go on tour. It wasn't permitted for students to work professionally or to tour, but I did it anyway. I was always announcing that somebody in my family, a distant relative in California or somewhere, had died, and I had to go off for a week. And they all knew what was happening.

Argot. Louis Falco Dance Company. Louis Falco & Sarah Stackhouse.
Photo: Jack Mitchell.

I danced with José Limón's company from 1960 to 1970. Even then, though, I also danced with Donnie McKayle's and Alvin Ailey's companies. In terms of movement style, José was a great influence. I felt his movement offered the most freedom and most potential in terms of my own interest in developing a dramatic dance language.

Merce Cunningham and John Cage have been major influences, and yet their styles are not styles I myself emulated. I was more interested in developing my own style of movement. What affected me in their work was the freedom of their thinking, something like a Zen philosophy which they incorporated into the medium. I've tried to incorporate that kind of freedom into my own work and to encourage it in my company members.

In the evolution of my work, I feel I've gotten closer and closer to what I want it to be about. I've gone through many periods where it looks like one thing, then it looks like another and to me, that's not contradictory. It's just how large my world is. It's a matter of how much, how many different areas of experience I can include in my life. Each time I do a piece I try to make it an exploration of something I'm curious about, that I haven't seen before. I try to give myself new information.

When I'm looking at someone else's work, whether it's a painting, a movie, a ballet, it doesn't matter, I'm looking for something I haven't seen before. Not that anything is new or original, but I'm looking for it in such a way that it'll show me something new. I try to do that in my own work and sometimes I realize it and other times I don't.

One of the main things I set out to do was to deal with dancers on the stage so that they maintained their identities as individuals. I grew up in a modern dance world where choreographers were gods and dancers were subservient expressions of a particular philosophy or school of thought.

Years back, if you danced with one company and took a class with another company, you were a traitor. You were married to those people. It all came out of insecurity and fear, an angry, tight feeling among the whole scene that always distressed me and alienated me on a certain level.

When I was dancing with José up at Connecticut College and I'd have an hour or two free, I'd go take a Graham class or Cunningham class. He would see that and get very angry, but to me it was absurd because I had made a major commitment to him. I was available for whatever hours he wanted me to rehearse, which were

Timewright. Louis Falco. Photo: Jack Mitchell.

normally from ten in the morning until ten at night, six or seven days a week.

One of the things I wanted to break down immediately in my own company was that kind of thinking. So I told my dancers, "Just because you're dancing with me doesn't mean your life becomes less, that you can only dance with me and nobody else and not do other projects." I tried to encourage them to do as many other things as possible, but on a certain level it became a contradiction or impossible because the company was so active and involved, it didn't give them much time to do anything else.

I didn't want people to look like dancers on stage. I wanted them to look like people who dance. I didn't want to see their hair in tight little buns and didn't think there was any reason why some of the most beautiful people in the modern dance world had to go on stage in ugly little leotards and tights and bad makeup, and look unattractive and grovel on the floor. I wanted that to change. I didn't think modern dance had to have that stigma. I wanted to make it more accessible.

I wanted strong individuals to work with me. I didn't want intimidation in the sudio. And I didn't want the pretentiousness of the dance world in which I grew up.

I wanted to make dances that were a part of our lives and I wanted to use the popular music we listened to while living those lives. So I made works like *Sleepers,* 1971, in which the score was the dancers themselves speaking, and it felt to me at the time like an authentic extension of my life.

Sleepers and *Caviar* seemed different to me from everything I had seen before and premiered during the same season at City Center. I made them at the point when my work really began to change and became more individual. It began to be more what I was thinking and feeling, and how I felt dance needed to evolve in relation to the increasing freedom that was affecting all of our lives.

The dialogue in *Caviar* was spoken as though it was a news broadcast. It changed with each performance according to that day's news. It was something of the times. When it was first done, we had a rock group and 30 singers on stage, and the orchestra in the pit. Marisol made foam rubber fish for us. *Caviar* was when we began to start flinging out the movement, throwing it away—the impulses from each other's bodies and all of the shaking and rubber quality, the abandonment of the individuals. It was showing the particular life style which I think was very important at that time. People were beginning to live like that and it was a reflection of our times. It was just being part of what our lives were—the music, the attitude on stage, the way people conducted themselves and behaved with each other.

What I found important about *Caviar* was that I had the freedom to start off with one idea and end up with another. I'd walk into the studio with a particular idea to work on, and after letting out movement for five or ten minutes, I'd go off in a totally different direction. I had the freedom to be able to face a room full of people and choreograph on the spot. That's how you make things, you have an idea and then you start putting it together and see if it supports that idea and takes it further.

In September 1981, I did a six-week series, aired every Saturday for RAI television on Channel 1 in Italy. *Imaginations* was an investigation into the mind of a man and how his investigation affected and altered his vision. *Bedroom* depicted the ways in

R.A.I. T.V. 1980. Louis Falco Dance Company. Louis Falco & Juan Antonio. Photo: Luciano Locatelli.

which a middle-class, middle-aged man attempted to retain his fantasies. *Transmissions* examined the effect of the energy outside oneself that one encounters throughout life and how that energy can channel one's own energy, resulting in conformity. *The Match* explored the dependencies that a man establishes as support for his life, dependencies which prevent him from the full use of his powers.

The Eagle's Nest was a work I made for La Scala in 1979–1980. The idea was stewing for about three to four years with a piece called *Saltimbocca,* which is food, and translated means "jump in the mouth." I have a lot of ballets named after food and that probably comes from the fact that my father was a chef and food was one of the most important things my family participated in: any time anything happened, whether it was good, bad, or indifferent, it was always around the dinner table. I don't know why I didn't get fat.

Like *Saltimbocca,* I started *Eagle's Nest* with a family structure. It started off at Ellis Island, with two young people arriving from Italy and coming to America with fantasies, needs, and explorations of what they thought they were going to realize in this country. And then ultimately it became what they had to do to make their lives work and to survive.

When we were making the ballet, we were thinking of a film. As I wrote it down, it was as though I was choreographing from the perspective of a lens. What I wanted was a long shot starting from the clouds, dealing with the view of an eagle hovering over the city, and then coming in for a close-up, until eventually it became a sparrow's view, and ultimately it became the view of the people walking on the street.

As the camera is panning down, going from the rooftops, we see the eagle, lying in a huge brass bed on top of the Twin Towers [of the World Trade Center] overlooking all of Manhattan. It's his territory, his domain, and he wakes up. "Ah, another day, what am I gonna do with it?" And he throws off the covers and very sensually slides out of the bed and starts bathing himself using a pitcher and basin, then wipes himself with a towel. The eagle is obviously a symbol of America, representing an image of great sensuality and power.

Then he starts filling out the space as he leaves the bedroom which is the top of the building and you see from a distance, all these immigrants coming forward, which is Ellis Island, as if he came down from the Twin Towers and went out to Ellis Island.

And then you see 150 people coming forward with luggage and weighted bags and it was quite wonderful at La Scala, with the stage going so far back and the progression of all these people coming forward, with the eagle circling and opening up that space. Finally when they do come forward, we see a drop come down and that focuses our attention on the individuals arriving in the country.

Eagle's Nest is important to me because of its political and social statements. I do see people as a thrust of what their lives are about. In *Eagle's Nest,* those lives were motivated either as a whore or as a martyr. For the purpose of this piece, we dealt with these two characters who came over from Italy. The woman was compelled by whoredom and the man by martyrdom. Whoredom has to do with getting rewards on earth, martyrdom with getting rewards in the heavens after death.

Offhand I think anything I do would reflect the state of our culture, since I'm living in it. That's all I can do. I am a reflection of what I'm being shown. I think anything anyone makes, anything anyone does is always automatically that. It's a reflection of their personalization of information. In *Eagle's Nest,* I tried to go beyond that personalization to something more universal, something that shows the overwhelming courage it takes to survive in the face of one's dreams.

The concept for the *Eagle's Nest* was worked out between Rocco Bufano and myself. Later Michael Kayman came in and wrote the music and Bufano did the scenery and costuming. What was interesting about working with Bufano was that we talked so much and were so involved, we couldn't tell at a certain point where the ideas came from and what belonged to whom. The entire project was really two people pulling and tugging, two minds pushing a project forward. I consider it to be one of the most positive collaborations I've ever experienced.

In the beginning we worked very closely with Michael Kayman before we left for La Scala. We did it in two periods: one was for one month and the other for six weeks, with about a month and a half broken up in between.

Eagle's Nest was made as if we were constantly rearranging the pieces of a puzzle. We would ask, "Is the movement telling us anything new, dramatically is it taking us further?" A lot of it looked very balletic and that's simply because La Scala dancers are balletically trained. Sometimes things enter into a work whether you anticipate them or not, and they are all worthy of consideration.

Working with one's own company is the best way to learn to make choreography. It is a situation that allows you the opportunity to make mistakes. However, it wasn't until I began to choreograph outside the company, like at La Scala, Paris Opera, Netherlands

Dance Theater, or even more commercial situations like the MGM film *Fame,* that I feel my work took off in a whole new direction. Freed of both the insular nature of my own company and the responsibility of maintaining that company, I was able to discover another kind of freedom. I think it has something to do with experiences after the death of parents.

September 15, 1980, with revisions in 1985

All works were created by Louis Falco unless otherwise indicated.

Year	Title of Work	Place and Details
1967	*Argot*	92nd Street YM-YWHA, New York City. Single performance of the newly founded Louis Falco Dance Company. Music by Bartok. Duet performance. 12 minutes.
1968	*Huescape*	Performed in New York City, Massachusetts, Colorado, and Washington, D.C. Music by Schaeffer/Baschet. Performed by 3 dancers. 15 minutes.
1969	*Timewright*	Performed in New York, Missouri, Ohio, Illinois, and Pennsylvania; Spoleto Festival, Italy. Music by Alcantara. Performed by full company. 25 minutes.
1970	*Caviar*	Performed in New York, Ohio, Michigan, and New Jersey. Music by Cole. Performed by full company. 30 minutes.
1970	*Ibid*	Performed in New York, Ohio, Michigan, and New Jersey. Music by Alcantara. Performed by 7 dancers. 8 minutes.
1971	*Sleepers*	Performed in New York, Pennsylvania, New Jersey, Florida, Wisconsin, Illinois, Massachusetts, Washington, D.C., and Caramoor Festival. Experimentation, in *Sleepers*, with dialogue spoken by the dancers. Performed by 4 dancers. 30 minutes.
1971	*First Base* (created by Juan Antonio)	Performed in New York, Pennsylvania, New Jersey, Florida, Wisconsin, Illinois, Massachusetts, Washington, D.C., and Caramoor Festival. Performed by 2 dancers. 23 minutes.
1972	*Soap Opera*	Performed in New York, California, Arizona, Massachusetts, Pennsylvania, Connecticut, Delaware, North Carolina, Ohio, Missouri, Mississippi, Louisiana, and Illinois; Guadalajara and Mexico City, Mexico. Music by Alcantara. Performed by full company. 30 minutes.
1973	*Avenue*	Performed in New York, Michigan, Maryland, California, Pennsylvania; Montreal; West Berlin; Rotterdam, The Hague, Amsterdam, and Utrecht; London; Nice, France. Music by Vertical Burn. Performed by full company. 25 minutes.
1973	*Twopenny Portrait*	Performed in New York, Michigan, Maryland, California, Pennsylvania; Montreal; West Berlin; Rotterdam, The Hague, Amsterdam, and Utrecht; London; Nice, France. Music by Alcantara. Duet performance. 14 minutes.

Year	Title of Work	Place and Details
1974	*Storeroom*	Performed in New York, Ohio, Michigan, Minnesota, Florida, Connecticut, Nebraska, Illinois; Montreal and Downsville, Canada; Amsterdam, The Hague, Rotterdam, Eindhoven; Paris. Music by Nurock. Performed by 7 dancers. 38 minutes.
1974	*I Remember* (created by Antonio)	Performed in New York, Ohio, Michigan, Minnesota, Florida, Connecticut, Nebraska, Illinois; Montreal and Downsville, Canada; Amsterdam, The Hague, Rotterdam, Eindhoven, Paris. Performed by 6 dancers. 25 minutes.
1975	*Pulp*	Performed in New York, North Carolina, South Carolina, Delaware, Minnesota; Paris. Music collage. Performed by full company. 90 minutes.
1976	*Champagne*	Performed in New York, Michigan, Indiana, Colorado, California, Kansas, and Arizona; Hamburg, Frankfurt, Darmstadt, Berlin, and Heidelberg, West Germany; Bergen, Norway. Music collage. Performed by full company. 30 minutes.
1976	*B-Mine*	Performed in New York, Michigan, Indiana, Colorado, California, Kansas, and Arizona; Hamburg, Frankfurt, Darmstadt, Berlin, and Heidelberg, West Germany; Bergen, Norway. Music by Jarrett. Performed by 6 dancers. 18 minutes.
1977	*Hero*	Performed in New York, Vermont, Maine, Florida, Texas, and Connecticut; Vienna; Orleans, Angers, Nantes, Rennes, Montbeliard, and Paris, France. Music by Tulsa. Performed by 6 dancers. 27 minutes.
1977	*Tiger Rag*	Performed in New York, Vermont, Maine, Florida, Texas, and Connecticut; Vienna; Orleans, Angers, Nantes, Rennes, Montbeliard, and Paris, France. Music by Kamen. Performed by 6 dancers plus 18 extras. 30 minutes.
1977	*Coasting* (created by Antonio)	Performed in New York, Vermont, Maine, Florida, Texas, and Connecticut; Vienna; Orleans, Angers, Nantes, Rennes, Montbeliard, and Paris, France. Music by Jarrett. Duet performance. 14 minutes.
1978	*Escargot*	Performed in New York, Pennsylvania, Rhode Island, Indiana, New Hampshire, Georgia, Minnesota, Connecticut, and Washington. Music by MacDonald. Performed by 6 dancers. 20 minutes.
1978	*Imago* (created by Antonio)	Performed in New York, Pennsylvania, Rhode Island, Indiana, New Hampshire, Georgia, Minnesota, Connecticut, and Washington. Music by Brahms. Performed by 7 dancers. 18 minutes.

Year	Title of Work	Place and Details
1978	*Djin* (created by William Gornel)	Performed in New York, Pennsylvania, Rhode Island, Indiana, New Hampshire, Georgia, Minnesota, Connecticut, and Washington. Music by Rimbaugh. Performed by 5 dancers. 18 minutes.
1979	*Early Sunday Morning*	Music by Sanborn. Solo performance. 20 minutes.
1979	*Saltimbocca*	Music by Sahl. Performed by full company. 30 minutes.
1979	*Tournament* (created by Antonio)	Music by Campuzano. Performed by 3 dancers. 16 minutes.
1980	*Kate's Rag*	Music by Joplin. Performed by 7 dancers. 35 minutes.
1980	*Service Compris*	Music by Faithfull. Performed by 6 dancers. 14 minutes.
1981	*Black and Blue*	Music by Nilsson/Newman. Performed by 7 dancers. 35 minutes.
1981	*The Other One* (created by Antonio)	Music by Piazzola. Performed by 5 dancers. 25 minutes.
1982	*Little Boy*	Music by The Band. Duet performance. 15 minutes.

R.A.I. TV, 1980. The Match. Louis Falco. Photo: Francette Levieux.

Douglas Dunn

Photo: Peggy Jarrell Kaplan.

DOUGLAS DUNN

Douglas Dunn performed with Yvonne Rainer & Group (1968–1970), with Merce Cunningham and Dance Company (1969–1973), and with Grand Union (1970–1976). In 1971 he began presenting his own work; in 1976 he worked on and performed *Lazy Madge,* an ongoing choreographic project for ten dancers; two years later he began touring with Douglas Dunn & Dancers. In 1978 and 1981 the company was invited to the Festival d'Automne in Paris.

Dunn's commissioned works include *Celeste,* set by Tal Streeter, for the American Dance Festival, 1977; *Relief,* for the Repertory Dance Theater, Salt Lake City, Utah, 1979; *Suite de Suite,* with music by Eliane Radigue, set by Christian Jaccard, for the Ballet Théâtre Français de Nancy, 1980; *Pulcinella,* for the Ballet de l'Opéra de Paris (co-sponsored by the Festival d'Automne), also 1980; and *Cycles,* with music by Steve Lacy, for the Groupe Recherche Choreographique de l'Opéra de Paris, 1981. In 1982, Susan Dowling of WGBH New Television Workshop commissioned *Secret of the Waterfall,* a videodance made in collaboration with film maker Charles Atlas and poets Anne Waldman and Reed Bye. A year later the Institute of Contemporary Art in Boston commissioned and presented *Second Mesa,* a collaborative museum event with Douglas Dunn & Dancers; John Driscoll and Richard Lerman, musicians; and Jeffrey Schiff, sculptor.

Douglas Dunn has received choreographic grants from the Creative Artists Public Service (CAPS) program, the New York State Council on the Arts, and the National Endowment for the Arts, and a fellowship from the John Simon Guggenheim Memorial Foundation.

DOUGLAS DUNN

Three Interviews

I

DD Nice place. Great view

DD It's on loan

DD Shall we begin

DD By all means

DD How long have you been dancing

DD Forget it

DD Why did you choose dancing

DD The question doesn't come up. It's historical. I'm not interested

DD What interests you

DD The business of arranging energy

DD (pause) Business

DD Yes. A good businesslike word, don't you think, like the ones business people use. The way they talk to each other they build up a kind of trust. I'll relate to you as a stereotype if you'll return the favor. Off they go getting business done. So in the business end of the operation I try to call things by their proper names. Otherwise they think you're crazy & then you never realize an image outside your head & then you ARE crazy. I carry a regular business card

DD Then I take it you no longer dance for other choreographers

DD Right. For a while there I thought I was going to BE some of those other choreographers. They showed me a lot. Sometimes I thought I saw everything. Of course I did not. Now I spend time thinking about oh, shall we say, Houdini

DD What was that

DD Houdini

DD No, that noise

DD I missed it

DD (pause) Tell us a little about your work

Douglas Dunn. Photo: Susan Dunn.

DD Why not. In *Time Out* I discovered an inverse proportion between outer & inner movement. Slowing down the body made the head swim. This piece also got me past condescension toward audience. Since then I've worked as if everyone can understand everything. This thinking leads to crystal clear images. In *Four for Nothing* I took the problem of inner movement more consciously in hand & juxtaposed to it an image of the body-person as weight placed on a spectrum running from high tension to extreme relaxation. Body weight as a metaphor for body weight. These elements are present in all dancing; here they sound the tonic note

DD I see

DD Following these tendencies to their logical & intuitional conclusions brought me to *101:* the image of stillness set on a structure that gives evidence of great activity. *101* is full of innumerable ambiguities, even paradoxes, that are becoming the source of many things

DD Like the title

DD Yes. The most literal & the most expressionistic in one. During the seventh week of performance I amused myself imagining the piece elsewhere & became aware how specific lying in New York is, how different it would be lying in Paris or in San Francisco

DD Stillness seems to be an important part of your work. Could you tell us about that

DD (very long pause) There's nothing to it

DD Why don't you ask me a question

DD What do you do

DD I'm self-employed. (pause) What do you think about acting

DD Not acting like a celebrity when you're not one is difficult. Becoming a celebrity so you can not act like one is less difficult

DD Our time is almost up. Is there anything you'd like to say before I go

DD Yes. I'd like to emphasize to the public how much I enjoy what I do & what happens as I do it

DD Wonderful

II

DD How are you today

DD I feel . . . slow. I feel like . . . making slow moves

DD Is that because it's hot out

DD Do you remember the time, we were on tour, trying to get the car up a hill, & Jimmy put his leg out, & pulled a muscle

DD Yes, & you had to learn his part & do his part & your part both. Let's talk about something that would be of interest to an imagined listener

DD I remember there was no way to cross over without going outside. It was sultry, there was wet grass. I thought I might step on a frog or something. Then coming in the door I tripped & hit my head on some pipe or other. Ha! I went on. Blood was

Elbow Room. Douglas Dunn & Dancers. Diane Frank, Susan Blakensop, Bill Young. Photo: Beatriz Schiller.

running down my forehead into my right, no my left, no my right eye. Someone said after, how interesting to change the make-up in the middle like that

DD Yes. Wow. You know, this is your chance to catch those who don't know you up on what you've been doing. In the first interview you only reached 1974. People might get the idea you're more interested in lying down than in dancing. What about the hour-long solo from '75, *Gestures in Red.* Or *Lazy Madge:* Certainly a two year project with a dozen dancers is worth saying something about

DD When I complained in England about the cold in the performance area, they brought in a jet engine. I mean, it looked like one. It had a huge fan, & it spurted fire. It was supposed to blow hot air all over the place. Maybe it was a giant flame-thrower.

Elbow Room. Douglas Dunn & Dancers. Douglas Dunn, Paul Engler, Bill Young, Deborah Riley. Photo: Beatriz Schiller.

They had it on all day. By curtain it was two degrees warmer, or less. Some guy after 10 minutes walked down the creaky bleachers cussing & everyone booed him. I loved it so much I almost showed it

DD   Since 1978 you've been making shorter pieces, twenty or thirty minutes mostly. What caused this shift away from the occasion-oriented, often site-specific, evening length works, to the more conventional repertory format

DD   How about in Florence when my back was hurting & Teresa would be standing there after the show holding a bag of ice fresh from the cafe next door. I'd take it to the restaurant & put it between my back & the chair. By the end of the meal there was a puddle of water under the chair & sometimes my feet were wet. Or in, where was it, Toulon, outdoors, when the deck was so hot . . .

DD   Excuse me, but you're really going off. You haven't even mentioned your *Pulcinella,* or the GBH Video, or the ICA piece. If you really have nothing helpful to say about what you've been doing, maybe we ought to . . .

DD   . . . boy everyone really jumped high in THAT performance

DD   . . . stop for today

DD Know the perceived . . .
DD . . . itself
DD Work with faith . . .
DD . . . in direct . . .
DD . . . immediate apprehension
DD Focus attention . . .
DD . . . away from imagined audience . . .
DD . . . desire, disarm, pay . . .
DD . . . attention
DD Set up . . .
DD . . . decision-making . . .
DD . . . a framework a . . .
DD . . . set of rules
DD Circumvent insistent . . .
DD . . . predilections . . .
DD . . . ignore judgments if . . .
DD . . . they're rational . . .
DD . . . residues . . .
DD . . . of already used . . .
DD . . . intuitions
DD Make something . . .
DD . . . new with a new . . .
DD . . . experience
DD . . . liberate . . .
DD . . . previously untapped . . .
DD . . . intuitive resources . . .
DD . . . along the way
DD Dance daily . . .
DD Make, break . . .
DD . . . kinesthetic habit
DD Invite others . . .
DD . . . to witness . . .
DD . . . not the same . . .
DD . . . thought or . . .
DD . . . feeling
DD Restrain desire . . .
DD . . . to be seen . . .
DD . . . by many by . . .
DD . . . certain . . .
DD . . . by few
DD Dance . . .

DD . . . in the world . . .
DD . . . not . . .
DD . . . in the . . .
DD . . . information . . .
DD . . . made up . . .
DD . . . about it
DD Make . . .
DD . . . the space . . .
DD . . . make . . .
DD . . . *Coquina*
DD Speak
DD Shoot . . .
DD . . . your mouth off
DD Hide . . .
DD . . . not . . .
DD . . . your heart . . .
DD . . . answer all . . .
DD . . . her questions

July 1984

Date	*Title of Work*	*Place and Details*
June 1971	*One Thing Leads to Another*	61 Crosby Street, New York City. Collaboration with Sara Rudner. Evening-length duet.
1971	*Dancing Here*	Merce Cunningham Studio, New York City. Collaboration with Pat Catterson. Evening-length duet.
1972	*Co-incidents*	Merce Cunningham Studio, New York City. Collaboration with David Gordon. Evening-length duet.
1972	*Mayonnaise, Part I*	Film with Charles Atlas.
October 1973	*Nevada*	New School for Social Research, New York City. Solo performance.
December 1973	*Time Out*	Exchange Theater for the Arts, New York City. Evening-length solo.
January 1974	*Four for Nothing*	508 Broadway, New York City. Evening-length work with Laleen Jayamanne, Epp Kotkas, David Woodberry.
April and September 1974	*101*	508 Broadway, New York City. Performance Exhibit. Solo. 7 weeks.
1974	*101*	Film with Amy Greenfield.
October 19, 1974	*Octopus*	New School for Social Research, New York City. Group work with Epp Kotkas, Sara Rudner, Howard Vichinsky, David Woodberry.
1975	*Part I Part II*	508 Broadway, New York City. Collaboration with David Woodberry. Evening-length duet.
May 14, 1975	*Gestures in Red*	Merce Cunningham Studio, New York City. Evening-length solo.
October 23, 1976	*Early and Late*	Styrian Autumn Festival, Graz, Austria. Occasional evening-length solo.

Date	Title of Work	Place and Details
1976–1977	*Lazy Madge*	Danspace, St. Mark's Church, New York City, June 1, 1976. Two-year ongoing choreographic project with David Woodberry, Ellen Webb, Michael Bloom, Diane Frank, Christina Grasso-Caprioli, Meg Eginton, Jennifer Mascall, Daniel Press, Ruth Alpert, Susan Dunn, and Dana Roth.
August 1977	*Celeste*	Connecticut College, New London. Commissioned by American Dance Festival. Set, skydivers, and score by Tal Streeter. Outdoor-indoor group work for 30.
October 7, 1977	*Solo Film and Dance*	Stanford University, Palo Alto, California. Evening-length solo (films by Charles Atlas and Amy Greenfield).
April 20, 1978	*Rille*	Brooklyn Academy of Music, New York City. Evening-length group work with Graham Conley, Christopher Crawford, Kyle deCamp, Diane Frank, Deborah Riley, Marta Renzi.
1978	Douglas Dunn & Dancers	Douglas Dunn, Diane Frank, Deborah Riley, Steve Spencer, and Graham Conley.
October 9, 1978	*Lazy Madge II*	University of California, Berkeley. Group work with Diane Frank, Deborah Riley, Steve Spencer, and Graham Conley.
October 9, 1978	*Rille*	University of California, Berkeley. Music by David Berman. Group work with Diane Frank, Deborah Riley, Graham Conley, and Steve Spencer.
October 9, 1978	*Coquina*	University of California, Berkeley. Music by Robert Ashley. Costumes by Charles Atlas. Group work with Graham Conley, Diane Frank, Deborah Riley, Steve Spencer.

Date	Title of Work	Place and Details
May 20, 1979	*Foot Rules*	Akademie de Kunst, Berlin, West Germany. Music by John Driscoll. Costumes by Mimi Gross. Evening-length duet with Deborah Riley.
July 6, 1979	*Echo*	Summergarden, Museum of Modern Art, New York City. Music by John Driscoll. Costume by Charles Atlas. Occasional solo.
October 1979	*Relief*	Commissioned by the Repertory Dance Theater, Salt Lake City, Utah. Music, "Bottom Coasting," by John Driscoll. Costumes by Marina Harris. Group work with members of the Repertory Dance Theater.
February 1980	*Suite de Suite*	Commissioned by the Ballet Théâtre Français de Nancy, France. Music by Eliane Radigue. Costumes and decor by Christian Jaccard. Group work with members of the Ballet Théâtre Français de Nancy.
April 1980	*Echo*	The Kitchen, New York City. Music by John Driscoll. Costumes by Charles Atlas. Set by Mimi Gross. Group work with Susan Blankensop, Grazia Della-Terza, Diane Frank, Alice Kaltman, John McLaughlin, Deborah Riley, Steve Spencer, and Megan Walker.
1980	Douglas Dunn & Dancers	Susan Blankensop, Grazia Della-Terza, Douglas Dunn, Diane Frank, John McLaughlin, and Deborah Riley.
November 18, 1980	*Pulcinella*	Théâtre Champs-Elysées. Co-commissioned by the Ballet de l'Opéra de Paris and the Festival d'Automne. Music by Stravinsky. Costumes by Norbert Schmucki, after an idea by Douglas Dunn. Group work with members of the Ballet de l'Opéra de Paris.

Date	Title of Work	Place and Details
April 1981	*Cycles*	Théâtre de la Ville. Commissioned by the Groupe de Recherche Choréographique de l'Opéra de Paris. Music, "The 4 Edges," by Steve Lacy.
June 20, 1981	*Walking Back*	The Dance Center, New York City. Music by John Driscoll. Occasional dance for Douglas Dunn & Dancers.
July 24, 1981	*Holds*	Harvard University, Cambridge, Massachusetts. Music by John Driscoll. Occasional dance for Douglas Dunn & Dancers.
August 1, 1981	*Châteauvallonesque*	Châteauvallon, France. Occasional dance for Douglas Dunn & Dancers.
November 1, 1981	*Skid*	Festival d'Automne, Paris. Music, "Fishs Eddy," by John Driscoll. Costumes by Mimi Gross. Group work for Douglas Dunn & Dancers.
November 1, 1981	*View*	Festival d'Automne, Paris. Music, "Lums Pond," by John Driscoll. Costumes by Charles Atlas. Group work for Douglas Dunn & Dancers.
November 1, 1981	*Hitch*	Festival d'Automne, Paris. Music, "Median Strip II," by Linda Fisher. Costumes by Charles Atlas. Group work for Douglas Dunn & Dancers.
May 20, 1982	*Game Tree*	Danspace, St. Mark's Church, New York City. Music, "Aurora," by Linda Fisher. Evening-length group work for Douglas Dunn & Dancers.

Date	Title of Work	Place and Details
September, 1982	*Secret of the Waterfall*	Videodance for Douglas Dunn & Dancers, shot on Martha's Vineyard, Massachusetts. Produced by Susan Dowling, WGBH New Television Workshop. Directed by Charles Atlas. Poetry written and performed by Reed Bye and Anne Waldman. Costumes by Charles Atlas.
January 15, 1983	*Second Mesa*	Institute of Contemporary Art, Boston. Commissioned by the I.C.A. for Douglas Dunn & Dancers. Music by John Driscoll, with additional music by Richard Lerman. Sculpture by Jeffrey Schiff. Curated by Elizabeth Sussman.
January 21, 1983	*Secret of the Waterfall*	541 Broadway, New York City. Adaptation of videodance for live performance. Poetry written and performed by Reed Bye and Anne Waldman. Design by Charles Atlas and Mimi Gross.
May 23, 1984	*Elbow Room*	Joyce Theater, New York City. Music, "Speechless," by Linda Fisher. Lighting by Patrick O'Rourke. Costumes by Mimi Gross. Group dance for 7.
May 23, 1984	*Pulcinella: Ballet in One Act*	Joyce Theater, New York City. Music by Stravinsky. Costumes and set by Mimi Gross. Lighting by Patrick O'Rourke. Reset on Douglas Dunn & Dancers and 8 guests.

Date	*Title of Work*	*Place and Details*
October 1984	*1st Rotation*	Minneapolis. Group work commissioned by the Walker Art Center and the New Dance Ensemble. Danced by members of the New Dance Ensemble. Music by Steve Kramer. Costumes by Beth Sidla.
November 1984	*Futurities*	Lille, France. Evening-length duet made in collaboration with Elsa Wolliaston, in piece conceived by Steve Lacy. Music by Steve Lacy. Text by Robert Creeley. Set by Kenneth Noland.
December 1984	*2nd Rotation*	Grenoble, France. Choreographed for Douglas Dunn & Dancers and four guest dancers. Music by Linda Fisher.
March 1985	Douglas Dunn & Dancers	Diane Frank, Grazia Della-Terza, Deborah Riley, Susan Blankensop, Paul Engler, Bill Young, Douglas Dunn.
March 1985	*Jig Jag*	The Dance Center, New York City. Dance for Douglas Dunn & Dancers. Music by Ron Kuivila. Costumes by David Hannah.
March 1985	*3rd Rotation*	The Dance Center, New York City. Dance for Douglas Dunn & Dancers. Music by Linda Fisher. Costumes by David Hannah.

Mel Wong

Photo: Peggy Jarrell Kaplan.

MEL WONG

Mel Wong was born in Oakland, CA, where his interest in gymnastics led him to dance. He performed with the Pacific Ballet Company, the Oakland Civic Light Opera Association, and the Oakland Civic Ballet Company; he was a Ford Foundation scholarship recipient for two years at Balanchine's School of American Ballet. Wong has a B.A. from San Francisco State University and an M.F.A. in the visual arts from Mills College, where he received the Catherine Morgan Trefethen fellowship in art. He is a few credits short of a second master's degree in dance from UCLA, because he left to join Merce Cunningham and Dance Company in 1968, performing internationally through 1972.

Mel Wong has been choreographing and performing his own work since 1970; he formed the Mel Wong Dance Company in 1975. Since then he has choreographed over 80 dances. His company has performed in most of the major dance series in New York City, as well as in Asia and in the United States.

Wong has taught at the American Dance Festival for three summers, Québec Été Danse, Harvard Summer School, SUNY, Purchase, Cornell, Trinity College, and NYU. He has conducted master classes and workshops throughout the world. His dances can be seen in the repertoires of Workcentrum Dans, the Modern Dance Theatre of Hong Kong, and EDAM, Vancouver, B.C. His work as a visual artist has been exhibited throughout the United States. Wong is the first Chinese American to receive a Guggenheim Fellowship in Choreography. Other awards include grants from the Foundation for Contemporary Performance Arts, the Jerome Robbins Foundation, the National Endowment for the Arts, the New York State Council on the Arts, and three from the Creative Artists Public Service (CAPS) program.

MEL WONG

Other Realms

I am interested in an awareness of another energy, a God or life force that permeates the universe. Art transcends everyday life in a spiritual sense so that the separate parts together become something beyond their own literalness. I'm interested in finding another energy we have yet to actualize on earth, and I try to depict this through movement. This to me is spirituality. Nature, mountains, trees, oceans, waterfalls, creatures, space travel, living in space—by permeating another kind of energy all these things take me beyond earthly thoughts into another realm.

My work reflects who I am and my dances use symbolism as a means to trigger the imagination of the viewer. The props and gestures are intended as universal, time-eternal symbols, each meaning something different according to the individual's experience. Though the overriding concept is very specific to each piece, the "meaning" in the choreography is abstract so that the audience can relate to it creatively.

A good piece has universal meaning. Within that there will be ideas pertinent to some individuals and not to others. My choreography doesn't necessarily set up something for the audience to realize, but I do choreograph about things meaningful to me that relate to contemporary life, such as the direction or emphasis people place on life, and I might try to suggest a change. Art gives hints about life and it functions in many ways. I believe that art does have a certain meaning, and I am trying to convey concepts or ideas which relate to life.

Choreography is not merely a challenge to me, but rather something I love to do. Each time, I try to be honest with myself, as honest as I can be. I view art as a cleansing process both for the viewer and definitely for me as an artist. My objective is to find something for myself, a new kind of relationship I have never before explored. I try to find something about the unknown, which for me is the universe and its spirituality, about existence in other realms. I'm trying to project this idea into my work while also expressing something about life on earth and its relationship to other parts of the world or universe. Though it sounds like an overwhelming task, that's what I'm exploring. And the greatest challenge for me is to feel satisfied within myself, to feel that I have found new relationships while making a statement.

I would also like to help people viewing my pieces to come to an understanding of—I hate to use the word because it's so closed and boxed in—but religion, in the sense of the unknown. I think of it more in terms of a spiritualism which holds no limits to one's spiritualness. Many times religion is limited because there are certain dogmatic rules and doctrines. For me, God can be an energy. I could call Him or Her God, Buddha, or Tao, but the simplest way to say it is that I'm searching for an unknown to help me become one with the universe. And while on my path, on my journey of finding this mysterious thing, or energy, or whatever, I would like to expose other people to my ideas.

Before I choreograph I usually read a lot about everything, from philosophy and humanitarian subjects to science fiction and *Consumer Report.* I don't necessarily set up a problem and try to resolve it, but I focus on an idea which is a mystery to me and start from there. I try to put myself in a mood or mindframe and act upon that mood.

I try to put myself in a state of awareness on a subconscious level, where the subconscious level becomes conscious through my movements. I love to daydream, and when I do, I'm really working —I'm letting the process begin to happen. That's how I work. As in the visual arts, my choreography is best when everything happens intuitively and spontaneously, and then crystallizes in my mind. I choreograph directly onto the dancers, then look at it and make changes or add onto it. In that way the piece evolves.

I think I have an Asian attitude of accepting what happens in my work and dealing with it. When I was going to art school, the style of painting was abstract or nonobjective. I would start making forms and shapes and sometimes, mysteriously, interesting shapes came up that I wasn't even aware of consciously. And I would accept that, look at it, and if it moved me and worked well within the context of the picture, I wouldn't rub it out because it wasn't premeditated, but accept it and incorporate it into the work.

That happens frequently in my choreography. Many times special things just happen and I accept them and they take me into another direction. Often when I'm choreographing it seems as if I'm not even doing it, somebody else is—and I really like that. Nothing is premeditated and there is no predetermined message to the audience. Each individual movement, for me, signifies a certain kind of abstract meaning, or gives a new relationship to movements, or a new way to view something, but it doesn't necessarily have to be defined. Much like hearing Bach or Beethoven, reacting to a color or seeing the ocean or mountains—my work strives to convey an intuitive feeling which is individualized by the viewer. There is no one interpretation.

Juxtaposed with abstract movement there are dancers performing rituals. People get confused and don't know how to react when they first see this, until they train themselves to realize that within the movement are certain gestures, related and interwoven in the phrases. Then they can more clearly understand the ritualistic tasks.

It's like the first time you listen to Stravinsky or John Cage, or see a nonobjective painting such as a Jackson Pollack—it's a mishmash. You have to learn how to form it and shape it and understand it. And then you say, "Oh, there *is* a structure. I get it!" The same applies to viewing dance. The way I work, you have to look at the whole stage and the juxtapositioning of the visual arts with the movement, rather than at one or two dancers.

In this age people can comprehend and digest information more quickly than people 100 years ago. A few generations back they stayed within a 15- to 20-mile radius, but now they travel all over the earth. This space-time concept is a reflection of our culture. Because there are more stimuli constantly bombarding us, the mind is forced to assimilate faster. On a space ship, one can't look at one monitor to know what the craft is doing. All the monitors and information must be focused on as a whole rather than separately.

I feel that dance should be viewed similarly and I put more information in, in less amount of time. Some critics say that my work is too dense, but this is the reason why. I work very fast to stimulate the spinal reflex so that the brain doesn't have a chance to analyze the movement, and it becomes a primordial instinct of learning and viewing.

It's like when you put your hand on a hot stove, you don't say, "Well, if I don't take it off, I'm going to burn my hand and have blisters." You automatically take it off. And that's what I work on— to train the eye to take in more information. Visual information can be assimilated faster than verbal, and once the reflex is stimulated, you comprehend a lot faster.

Time also slows down once an accelerated way of working or viewing has been learned. On a time continuum of A to B, if you're used to comprehending 3 kinds of information within that time and all of a sudden you're confronted with 12, you have to do something.

You may average only 6 or 7, but you have learned that much faster. In a sense, your mind has slowed down to analyze and comprehend the information, but in reality it has speeded up. Another example is a t'ai chi or kung fu master who can repel eight attackers at once. His mind has slowed down so that he can make decisions, but in reality it's going very fast. I think the same thing can happen when learning or viewing dance. The mind must slow down to work quickly, to comprehend everything, because time is so fleeting.

Maybe in the beginning I thought of myself as an experimental choreographer, but now I don't think about it. I'm not concerned with what kind of choreographer I am. Labels limit. Besides, an old idea can, in essence, be a new one. Postmodern dance, movement for movement's sake, with no other connotations but that, doesn't interest me anymore. Besides, I believe that movement does evoke emotion.

I studied dance with a number of people and something in my own movement, choreography, or in teaching has been retained from each one of them. In California I studied with Marc Wild, Carolyn Parks, Raoul Pausé, Alan Howard, Harold Christensen, Mia Slavenska, Carmelita Murachi, Victor Anderson, Frank Shaw, and Bill Ross. I even continued to practice my dancing when I was doing two years' active duty on a radar picket ship in the U.S. Navy (I worked it so that I didn't have to shoot a gun, but I did have to convince the sailors that it was okay for males to dance, and it ended up that quite a few of them wanted to learn!). Later, in New York, I received a scholarship to Balanchine's School of American Ballet, and also studied at the New York School of Ballet with Richard Thomas and Barbara Fallis, as well as American Ballet Theater School and at the Joffrey.

I studied modern dance in California at San Francisco State University, at Mills College, where I got an M.F.A. in the visual arts, and at UCLA, where I worked on a master's degree in dance. I also studied at Ann Halprin's Dancer's Workshop. In 1967 I went to New York City to take a Christmas course with Merce Cunningham. In 1968, he wired me a telegram asking me to join his company, and I performed as a member of the Merce Cunningham and Dance Company from 1968 to 1972.

Cunningham was the greatest influence on me, even before I joined the company. In 1962, when I first saw his work, I thought it was off the wall, but even then I got a feeling that I would work with him someday. By seeing Merce, I realized that the visual arts had a more unique relationship with modern dance than with ballet. His philosophy of discovering new and different ways to move, his criteria for making dance, the movement in relationship to the art objects, the rhythm, grouping and spacing, was all very different. It served as an important example which taught me not to be afraid to put anything together, to juxtapose elements.

Certainly my background with ballet and the Cunningham school has been influential, but I have tried to find my own way of moving. The breath, curves, lyrical movement, roundness, flow, the use of gravity and a controlled but loose, floppy abandon are important to me. My concern is for the total phrase and its flow, on the way the dancers move through space, rather than on the individual parts.

I choreograph in many different ways: by making drawings and beginning movement from them, or by having images in my mind which I try to reproduce. I like to make relationships between visual arts and dance so that the visual art objects (sculpture, paintings, movies, slides) express the same kind of idea as the movement, and it all functions as a whole. These elements give the audience more flexibility in projecting their own feelings, ideas, or reactions about the imagery and meaning in the pieces. I don't like a stage set where the set is not an integral part of the piece, where it's just decor. I want all of the elements, the visual arts, the music, and the dancing, to function as one.

I also make drawings relating to the piece, which give another dimension to the kind of feeling I want to communicate in my dances. Even though the drawings are separated from the actual dancing on stage, hopefully the same feeling or image is conveyed.

I have definite musical ideas which I want to create a spatial mood or ambience to help the movement propel itself. For many years now I've been working closely with composers Rob Kaplan and Skip La Plante. Although I don't dictate what kind of music they play, we have lengthy discussions about what I want to say. I hate to lock myself into any mode of choreographing because I have done it so many different ways.

Gesture and symbolism are used by me as a means to reflect the past as well as the present. Symbols from both Western and Eastern cultures are frequently incorporated in my dances. These have included bread, wine, birds, fish, snakes, candles, lanterns and other lights, rocks, water, smoke, incense, cloth, rope, sand, mirrors, books, geometric shapes, colors, and numbers, among others. Each of these symbols signifies something to the individual, according to his or her experience with the objects and gestures. It could act upon one's subconscious as well.

For example, in *Salt,* 1979, there was a man coughing and collapsing as he moved and spoke about his two apartments, wife, and business. The act of coughing could be interesting in a literal sense, or it could also be viewed symbolically—that the man was coughing because of his life style, a symbol of sickness and decadence.

In *A Town in Three Parts,* 1975, and *Harbor,* 1978, there were 35 trays of water, 14 by 14 inches, and 3 inches deep. The dancers moved within these trays, creating a sculpture, and the light shone onto the water, emitting a shimmering aura onto the backdrop. I have also used aquarium containers on stage, filled with colored water. In *Harbor,* one was red, one blue, and another yellow. When Chlorox was poured into the aquarium, the colors became clear. This has a certain symbolic meaning to me, an act of purification. Nudity also symbolizes purity and spirituality to me, and primary colors and numbers have symbolic significance too.

Streams. Mel Wong Dance Company. Valerie Bergman, Rosemary Camera, Susan Alexander. Photo: © Johan Elbers 1986.

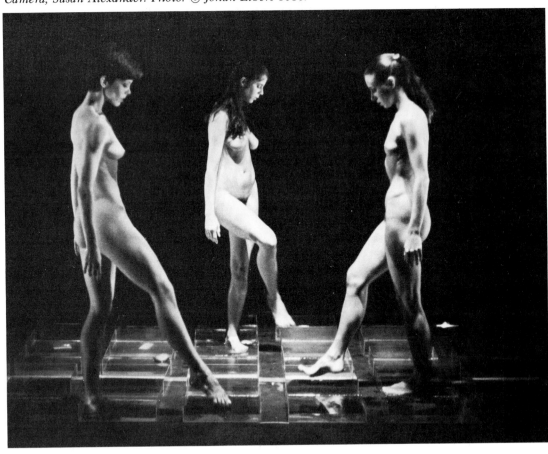

By creating an environment in space for the dancers to move in, images are created. To do this, I've used trays of water, ramps, walls, strings, torches, and different kinds of lighting—gas, candles, and railroad lanterns—and even an electric train.

In *ZIP CODE,* 1972, a 12-hour dance, the space was changed by incense in a huge Plexiglas box. The audience watched the box first fill up with smoke, and then they saw it dissipate as the box was lifted. In *Catalogue 34,* 1973, the dance occurred simultaneously on three levels. The audience could view the other levels on video, so it was like three-dimensional chess. There were sculptures made out of wax, melted by torches during the performance, thus creating another kind of image. There were also booklets which instructed the audience to perform certain tasks (e.g., "hold your breath for ten counts," or "clench your fist"), and they documented dances previously choreographed on a highway with cars speeding by. The same choreography was repeated in the performing space, a different environment.

What I am exploring is new relationships between dance and the visual arts. Visual art objects, for me, give another kind of image and information as another way to relate to movement. In my earliest choreography, often the visual art would dominate the pieces. The movement was not as complex. Now the movement flows more, the choreography is more intricate. Now there are many focuses within the choreography and with its relationship to the visual arts. It is up to the audience to let whatever interests them dominate.

Salt was a piece performed in the Cunningham Dance Studio in June 1979, with video by Dennis Diamond. There was an exhibit related to the piece in another studio which contained drawings as well as sculptures of feet, arms, and faces, made out of plaster.

A cardboard wall, 50 feet long by 8 feet high, divided the dance space and the audience in half. On one side was "earth"; the other, "space." The events in each section took about half an hour and at the end, the audience was instructed by guides to go through a door in the wall to watch the action on the other side.

Dialogue occurred on both sides. It interests me to have events happening simultaneously—the audience could hear hints of what was happening on the other side, and in this way another dimension or a different relationship was added to the piece.

On the earth side, a guide from the future related that it was the year 2000, and a few months later the earth would disintegrate. The people on earth were trying to figure out what fell out of the sky. They were speculating about the possibility of the earth's disintegration, even though there was "enough of everything on earth to supply the people for the next 10,000 years."

Peaks. Mel Wong Dance Company. Hope Mauzerall, Gayle Ziaks, Susan Alexander, Valerie Bergman. Photo: © Johan Elbers 1986.

A woman washed her hair. The guide related: "During earth's history, washing hair and cleansing the body had some sort of meaning."

On the space station side, dancers were "searching for the cause of the earth's destruction." A dancer fluttered her fingers with her arms outstretched, lowering them from shoulder height, while another related that this action was a symbol for water. "It's an important clue to the earth's destruction because during the earth's development, the people acquired the use of symbolism, but it was lost towards the end of the twentieth century. During the final years on earth, new symbols were never adopted to replace the old and forgotten ones."

It was also suggested that the earth's disintegration was due to the changing of the poles, or because the "earth drifted into cosmic dust which blocked the sun's rays and caused an ice age." But everyone knew that *"it* was the people." "But I think we all know that it *was* the people."

There was an asteroid section where both the past and the future could be seen at once. "We see the people of the spaceship and the people of earth. The people of the past and the people of present. We are entering another cosmos."

The movement on the earth side was more tribal, with mundane gestures such as someone smoking a cigarette, or children playing hopscotch. On the space side the movement was lighter, with emotionally detached gestures and unison group dancing.

Booklets were given to each spectator and videos instructed page turns. The booklets contained images of earth and space, which conveyed certain feelings related to different sections of the piece. The booklets could be viewed as visual correlations to the movement imagery.

Video on the earth side presented symbolic images of bread, wine, and candles. On the space side it scanned the New York City skyline from the top of the World Trade Center. During the second half of the piece, the wall was removed, and the video was placed at the edge of the stage. To me it conveyed another relationship to the piece, and it also broke up the space, thus changing the dance space.

It projected different colors: red, green, blue, and yellow. Red could symbolize danger (blood), or the energy of the life force, both love and hate. Green could be the earth and its vegetation. Blue has spiritual connotations symbolizing the heavens and heavenly love, and yellow may mean either the sun and divinity, or deceit. Colors have dual meanings, as do most things in life.

Throughout the piece there appeared geometric symbols: a triangle (the Trinity, or beginning, middle, and end), a square (earth), and a circle (completeness, the universe). The audience may or may not have been aware of these, but they were there and existed. And they related to the dancing in various ways. At the very end of the piece, dancers came out with mirrors, put them on the floor, and reflected these images to the audience, thus ending the dance.

In the second half, when the wall was taken down, it was all movement, which gave a feeling of releasing energy from another world, or an awareness of another energy from another world. I suppose it could be called the emotion of hope, that we are optimistic about the world and that life will continue. This was conveyed especially when the dancers were out on the balcony of the Cunningham studio, waving into space, while the studio lights inside were dim. And then some of the dancers came back in and reflected the symbols to the audience, so that they could see that the symbols were always there, just as the energy throughout history has always been there.

What I said in 1979 still applies to my thinking now, in 1985—perhaps even more so, because I feel that mysteries of the universe are beginning to open up. It seems to me that many artists of the sixties generation are giving back to the people what they learned through experimenting with meditation, drugs, reading from spiritual books, free love, the "back to nature" life style, and the general attempt to go "to the source," to the roots of living. Artists such as Steven Spielberg, George Lucas, and Ron Howard in the film industry, John Lennon and Philip Glass in music, Robert Wilson in theater, James Turell in light sculpture, and even Shirley MacLaine in her books, are educating and exposing people to a new energy or outlook.

A lot of dancing seems to be behind in this aspect because it is

Mel Wong at the Great Wall. Photo: Connie Kreemer.

following the punk trend, popular iconography having to do with TV-type entertainment, social discourse, sex, personal relationships, or pyrotechnical feats. My pieces have always expressed something about humanity and spirituality, but the *Buddha* series, beginning in 1984 with *Sitting Bull Meets Buddha in the Reading Room* (which included 43 dancers, 3 motorcycles, 2 horses, and 100 balloons), has blended Eastern and Western spirituality more overtly. The premiere of *Buddha Meets Einstein at the Great Wall*, 1985, furthered that, using music of Philip Glass, from the album, "KOYAANIS-QATSI." Then my last piece, *Buddha at The Mount*, was again a blending of Eastern and Western spirituality, but this time using Mozart's requiem—the great Mass in C Minor. This piece concentrated more on Christian symbolism, with the "Mount" signifying Jesus at the Mount of Olives.

I seem to be becoming more literal, direct, and obvious, yet still have abstraction in the movement, blending very technical dancing with theater—though the emphasis remains primarily on the dancing. I don't know why I'm more literal now—I don't understand it. I always do a little meditation before I start a new piece, and for some reason it just feels right now, to be more literal, so I go with that impulse. It's like with using Mozart's mass—before it didn't feel right, but now it does.

We don't question Mount Shasta, the Grand Tetons, or the Gobi Desert—they exist and give out energy for those who want to receive it. That's what I'm doing with my pieces—they are there for those who want to look.

October 1, 1979,
with additions
in August 1985

Date	Title of Work	Place and Details
1970	*Dance for One Mile*	Various streets, New York City. Performed by Mel Wong Dance Company.
1970	*Subway Piece*	Various subway stations, New York City. Performed by Mel Wong Dance Company.
June 1971	*Continuing Dance Project*	Cubiculo, New York City; Prospect Park, Brooklyn, New York City; Statue of Liberty, New York Harbor. Performed by Mel Wong Dance Company. 20 minutes.
August 1971	*Water Walk*	Cubiculo, New York City. Performed by Mel Wong Dance Company. Lighting by Blu. 25 trays filled with water. 15 minutes.
October 1971	*Wax Walk*	Cubiculo, New York City. Lighting by Blu. Performed by Mel Wong Dance Company. Wax sculptures that melted. 13 minutes.
October 1971	*Ramp Walk*	Cubiculo, New York City. Performed by Mel Wong Dance Company. Lighting by Blu. Ramp on 45-degree angle, 9 feet high, 8 feet long, 4 feet wide. 12 minutes.
June 1972	*ZIP CODE*	Washington Square Methodist Church, New York City. Music by Gordon Mumma. Performed by Mel Wong Dance Company. Lighting by Blu. 12 hours, 6 P.M. to 6 A.M.
September 1973	*Catalogue 34*	Herbert F. Johnson Museum of Art, Cornell University, Ithaca, New York. Music by Gordon Mumma and Pauline Oliveros. Performed by Mel Wong Dance Company. Mixed media, paintings, sculpture, video, slides. 2 hours, 30 minutes.
1974	*Four or Five Hours with Her*	Cornell University, Ithaca, New York. Performed by student repertory. Mixed media, video, sculpture. 15 minutes.
1975	*Rocktown*	State University of New York, College at Purchase. Sound collage. Performed by student repertory. Mixed media, video. 45 minutes.
1975	*A Town in Three Parts*	Cathedral of St. John the Divine, New York City. Performed by Mel Wong Dance Company. Mixed media, with 14 dancers. 4 hours.

Date	Title of Work	Place and Details
December 1975	*Bath*	State University of New York, College at Purchase. Music by Denman Maroney. Performed by student repertory. Mixed media. 45 minutes.
1976	*Wells*	Wells College, Aurora, New York. Performed by Mel Wong Dance Company.
June 1976	*Breath*	St. Peter's Church, New York City. Music by Denman Maroney. Performed by Mel Wong Dance Company. Lighting by Andy Tron. Mixed media. 1 hour, 15 minutes.
1976	*C-10-20-W*	American Dance Festival. Connecticut College, New London, Connecticut. Music by Skip La Plante. Performed by student repertory. Multimedia, with 18 dancers. 45 minutes.
December 1976	*Glass*	American Theatre Laboratory, Dance Theatre Workshop, New York City. Full production. Music by Beethoven and Skip La Plante. Performed by Mel Wong Dance Company. Environmental sculptures, video, paintings, with 13 dancers, 3 children. 3 hours.
May 1977	*Quick Run*	State University of New York, College at Purchase. Music, singing, and dialogue by Mel Wong. Performed by student repertory. Mixed media, three different environments, with 37 dancers. 12 hours, 8 P.M. to 8 A.M.
June 1977	*Envelope*	Merce Cunningham Studio, New York City. Performed by Mel Wong Dance Company. Music by Skip La Plante. Video, program booklet of drawings. 1 hour, 30 minutes.

Date	Title of Work	Place and Details
July 1977	*Trees*	American Dance Festival, Connecticut College, New London. Music by Skip La Plante. Dialogue by Mel Wong. Mixed media. 1 hour, 30 minutes.
July 1977	*I Was Flying the Other Day*	American Dance Festival, Connecticut College, New London. Music by Skip La Plante. Six 3-minute pieces.
March 1978	*Harbor*	American Theatre Laboratory, Dance Theater Workshop, New York City, full production. Music by Skip La Plante. Performed by Mel Wong Dance Company. Drawings exhibited. 1 hour, 45 minutes.
1978	*The Organization, Performed by the Organization: We Are Looking for the Letter*	State University of New York, College at Purchase. Music by J. S. Bach. Dialogue by Mel Wong. Performed by student repertory. 25 minutes.
November 1978	*You See It All Started Like This . . .*	Dance Umbrella Entermedia Theater, New York City. Music by Skip La Plante and Rob Kaplan. Performed by Mel Wong Dance Company. Lighting by Andy Tron. Mixed media. Dialogue, drawings exhibited, film, slides, paintings, and sculptures. 1 hour, 30 minutes.
December 1978	*Door 1, Door 2, Door 3*	State University of New York, College at Purchase. Music by Rob Kaplan. Performed by student repertory. 27 minutes.
1979	*Epoxy*	State University of New York, College at Purchase. Sound collage. Performed by student repertory. Mixed media. 15 minutes.

Date	Title of Work	Place and Details
June 1979	*Salt*	Merce Cunningham Studio, New York City. Music by Rob Kaplan. Performed by Mel Wong Dance Company. Video by Dennis Diamond. Program booklet, drawings and sculpture; 50-foot wall dividing dance space. 1 hour, 20 minutes.
November 1979	*Peaks*	Dance Umbrella, Camera Mart/Stage One, New York City. Music by Rob Kaplan. Performed by Mel Wong Dance Company. Mixed media. Drawings and sculpture exhibited. 1 hour, 15 minutes.
May 1980	*Wings-Arc*	Music by Skip La Plante. Stones and logs. 30 minutes.
	Streams	Music by Rob Kaplan. Performed in 30 plexiglass trays of water. 8 minutes.
May 1980	*Phones*	Music by Rob Kaplan. 19 minutes.
		Three dances, *Wings-Arc, Streams,* and *Phones,* all presented at Performing Arts Center, Emanu-El Midtown YM-YWHA, New York City. Performed by Mel Wong Dance Company. Costumes designed by Allison Lances. Lighting by Colman Rupp. Drawings exhibited.
June 1980	*Untitled*	Lecture-demonstration, George Washington University, Washington, D.C. Music by Rob Kaplan. 45 minutes.
August 1980	*Bouncing*	Pepsico Summerfare '80, State University of New York, College at Purchase. Music by Rob Kaplan. Performed by students. 19 minutes.
January 1981	*Palms*	YM-YWHA, West Orange, New Jersey. Music by Rob Kaplan. Costumes by Gabriel Berry. Performed by Mel Wong Dance Company. 21 minutes.
May 1981	*Merge*	Music by Rob Kaplan. Video by Dennis Diamond. 30 minutes.
	Shuttle	Music by Skip La Plante. Props by Mel Wong. 15 minutes.

Date	*Title of Work*	*Place and Details*
May 1981	*Solo 1, Solo 2, Solo 3*	3 minutes each.
		Three dances, *Merge, Shuttle,* and *Solo,* all performed at Hunter College Playhouse, Hunter College, New York City, by Mel Wong Dance Company. Costumes by Gabriel Berry. Lighting by Colman Rupp.
January 1982	*Seasons*	Trinity College, Hartford, Connecticut. Music by Beethoven. Solo for Connie Kreemer. Lighting by John Woolley. 7 minutes.
March 1982	*Prologue A, B, C*	Music by Rob Kaplan. 7 minutes.
	Migration	Music by Rob Kaplan. 15 minutes.
	Telegram	Music by Rob Kaplan and Skip La Plante. 19 minutes.
	From Connecticut to New York	Music by Skip La Plante. 7 minutes.
	Desert Ghosts	Music by Skip La Plante. 25 minutes.
		Five dances, *Prologue, Migration, Telegram, Connecticut,* and *Desert Ghosts,* all presented at Riverside Dance Festival, New York City. Performed by Mel Wong Dance Company. Costumes by Gabriel Berry. Lighting by Blu. Mixed media. Drawings exhibited.
May 1982	*Catch*	The Dance Place, Washington, D.C. Music by Rob Kaplan. Performed by Mel Wong Dance Company. Costumes by Gabriel Berry. 15 minutes.
December 1982	*Zephyr*	Riverside Dance Festival, New York City. Music by Skip La Plante. Costumes by Gabriel Berry. Lighting by Blu. Solo for Gayle Ziaks. 5 minutes.
December 1982	*Paris*	Riverside Dance Festival, New York City. Music by Skip La Plante. Performed by Mel Wong Dance Company. Costumes by Gabriel Berry. Lighting by Blu. Abstract 12-foot sculpture.

Date	*Title of Work*	*Place and Details*
May 1983	*Jade*	La Mama E.T.C., New York City. Music by Skip La Plante. Mixed media, with 36 performers. Costumes by Gabriel Berry. Lighting by Blu. 1 hour, 20 minutes.
July 1983	*Untitled*	Music by Poulenc. 12 minutes.
	Untitled	Music by Haydn. 25 minutes. Two *Untitled* dances performed at Lac du Nations, Sherbrooke, Canada, by members of Qúebec Été Danse.
October 1983	*Eclipse*	Music by Rob Kaplan. Solo for Mel Wong. 7 1/2 minutes. Performed at the Asian Arts Festival, City Hall, Hong Kong.
May 1984	*Future Antiquities*	The Whitney Museum of American Art at Philip Morris. Music by Ron Kuivila. Collaboration with environmental light sculptor Cathey Billian. Performed by Mel Wong Dance Company. Costumes by Gabriel Berry. 1 hour.
March 1985	*Buddha Meets Einstein at the Great Wall*	Asia Society, New York City. Collaboration with computer video artist Ron Rocco and architect Michael Janne. Performed by Mel Wong Dance Company. Costumes by Gabriel Berry. Lighting by Blu. 1 hour.

Commissioned Choreography

Date	*Title of Work*	*Place and Details*
1974	*Watertown*	Harvard Summer School Dance Center, Cambridge, Massachusetts. Mixed media. 1 hour, 20 minutes.
January 1978	*Winds*	State University of New York, College at Purchase. Music by Michael Blair. 20 minutes.
August 1979	*Windows*	Werkcentrum Dans, Rotterdam, The Netherlands. Music by Rob Kaplan. 27 minutes.
August 1980	*Kiezelstenen (Pebbles)*	Werkcentrum Dans, Rotterdam, The Netherlands. Music by Rob Kaplan. 24 minutes.
November 1980	*Imprint*	Solo for Junko Kikuchi, Japan House, New York City. Music by Rob Kaplan. 8 minutes.

Date	Title of Work	Place and Details
June 1981	*Rush*	Solo for Douglas Bolivar, Dancers in Repertory. Japan Society, New York City. Music by Rob Kaplan. 6 minutes.
July 1981	*Jelly Bean (Red)*	7 minutes.
	Jelly Bean (White)	19 minutes.
	Jelly Bean (Blue)	3 minutes.
		Three *Jelly Bean* dances commissioned by New York University, New York City. Music by György Ligeti and Rob Kaplan.
November 1981	*Towers*	State University of New York, College at Purchase. Music by Rob Kaplan. Mixed media. 20 minutes.
March 1982	*Landings*	Basement Workshop, Morita Dance Company, New York City. Music by Rob Kaplan and Skip La Plante. 20 minutes.
June 1982	*Early Days*	92nd Street YM-YWHA, New York City. Music by Michael Cherry. 12 minutes.
July 1982	*Manhattanville Summer Piece*	Manhattanville College, Purchase, New York. Music by David Yokum. Performed by students. 20 minutes.
April 1983	*Running Times*	Manhattanville College, Purchase, New York. Music by Charles Blenzig. Performed by students. 16 minutes.
May 1983	*Ariel*	George Mason University, Fairfax, Virginia. Music by Rob Kaplan. Performed by students. 15 minutes.
June 1983	*Scenario on a Bridge*	Brooklyn Anchorage, New York City. Commissioned by Creative Time, Inc. Collaboration with architect Micheal Janne for the Brooklyn Bridge centennial celebration. Music by Rob Kaplan, Bob Kuttruf, Skip La Plante. Performed by the Mel Wong Dance Company. Costumes by Gabriel Berry. 1 hour.

Date	*Title of Work*	*Place and Details*
October 1983	*Breakwater*	20 minutes.
	Running Lights	25 minutes.
	Twilight	16 minutes.
		Three dances commissioned by Modern Dance Theatre of Hong Kong, Asian Arts Festival. Performed at City Hall, Hong Kong. Music by Rob Kaplan.
September 1984	*Sitting Bull Meets Buddha in the Reading Room*	Neuberger Museum, Purchase, New York. Music by Skip La Plante. Choreographed outdoors around Siah Armajani's sculpture *Reading Room III.* Performed by 43 students at State University of New York, College at Purchase, with 3 motorcycles and 2 horses. 55 minutes.
July 1985	*Buddha at the Mount*	Western Front, Vancouver, B.C. Music by Mozart. Performed simultaneously outdoors and indoors, by EDAM (Experimental Dance and Music) and 10 performers. 25 minutes.

Catalogue 34. Mel Wong. Photo: Randi Korn.

Lucinda Childs

Photo: Peggy Jarrell Kaplan.

LUCINDA CHILDS

Lucinda Childs began her career as a choreographer and dancer in 1963 as an original member of the Judson Dance Theatre in New York. A decade later she formed the Lucinda Childs Dance Company, for which she has choreographed over 25 large-scale ensemble works and solos.

In 1976 Childs collaborated with Robert Wilson and Philip Glass on *Einstein on the Beach;* she received a Creative Artists Public Service award for her choreography and a Village Voice Obie award for her performance in the opera. Since 1979, Childs has concentrated on creating large-scale collaborative productions. The first of these, *Dance,* 1979, was supported by a Guggenheim Fellowship. The third, *Available Light,* was commissioned by the Museum of Contemporary Art in Los Angeles, where it premiered in 1983. Anna Kisselgoff of the *New York Times* called it both a "major breakthrough" for Childs and a "major work altogether."

The following year, 1984, Childs was commissioned by the Pacific Northwest Ballet to choreograph a ballet titled *Cascade,* with music by Steve Reich. In the same year she was also invited by the Paris Opera Ballet to create *Premiere Orage.* In December of 1984 Childs appeared in the revival of *Einstein on the Beach,* which featured new dances for Acts II and III, choreographed by Childs and performed by her dance company.

The Lucinda Childs Dance Company is supported in part by the Dance and Inter-Arts programs of the National Endowment for the Arts and by the New York State Council on the Arts.

LUCINDA CHILDS

After graduating in 1962 as a dance major from Sarah Lawrence College, where I studied with Bessie Schönberg, I became a student at the Cunningham studio in New York. There I came in contact with Yvonne Rainer, also a Cunningham student. Judith Dunn, a member of Cunningham's dance company who had been one of my teachers at Sarah Lawrence, encouraged me to see Rainer's performances. In the summer of 1962 I saw Rainer's *Ordinary Dance* at the Judson Memorial Church. The piece was entirely made up of simple gestures, and Rainer spoke while performing them. What impressed me was that she was able to sustain a sensibility that other choreographers whose work I admired, such as Merce Cunningham, Katherine Litz, and James Waring, only cared to touch on in their work.

The following fall I decided to join the Judson Dance Theatre, which Yvonne Rainer had recently co-founded with Steve Paxton. A major influence was, of course, John Cage. The composer Robert Dunn had been working with many members of the group on adaptations and interpretations of Cage's ideas. I participated in Dunn's last series of workshops, and I developed my own approach using objects and, in some cases, monologues that made intermittent reference to what I was doing.[1] My involvement with objects was subordinated to formal concerns with respect to time and space, in order to arrive at a tension equivalent to any highly structured choreographic form, while consisting solely of nondance movements.

During the period between 1963 and 1966, I created 13 works, mostly solos, of which *Carnation* (1964) has been the most frequently performed. *Street Dance* (1964) is one of the most important works from this period, as some of the main ideas generated in this piece have reemerged in my later work. *Street Dance* was performed on

[1]See "Lucinda Childs: A Portfolio," *Artforum*, February 1973.

a street in lower Manhattan for a group of spectators who were observing from a loft window. While the spectators were not able to see in exact detail what the performers on the street were doing, information about these details was played back to them on a tape which was perfectly synchronized with each of the performers' actions. The spectator was thus called upon to envisage, in an imagined sort of way, visual information that existed beyond the range of his actual perception. This idea comes up again and again in my work in the seventies when the same material is constantly introduced from a different point of view. Each time it is seen again, it is slightly removed from its original mode of presentation. This in turn sets up a field of cross reference for the spectator to engage in.

This was a difficult and perplexing period as I struggled to establish a plausible aesthetic expression in the midst of a welter of contradictory influences.[2] The making of each work felt like a rigorous exercise in problem solving, in which I was operating under an extraordinary self-imposed handicap. I was like someone religiously determined to make an omelette with anything but an egg. During "Nine Evenings of Theatre and Engineering," in 1966, I had the experience of collaborating with engineers from Bell Laboratories to create a work titled *Vehicle.* While the process of collaboration has played a major role in my later work, I was starting to have my doubts about the self-imposed strict observance of broken rules. A major influence at this time came from the world of the visual arts. I was particularly impressed by the paintings of Jasper Johns, Barnett Newman, and Frank Stella. In my own work, I continued to make dances with nondance movement, but I decided to abandon objects and monologues as a framework to put them in.

The result was a work for three dancers called *Untitled Trio.* Working with grid patterns and simple geometric shapes, I continually manipulated the relationship of one dancer to another, so that individual phrase patterns could be seen in increasingly complex configurations as they were counterpointed against each other. The shifts from one variation to another, at times imperceptible, never revealed the underlying structure. Nor was that structure important in and of itself—or dictated by any system, serial or other. This approach opened up for me a vast new range of possibilities, and I stopped performing at this point in order to explore them.

In 1973 I formed my dance company. The previous year I had seen a performance given by Judy Padow and Batya Zamir, who

---

[2]In 1963–1964 I was also a member of the James Waring Company and appeared in works by Merle Marsicano, Beverly Schmidt, and Aileen Passlof.

Lucinda Childs. Photo: Thomas Victor.

were working with some of the same problems that I had been exploring. What impressed me was that most of the rich movement ideas that came out of their working together derived from an extremely restricted range of movement, elaborating primarily on change of direction in walking.[3] I was fortunate to have Judy Padow as a member of my company until 1979.

Starting with a revised version of *Untitled Trio* in 1973, I created 16 dances—solos and works for small ensembles—between 1973 and 1978. Of these dances, all between 10 and 13 minutes long, *Particular Reel* (1973), *Radial Courses* (1976), *Melody Excerpt* (1977), and *Interior Drama* (1977) still remain in the company's repertory. *Calico Mingling* and *Katema* have been documented by the film makers Babette Mangolte and Renato Berta.

[3]See my "Notes on Judy Padow," *Dance Magazine,* November 1974, and "Notes on Batya Zamir," *Artforum,* June 1973.

The dances from this period were performed without musical accompaniment, as I found that the sounds made by the footwork of the dancers had a musical quality of their own. The effort involved in keeping a consistent steady tempo among the dancers took tremendous concentration. Each dancer's part was meticulously recorded on a score, which illustrated in time frame intervals the overhead view of each dancer's path in space.

In early 1975, I saw Robert Wilson's *A Letter to Queen Victoria* in New York on Broadway at the Anta Theatre. It was the first theater performance that I had seen since my childhood that revived my enthusiasm about acting. Several months later Wilson invited me to participate in his new production with Philip Glass, *Einstein on the Beach*. I collaborated as both performer and choreographer. What was especially pleasing to me in my involvement with this five-hour long, full-scale production was to bring to it the kind of performance quality that I had developed as a dancer in the sixties, and to choreograph a solo section to Philip Glass's music. *Einstein on the Beach* was presented in New York at the Metropolitan Opera House in November 1976 and toured in Europe. When *Einstein on the Beach* was revived in 1984 at the Brooklyn Academy of Music, I re-created my leading role, but also choreographed the "Field Dances" for Acts II and III, which were performed by members of my dance company.

I worked with Wilson again during 1977 and 1978, appearing with him in his two-act play, *I Was Sitting On My Patio This Guy Appeared I Thought I Was Hallucinating.* This production was presented at the Cherry Lane Theatre in New York in May 1977 and also toured through the United States and Europe.

Dance, a full-length evening work, was the first in a series of collaborative works that I have begun to create since 1979. *Dance* was commissioned by Harvey Lichtenstein for the proscenium stage of the Opera House at the Brooklyn Academy of Music. Philip Glass composed the music for all five parts of *Dance,* and the visual artist Sol LeWitt designed the decor.

I had become familiar with Glass's music through working on *Einstein on the Beach,* but I found that even for the solo section that I choreographed for the opera, I preferred to work within the structure of the music, rather than treat the combination of his music and my dancing as some sort of collage. The fact that our work was compatible aesthetically emphasized, from my point of view, the need for a strong concern with how the two structures were put together. The choreography was developed in strict relation to the musical score, sometimes matching the metric intervals in Glass's music, and sometimes overlapping those intervals with different counts. A score for each of the five parts indicated the

Dance #3. Lucinda Childs Dance Company. Cynthia Hedstrom, Graham Conley, Daniel McCusker, Judy Padow. Photo: Lois Greenfield.

exact relationship of each dancer's movements to the music. The punctuated exits and entrances of dancers to and from the wings of the proscenium stage made for a kind of visual counterpoint, as they plunged in or out of sight on a given down beat in the music. This was especially apparent in the opening *Dance #1* from *Dance,* when the dancers swept across the space in pairs on horizontal paths with increasingly complex combinations of 12-count, 24-count, and 48-count phrases.

LeWitt chose to introduce film as a visual element that functioned as an integral part of the dancing. He filmed parts of three of the five dance sections in 35-millimeter black and white film. In performance the film projection was perfectly synchronized with the dancers on stage so that when the dancers on film appeared, they were always at that same point in the dance. At times the film image seemed to chase the dancers, sweeping across the stage along with them. Through shifts in the camera angle and changes of scale (the dancers seen sometimes in close-up, sometimes in long shot), the spectator's point of view was subjected to an ingenious series of manipulations. Sometimes LeWitt projected the film directly above the dancers on the same scale, creating a perfect double set of dancers; with split-screen images he displaced them further to the left and right; and he even enclosed image within image.

Dance #3. Lucinda Childs Dance Company. Ande Peck, Megan Walker.
Photo: Lois Greenfield.

My second evening-length collaborative work, *Relative Calm*, was also commissioned by the Brooklyn Academy of Music in 1981. The music was composed by Jon Gibson and the lights and decor were by Robert Wilson. Each of the four sections is a pictorial representation of a time of day. In the first section, "Rise" (dawn), eight dancers in white are positioned on a wide diagonal in the blue light of a lingering starry night designed by Wilson. The dancers pass between each other in pairs or four at a time, traveling continuously up and down the full length of the diagonal, each adhering to a particular diagonal path. The opening phrase is slow and continuous, and as each dancer in turn picks it up, the phrase is continued among them like a ripple.

The second section, "Race" (midday), is a quartet. Wilson used slides to project geometric images onto the cyclorama. A series of split-second geometric cartoons, programmed by computer to keep time to the music, popped into view behind a quartet of dancers, vigorously executing 17-count phrases. The four dancers were doubled in different ways against each other so that the phrase of one pair appeared to invade the space of the other, though never disturbing the fixed parallel relationship between each pair.

The third section, "Reach" (twilight), was a solo in which I was framed in a huge wedge of light that cut both stage and cyclorama diagonally in half. The solo elaborated on the turning variations introduced in the opening section but on the opposite diagonal. As each phrase increased in length and became more densely punctuated with turns, the overlapping layers of Gibson's soprano saxophone tones (initially sharp and percussive) blended together.

In the final section, "Return" (midnight), the eight dancers performed fragments of phrases from the second section. The dancers were positioned on stage in two diamond formations: a quartet of men on one side and a quartet of women on the other. A gradual invasion of one quartet's territory by the other began and developed in a cumulative fashion—at first one quartet in alternation with the other, and finally both quartets simultaneously building to a peak of complexity. Eight pools of white light were beamed down on the stage and flickered on and off, marking the in-place positions of the dancers, while huge geometrical light patterns—again, slide images programmed by computer to keep time with the music—flashed onto the cyclorama. As they increased in size, they eventually spilled out onto the stage itself.

In *Dance* and *Relative Calm* I continued to build phrases from simple movements, but the traditional dance vocabulary has begun to emerge. This vocabulary is essentially reinterpreted by me and my dancers in terms of the dynamic that we use. Each phrase has accents in it, but the accents are much less extreme than those I associate with other techniques. The dancers are either moving continuously or they are absolutely still. When they are moving continuously they maintain a vertical balance as they pass through one position to go on to the next. The turns have no preparation, and the momentum of each phrase is never broken until they stop. One sees in fleeting moments a typical dance position such as arabesque, passé, tendu plié, but the dancers are only momentarily arrested in these positions, or they merely pass through the end point of a position in the process of going on to the next one. Similarly, the arms are never fixed in one position or another but are used for control in executing changes of direction.

As a clear and precise articulation of the movement is absolutely crucial, I seek dancers who have strong backgrounds in either Cunningham or classical technique. In the sixties, classical training for the modern dancer was a more controversial issue, but by now it is a common practice and, in my opinion, an essential part of a modern dancer's training. I am particularly grateful to Maggie Black, who devotes a considerable amount of her time to guiding modern dancers; her help has made an enormous difference.

Without well-trained dancers, the subtle dynamics of my work would be lost. While the moderate dynamic that I use stays in a range that makes it possible for the dancers to span longer periods of time than in other kinds of work, the demands put on them in terms of concentration are enormous. For several years now Meg Harper, Nan Friedman, Steve Bromer, Michael Ing, and Garry Reigenborn have been working with me, and more recently Janet Kaufman, Raissa Lerner, Christine Philion, and Timothy Conboy have joined the company. Daniel McCusker was in the company from 1977 to 1983 and has begun to work as a choreographer on his own.

Since 1980, I have also been choreographing ballets for classically trained dancers. I have been invited twice by the Paris Opera Ballet: in 1981 I choreographed *Mad Rush,* with music by Philip Glass, and in 1984, *Premier Orage,* with music by Dimitri Shostakovich and a set by Roberto Platé. For the Pacific Northwest Ballet in Seattle, I choreographed *Cascade* in 1984 with music by Steve Reich (*Octet,* composed in 1979) and *Clarion* in 1986, with music by Paul Chihara. Extending in these works the style of my most recent repertory, I continue to explore rich and still untapped possibilities for merging the modern and classical idioms. I also find it challenging to work with the special capabilities of the classically trained dancer.

My third full-scale collaborative production, *Available Light,* was commissioned by the Museum of Contemporary Art in Los Angeles and had its premiere there in September 1983 in the "Temporary Contemporary" interim exhibition space. A split-level set was designed for me by the architect Frank Gehry (who also designed the "Temporary Contemporary"). The music was by John Adams, the costumes by Ronaldus Shamask, and the lighting by Beverly Emmons.

The result of my collaboration with Frank Gehry was quite comparable to the result obtained from working with Sol LeWitt in 1979. What both artists furnished for me was a visual construct that allowed me to develop one of the prevailing themes of my choreography: doubling. LeWitt achieved this in *Dance* through filmed images that I described earlier. Gehry achieved a comparable effect through the use of the split-level set, which consisted of two freestanding wood structures, one below and in front of the other. The stage area provided by the larger, lower structure corresponded in its dimensions to those of the average stage. The somewhat irregularly shaped structure in the rear provided a second upper stage for two or three additional dancers who, from behind and 5 feet above, picked up on different clusters of movement patterns of one or more of the dancers below them. The dancers on the upper level sometimes repeated movements exactly, sometimes with a delay in counts or in opposite directions or on opposite sides. I found it quite magical to observe the exchanges between doubling partners across the separation of the two structures. The dancers were rotated periodically in the course of the 50-minute work, so that all 11 dancers eventually danced on both levels.

Throughout the piece, dancers appeared or disappeared from three different points on the set. This treatment of dancers' exits and entrances originated in the "Temporary Contemporary" space and inspired Gehry's ingenious idea for the version of the set he designed for the proscenium stage at the Brooklyn Academy: the four tunnels under the overhanging upper level through which dancers almost magically appeared and departed. Although the theatrical adaptation of *Available Light* was an ambitious undertaking, it did prove possible to create a two-level stage for the proscenium space at the Brooklyn Academy of Music that had the same dimensions of floor space as the original set. In the end I preferred the version for the theater, as it was an important step in the collaboration toward making the piece work within the context of traditional theater architecture.

In the sixties the dances that I created called for miscellaneous performing environments. Now the challenge of presenting my collaborations on the traditional proscenium stage is as important to me as the collaboration itself. It would perhaps be reasonable to involve contemporary artists in theatrical collaboration by having them put their signatures on existing or known theatrical devices, such as drops, and traditionally constructed scenery. In my work I have categorically avoided this in order to bring the ideas of the artists together in a way that reflects their work in a plastic sense. The challenge to the artists is perhaps as great as the challenge to the audiences.

Portraits in Reflection, created in 1986, is my fourth full-length production for the company. The work is in four parts with music commissioned for each part for harpsichord and violin by the composers Michael Galasso, Michael Nyman, Allen Shawn, and Elizabeth Swados. The decor, designed by the photographer Robert Mapplethorpe, consisted of photographic equipment adapted for theatrical use, as well as projected images. The costumes were designed by Ronaldus Shamask, and the lighting by Gregory Meeh.

*January 8, 1982,
revised August 1985*

Date	*Title of Work*	*Place and Details*
January 30, 1963	*Pastime*	Judson Memorial Church, New York City.
June 23, 1963	*Three Pieces*	Judson Memorial Church, New York City.
June 30, 1963	*Minus Auditorium Equipment and Furnishings*	Gramercy Arts Theater, New York City.
November 10, 1963	*Egg Deal*	Judson Memorial Church, New York City.
February 10, 1964	*Cancellation Sample*	Surplus Dance Theater, Stage 73, New York City.
April 24, 1964	*Carnation*	Institute of Contemporary Arts, Philadelphia.
July 23, 1964	*Street Dance*	Studio of Robert and Judith Dunn, New York City.
August 12, 1964	*Model*	Washington Square Art Gallery, New York City.
January 29, 1965	*Geranium*	Alfred Leslie Studio, New York City.
March 12, 1965	*Museum Piece*	Judson Memorial Church, New York City.
May 23, 1965	*Screen*	Bridge Theater, New York City.
October 10, 1965	*Agriculture*	Once Festival, Ann Arbor, Michigan.
October 16, 1966	*Vehicle*	69th Regiment Armory, "Nine Evenings of Theater and Engineering," New York City.
June 11, 1968	*Untitled Trio*	Judson Memorial Church, New York City.
December 7, 1973	*Particular Reel* *Checkered Drift* *Calico Mingling*	Whitney Museum of Art, New York City.
March 8, 1975	*Duplicate Suite* *Reclining Rondo* *Congeries on Edges for 20 Obliques*	YMCA, Nyack, New York.
January 23, 1976	*Radial Courses* *Mix Detail* *Transverse Exchanges*	Washington Square Methodist Church, New York City.
June 8, 1976	*Cross Words* *Figure Eights*	St. Mark's Church, Danspace, New York City.

Date	*Title of Work*	*Place and Details*
November 3, 1977	*Plaza* *Melody Excerpt* *Interior Drama*	Brooklyn Academy of Music, New York City.
March 12, 1978	*Katema*	Stedlijk Museum, Amsterdam, The Netherlands.
October 17, 1979	*Dance*	Stadsschouwburg, Eindhoven, The Netherlands. Music by Philip Glass. Film and decor by Sol LeWitt. Full-length evening work.
March 31, 1981	*Mad Rush*	Centre Culturel, Soissons, France. For the Groupe Recherche Choréographique de l'Opéra de Paris.
November 16, 1981	*Relative Calm*	Théâtre National de Strasbourg, Strasbourg, France. Music by Jon Gibson. Lights and decor by Robert Wilson. Full-length evening work.
February 19, 1982	*Formal Abandon, Part I*	Tinel de la Chartreuse, Villeneuve-Les-Avignon, France. Music by Michael Riesman. Solo performance.
July 29, 1982	*Formal Abandon, Part II*	Loeb Student Center, Harvard University, Cambridge, Massachusetts. Music by Michael Riesman. Quartet performance.
July 8, 1983	*Available Light*	Festival de la Danse, Centre de Rencontres, Châteauvallon, France. Music by John Adams. Open-air version.
September 29, 1983	*Available Light*	"Temporary Contemporary," Museum of Contemporary Art, Los Angeles. Music by John Adams. Set by Frank Gehry. Costumes by Ronaldus Shamask.
November 29, 1983	*Formal Abandon, Part III*	Théâtre de la Ville, Paris. Music by Michael Riesman. Lighting by Gregory Meeh.
March 1, 1984	*Cascade*	Seattle Opera House, Seattle, Washington. For the Pacific Northwest Ballet. Music by Steve Reich.

Date	*Title of Work*	*Place and Details*
March 8, 1984	*Outline*	Whitney Museum of Art, New York City. Music by Gavin Bryars. Solo performance.
November 2, 1984	*Premiere Orage*	Palais Garnier, Opéra de Paris. For the Paris Opera Ballet. Music by Dmitri Shostakovich. Decor and costumes by Roberto Platé. Lighting by Serge Peyrat.
December 11, 1984	*Field Dances*	Brooklyn Academy of Music, New York City. Choreographed for Acts II and III of *Einstein on the Beach*, by Philip Glass and Robert Wilson.
January 28, 1986	*Portraits in Reflection*	Joyce Theater, New York City. Music by Michael Galasso, Michael Nyman, Allen Shawn, and Elizabeth Swados. Set by Robert Mapplethorpe. Costumes by Ronaldus Shamask.

Relative Calm, Part I: Rise. Lucinda Childs Dance Company. Tertius Walker, Daniel McCusker, Ande Peck, Priscilla Newell, Carol Teitelbaum, Meg Harper, Jumay Chu, Garry Reigenborn. Photo: Nathaniel Tileston.

Bill T. Jones & Arnie Zane

Photo: Peggy Jarrell Kaplan.

ARNIE ZANE

Arnie Zane is a native New Yorker, born in the Bronx and educated at the State University of New York at Binghamton. Zane's first recognition in the arts came as a photographer. In 1975 he was the recipient of a Creative Artists Public Service (CAPS) award in photography and has had shows of his work at The Kitchen, Dance Theater Workshop, and Pratt Institute. His dance photography has appeared in many publications, including the London *Vogue* magazine.

Arnie Zane's introduction into the dance world came in 1973 when he, Bill T. Jones, and Lois Welk formed the American Dance Asylum in Binghamton, New York. Since moving back to New York City in 1979, Zane has received a second CAPS award in choreography (1981) and two choreographic fellowships from the National Endowment for the Arts (1983, 1984). In 1980 Zane was co-recipient (with Bill T. Jones) of the German Critics Award for his work *Blauvelt Mountain.*

As Co-Artistic Director of Bill T. Jones/Arnie Zane and Company, Zane shares the choreographic responsibility for the company's repertory. In addition, his work has been seen in New York at Warren Street Performance Loft (*Pieman's Portrait,* 1980), at The Kitchen (*Cotillion,* 1981), at P.S. 122 (*Your Hero,* 1981), and at St. Mark's in the Bowery (*Garden,* with Johanna Boyce, 1981).

Prior to forming Bill T. Jones/Arnie Zane and Company, Zane and Jones toured extensively in the United States and abroad, appearing at the Kennedy Center in Washington, UCLA, the American Centre in Paris, the Dance Umbrella in London, and the Vienna Festival. A television project co-produced by WGBH-TV, Boston, and Channel 4 in London featured their work *Rotary Action.*

BILL T. JONES

Bill T. Jones, the son of a migrant farm working family, entered college as an athlete and actor in 1970. His first dance training took place at the State University of New York at Binghamton with Percival Borde in Afro-Carribean and West African forms. Subsequently Jones studied with Pearl Primus, Cor Poleman, Kei Takei, Erin Martin, Richard Bull, and Garth Fagan; he has performed with many of them as a guest artist.

Before forming Bill T. Jones/Arnie Zane and Company in 1982, Jones choreographed and performed as a soloist and duet company with his partner, Arnie Zane, touring nationally and internationally. During those years he toured Europe, performing at the Dublin Festival, Edinburgh Festival, and Vienna Festwocken, with appearances in Zurich, Stockholm, Brussels, Berlin, London, Paris, and Geneva, among others. Nationally, his work has been seen at the Kennedy Center in Washington, MoMing in Chicago, Roberson Art Center in Binghamton, and at numerous colleges and universities. From 1978 to 1981, Jones was an Affiliate Artist working extensively in high schools and art centers around the United States.

In 1979, Jones received the Creative Artists Public Service (CAPS) award in choreography; and in 1980, 1981, and 1982, he was the recipient of choreographic fellowships from the National Endowment for the Arts. His works can be seen in the repertories of Werkcentrum Dance Company and the Rezone Dancers. The commissioned work *Fever Swamp* has been in the repertory of the Alvin Ailey American Dance Theater.

Among Jones's film and video credits are *Break,* produced by KTCA-TV, Minneapolis, and *Rotary Action,* co-produced by WGBH-TV, Boston, and Channel 4 in London.

ARNIE ZANE

A Collaborative Intimacy

When Bill and I met, he was a very well-developed college athlete, state-level track champion, and I was an art history major at the university. I'd always been somewhat athletic, but never taken a dance class in my life. I was 25. We were good friends. One day Bill suggested I take a workshop in contact improvisation. The ad for it was very catchy; it was about lovemaking, wrestling, and anything that might make a person want to be physical. I had always loved the reality of social dancing and junior high school parties, so I decided to check out the workshop. Bill and I went, and it was like taking acid; on a physical level, it was a total liberating experience in the early seventies.

Then I took some Graham classes and Vaganova ballet, but I couldn't stand them. I'm too authoritarian to stand in rows, and don't like putting myself in that position. For five years I forced myself to take a regular technique class with Bill and Lois Weld and it caused many tears. I had a well-shaped body, which was strong, but fondu, rond de jambe? Well, I endured, and got the bug of making dances, which is now my passion.

Bill and I were members of the American Dance Asylum in Binghamton, New York, which was a collective of choreographers: Lois Welk, Jill Becker, and Donna Joseph. From 1974 to 1976 we worked together, took part in each other's works, and did about three major productions a year, with one person heading up the production.

By 1978 there were three of us left and the administrative weight was quite heavy on everybody, plus we were teaching classes. Bill had come to New York in 1977 to perform at the Clark Center. He did a solo and suddenly had press in the *New York Times* and other papers. Suddenly he had a career. We were living in Binghamton and were very suspicious of New York City. He was invited back the next year to the New York Dance Festival, and the same thing happened. Again there was very positive press, and again he was invited back. This time he took *Monkey Run Road,* which was our collaboration.

Monkey Run Road dealt with movement accumulation, but it was theatrical, almost like a play. Originally Bill was a black puppeteer and I was a black puppet, sitting on Bill's lap, but we pared the whole thing down by cutting out the black wigs and black makeup. We wheeled out a box, like a jack-in-the-box, and I stood in front of it, performing and speaking Dutch text. Bill performed abstract gestures and spoke about a memory from childhood, from the point of view of an 11-year-old boy. He spoke about the day the jets were dispatched to the Bay of Pigs crisis, and we pushed the box around on wheels. The music was like oscillating white noise, there were silences, and it was very minimal. The collaboration was long, rambling, and extremely austere. People thought it was an apocalyptic statement.

The mood of the nation at that time had an awareness of a potential nuclear crisis. When we finished the last concert, that night was the night of Three Mile Island disaster in Harrisburg, Pennsylvania. The dance was not intended to be heavy in that way—a lot of things just meshed—and people brought a lot of their own interpretations to it.

We aren't blind; we are aware of the differences of our physicality: a black man and a white man, short and tall, extreme differences in dance style. With all the prejudices people have, both positive and negative, they simply free-associate with the images we present.

One way we try to rise above that idea is to believe that we are just any two people who happen to be good friends making art. On a more fundamental level, when we make dances, often we each begin making material. We learned a long time ago that it's very difficult for us to do each other's movement. Bill's way of moving is difficult for me, and mine is difficult for him. Bill brings more traditional background to the movement than I do, so we get a catalogue of movements and information that begins to tell us how the whole thing should fall together.

I am not interested in improvisation as the performance act. All of my material comes from improvisation; but then I set the movement, and the process is videoed. Bill brings more personal dramatic expression to the dances than I, but we're both interested in structuralism. My approach to building movement is to integrate, shape, and change it, very much in a Cunningham-like way. I was a still photographer for many years and my passion in printing the still photograph was in making the print. For me, the passion in dance making is with the movement itself—how it's spaced on the stage. I'm not trying to get out any humanistic ideas. I could never begin to think like Bill in his *Social Intercourse.*

In a collaboration, we'll have ideas, a title maybe, or some hooks to latch onto, but then, ultimately, the movement always comes first. We go into the studio with our latest and most welcomed addition, the JVC portable video system, and we improvise to our hearts delight, then sit and scrutinize our improvisation and try to find new directions.

We've experimented with putting each other's movement phrases together—for example, putting his A next to my B, but what we decided was that it was too frustrating because we both have such strong feelings and values. For *Freedom of Information,* we decided to each do an entire section, 20 minutes a piece, and it worked, but it can look like patchwork. However, we share enough similarities so that there will always be a thread that unites.

Now we bring material to each other, then work on it together. In the past, during rehearsal, due to ego problems, we weren't very graceful in discussing our differences of opinions. It is difficult. As in any relationship, if you have faith in it continuing, or want it to, you compromise. With time, there's a natural resilience. Now we're courageous enough to confront this creative intimacy.

Becoming Bill T. Jones/Arnie Zane and Company was a big step for both of us. Before, we wanted our own outlets, our own performance egos. We experimented with every possibility of name, association, power, hierarchy, and structural level. I was once Arnie Zane and Dancers. Bill was Bill T. Jones and Company, and he was also Bill T. Jones alone. Another whole entity was Bill T. Jones and Arnie Zane, our duets, which we did for a long time. Neither of us wanted to stay either as a soloist or as a duo. This is the way we have grown, how we grow. Now we have a company, a shared company.

June 5, 1984

BILL T. JONES

Mainstream Religion

I was raised a Baptist-Methodist with a very important, deep religious upbringing which taught that we suffer here on earth because we get redemption on high. For me, religion is just trying to teach how to organize the world. Well, as a young teenager, I rejected it and abandoned a lot of those things. At the age of 14, I thought I'd discovered atheism and existentialism. Then, like many people in the late sixties or early seventies, I came back to religion in the form of Eastern religion; I shaved my head and became a vegetarian looking for peace and tranquility. I wanted nothing to do with the world, but that was not quite honest because I'm not a product of that culture. I remember the day I said I would like to abandon asceticism and embrace the world now. That, to me, meant embracing all that was about the senses, all that was about ambition, success, owning up to all of my foibles and diving in to make art. And that became my religion. As my art, choreography is now the organizing principle in my world.

I want to make fine vigorous dancing so that if you've never seen modern dance before, you will walk in and be charmed, like listening to music you've never heard before, when the sounds just fall together in an intriguing way. It doesn't have to be pretty, but at least intriguing. That, I would like my dancing to do. I want to make dances that are wild, outrageous, frightening, and yet beautiful; dances that are primeval, primitive, and yet streamlined—technical dancing with virtuosity still as elemental and poignant as maybe some of the things of Kei Takei. But at the same time, I want to see people flash feet and do masterful leaps and turns. Combine both. This is our legacy in the eighties; virtuosity is back, but it hasn't come back yet with full conviction.

I would like to become a force that is a voice of social consciousness which also brings people together, or at least brings them to questioning. I want to be in the mainstream. I'm not embarrassed about making dances many people can enjoy, but there will always be something controversial in the work, I won't compromise that. When you come to see Bill T. Jones/Arnie Zane and Company, it will be entertainment, it will have the trappings; there will be lights, there will be color, there will be attractive people up there doing things. There will be sensuality, questions, there will be some shock, there will be probably some violence, and some answers too, alternatives.

I have a friend who says he wants to be a household word like an Andy Warhol. I don't want to be an Andy Warhol, but I am a populist, I can't deny it. For example, after seeing the collaboration of Lucinda Childs, Philip Glass, and Sol LeWitt, I was so taken by the beauty and timelessness of their art that I said, "I want to make that kind of pure statement of art." My friend said, "But you're not an abstractionist and you're not Sol LeWitt, you're different." It could be reduced to Dionysian and Apollonian types, with me the Dionysian and Lucinda Childs the Apollonian. It's like two sides of the brain. My friend said that the world was fortunate to have us both, but I'd still like my work to become a bit more Apollonian.

Now that's pretty lofty. On a more practical level, I want to have a company of people who can do my work with the same conviction that I'm able to do it with, so that I can retire someday. Like many people, I feel pursued by aging and all the things to which a body is heir. A company gives an appendage, it makes you bigger and spreads you out more as a way to operate in the world.

My first role model was a brilliant speaker, my mother, a Southern Baptist. Every Christmas this woman would bring us all downstairs at five in the morning. Before we even approached the tree, we'd kneel around the room and she'd start a prayer of simple statements, prayers she'd heard throughout her own childhood. Then she'd improvise and come back to the statement, insistently, until she had worked in all of us. "Please pray for this one, and that one who was sick last week. . . ." It was like exorcism or something. And that ritualistic way of speaking was the model I drew on whenever I stood up in front of a group of people. I wanted to dig deep into myself, to touch them. It follows me. I'm rethinking it now because I feel it is too manipulative and predictable to know that a person is going to move to a point of absolute emotional hysteria.

Ever since I was 10 years old I wanted to be an actor and was involved in theater in upstate New York. I'd never heard of modern dance. I went to college at the State University of New York at Binghamton with the idea of becoming a professional actor and doing musical comedy and serious Broadway drama. While at the university, a relative of mine who was also there introduced me to

West African and Afro-Carribean dance. As a runner, I went to dance class as an excuse to get out of track practice. Of course, I assured my coach it caused me to sweat and work on my cardiovascular just as much as running!

The Afro-Carribean, West African dance was with Percival Borde. It was very important to see a large man move that way; it taught me a lot. In terms of movement style, I was very impressed by Mr. Borde. I remember him demonstrating the Watussi, which was taught to him by his wife, Pearl Primus. I'd never seen anything quite so beautiful, the way the arms moved and the way his weight came crashing down to the floor, the way he would sing to himself when he danced. That was a strong image.

Mr. Borde was a very important influence, but people who have often made the most impression on me have frequently been women. There was a woman with whom I studied, Pat Taylor Frye, who had formerly been with the Graham company, and who had left and gone back to California. She was a very beautiful, lyrical dancer who taught Graham- and Hawkins-based technique. For a young post-athlete, also bound, bound in the hips, it was very important. She taught me a great deal about relaxation.

I went to college with the notion that I was just going to hang out for awhile. My techniques were in Humphrey–Weidman, taught by Linda Grandy. There was also some Graham and a bit of Cunningham. Before I went to college, I had been hitchhiking around the country, like many people, "discovering America." I met Arnie Zane, who had lived in Amsterdam the year before. He said, "If you want to go someplace, why don't you go someplace you've never been? Go to Europe." Arnie knew people there and spoke the language. I was 19 and it was a good opportunity, so I left college during my first year, in 1971, and went to Amsterdam. I worked with a man named Cor Poleman, who taught what he called jazz ballet. I called it archaic jazz dancing, show dancing. To my mind at the time, it was like minstrel dancing, but it was good for discipline.

For me, Amsterdam was like the first hallucinatory drug one ever takes. I came back with a lot of information under my belt: number one, how much I didn't know about dancing, and two, how much I didn't know about art.

I went back to the university with a new kind of humility, but being at the State University of New York at Binghamton, I was disappointed and unhappy with the dance and theater departments. It was very oppressive, and they were doing things I was just not interested in doing. I transferred to the State University, College at Brockport, and that's where I worked with Kei Takei, Erin Martin, Dick Bull, and Garth Fagan. Kei Takei taught me a lot about putting movement together. Her elemental approach to choreography, the idea of forgetting about "dancing," of going for the very lifeblood of movement, hanging, falling, was very, very important, and it affected both Arnie and me.

My brother out on the West Coast had written a musical about the Civil War, which was going to be produced by the community theater. He said, "Hey, come out and be our choreographer." Though I had never choreographed a musical, I went to California. While there, I began working with Lois Welk, who is now the Artistic Director of the American Dance Asylum. She is the person who turned me on to contact improvisation as taught by Steve Paxton, and a good deal of my theory about improvisation came from her. She also took me to a workshop with Cliff Keuter which was very important. He was another man who was very lyrical and a confident mover—a good thing for a young dancer to see.

Contact improvisation has influenced my personal dance style and the way I construct partnering. I remember one memorable afternoon. We would have contact jams that would be two hours long. One particular jam was with a woman who was a former ballerina who couldn't have been more than 5 feet tall. I'm almost 6 feet. I think she weighed 85–90 pounds, and I weigh 175, but there was no problem the way she would lever me up on her back, or the way we'd go into the floor with my weight completely resting on top of her. It was very dynamic, and very, very exciting—like making love with somebody—a total experience. The possibilities seemed endless, and that was very important compositionally.

That was the basis of my partnering, but I think that it's somewhat removed now, because many other things have come into play. In terms of conceptualist influences, structuralist film making and modern music have been important. To this day, most of my friends are not dancers; the people I sit and talk about art with are visual artists or musicians. There was a wonderful film making department at the State University of New York at Binghamton which was dominated by independent nonnarrative film makers. They had a nonlinear approach to aesthetics, to hell with lyricism and flow. People like Michael Snow, Stan Brackage, Tony Conrad were dealing with lyricism found in dissonance and abrupt angularity. I learned a great deal about composition from them and have retained some of those influences.

I think there is something implicitly lyrical, squiggly, oozy, about my own particular dance style, but when I make dances I find they are often extremely angular, with one event crashing into another, two events overlaid as if they have nothing to do with each other.

Social Intercourse: Pilgrims Progress. Bill T. Jones/Arnie Zane and Company. Bill T. Jones & Rhonda Moore. Photo: Arnie Zane.

What is the greatest challenge of choreographing? To over-come personal clichés as well as general clichés. What am I trying to get across to an audience? I believe that a work of sculpture has a presence, so that when we suddenly come into a room and see a Brancusi, a Henry Moore, or a Louise Nevelson, that presence tells us something about ourselves. What does it do? What is it for? Well, it's a presence. It sits there. It is the way it is perceived. I would like to make art like that. I would like to become more and more a force that is a voice of social consciousness, something that brings people together, or at least brings people to questioning—to make works that deeply affect people and yet are cool and distant enough so that they can be observed like a sculpture, as a presence is observed. "Food for the eye," as Tobi Tobias once wrote.

What kind of choreographer do I consider myself? It's a mischievous question most of us would rather not deal with. Most of us would say it's irrelevant. Often the press, the publicity machine, the PR machine, sponsors, need to give you a tag. It helps that big faceless "other" out there, the other which is the audience. I guess I'm experimental because I try to put together disparate elements to see what happens, but I prefer to be called contemporary, which is a very humble way of saying that it's a work made now.

One concern I have is the accessibility question. Last year I was being considered to choreograph a Broadway show with Gregory Hines. They had seen something I did for Alvin Ailey which was a light, breezy audience pleaser, and they wanted to see more of the work I did. So they came to see *Freedom of Information* at the Brooklyn Academy. Though it was a successful piece, suddenly there were reservations about my style. Was I able to do what they wanted me to do? It just so happens they saw *that* work. Maybe if it had been something else, it might have been viewed differently. I don't want to be pigeonholed in a way that I couldn't choreograph a Broadway play. Hanya Holm did it, Balanchine did it, Jerome Robbins has done it. Yet we live in an era where our PR machine pigeonholes with labels. It's dangerous, and a choreographer shouldn't allow himself to think in those ways. I don't have any sacred cows. I'm willing to try any style.

How has my work evolved? My palate is wider now. My own dancing has deepened, has gotten richer. I have more steps in my command. I understand more about counterpoint, phrasing, nuances. On some levels I have more daring than I ever did, and on some levels I'm much more reserved than ever before.

The first piece I ever performed in public was *Sadhana* in 1970. It was actually three pieces about a man who takes his senses apart: his sight, his taste, his hearing. All of these things were symbolized by a group of dances. In *Bacon Fat and Porkchops,* it was a burlesque where I played all the parts. Bacon Fat was a vaudeville performer and Porkchops were his girls, his backup singers.

Even in *Bacon Fat and Porkchops* and *Sadhana* I was speaking in my dances. Perhaps now the dialogue is more refined. I haven't done my freewheeling, free-spoken improvisations for quite awhile. *Sisyphus,* in 1981, was one of the most successful pieces with speaking. The dialogue was roughly sketched, but the movement had been more formed. The main device was that the barely sketched movement and barely sketched dialogue would be revealed, created in front of the audience that night, right then and there.

It began as an autobiography and then it became fiction. The narrator, myself, talked about real events from his life. He went from age 5 to 14, 28 to 34, and 64. At the time, I was 29 or 30 years old, so the second half of the piece was all projected. The movement happened in seven areas and was repetitive, and in some ways, as my friend Senta Driver used to say, it was "noodling about," improvisationally, talking and moving. Of course, after performing it about 20 times, I found certain things worked in the narrative—for example, how I got the person from age 28, talking about something that happened last week on Fifth Avenue, to age 64, when he was about to have his leg amputated because of cancer of the hip socket. When I knew where I wanted to go, I found some things that helped me get there, and the piece became more and more congealed.

Lately I've been writing my monologues, scripting them. I'm a bit conflicted here because one reason I used to speak in public was that it was spontaneous poetry. For example, I could be a person on the street corner who shouted about the beauty of the world, while moving in an abstract way.

Now I want to save these words. I want to understand what I'm saying, because I can't remember some of my most powerful ones. Now I want to be able to reproduce, because there's this thing called "company," repertoire," and limited amounts of energy and time. Things must be made so that they can pay for themselves.

Also, in starting from scratch every night, some nights you're just not very good. If you're tired, you really need to have something, technique and your material, to fall back on. These things have helped me change my way of working, have refined it. Now I'm much more concerned with craft.

I made a piece for Alvin Ailey in 1983 and it was a piece for six men. When I saw those men, I felt, in a way, I was home. I had nobody to scream at. It was like once again being on the track field, the athletic fields. It was even deeper than that though, the kind of love I felt for them, the beauty in their way of moving and their personalities. I wanted to make something which was like a party. It was a hard party, very difficult, only ten minutes long, and when it was over, they would be lying on the floor.

Fever Swamp was a celebratory piece. I did want to see them dance, and that's what it was about. I wasn't thinking about social statement, I wanted to make a dance about fine vigorous dancing, which was a beautiful thing unto itself. Jack Anderson of the *New York Times* said it had no moral fervor, that it was nothing more than a crowd pleaser and a vehicle for six beautiful dancers. This says something. Not that I have lost an edge, but that now I don't have to wear my ideology on my sleeve, as I might have once.

The next thing I was offered in 1983, was a chance to do a piece for a small company downtown called the Second Avenue Dance Company (Codanco). When they asked me, I was working on a couple of different things at the time, and I said I would make something in my spare time. I did it in two weeks. It was called *Corporate Whimsey*. It turned out to be a large group dance with different things happening every moment. It was full of partnering, rambunctious and wild, and it was very rhythmic and colorful. It didn't finish at a shriek, it finished quietly. That was a breakthrough for me, to understand how to modulate the energy.

In *Freedom of Information,* 1984, I wanted to have the music already composed, to give me boundaries as if collaborating, even though the composer, David Cunningham, was not present. And that is another change that has acted upon my dance making. I listen more to the music now and actually try to hear it before I make the movement.

The major works I've done have been with Arnie Zane. A landmark duet we made was *Blauvelt Mountain,* which was the centerpiece of a trilogy in 1979. *Blauvelt* combined structuralism with personal introspective poetry, some social issues, but not as much as the world brought to it. It was an extremely rigorous piece in two sections. The set was a simple brick wall about 6 feet at its highest point. All the material could have been performed in about 15 minutes, but instead it was accumulated movement. The sequence was maybe 40 movements long, but the first 10 would be shown, then the first 10 plus 20, and so on, moving around in the space. It had some speaking in it, *sotto voce,* speaking in very low voices, almost word association games. And yet, the structure was unraveling all the time so it could be enjoyed on that level. The dance brought many disparate elements between two people together, like an urban clearinghouse: one who is short and white and one who is tall and black. When we did it in Berlin, we were awarded the German Critics Award.

Blauvelt Mountain. Bill T. Jones & Arnie Zane. Photo: Jim Jenkins.

One thing I've learned, is that the world brings a great deal of baggage to each performance. We didn't bring as much to *Blauvelt Mountain* as the world did. The dance had been made a year before we ever came to Berlin, even thought about going there, and suddenly I woke up one morning and we were going to premiere the piece in Berlin.

I said to Arnie, "I don't believe we're going to do this here." Because during the second act of *Blauvelt,* a cinder block wall is deconstructed by Arnie upstage and then reconstructed through the center of the space. And I said, "I don't believe we're going to build a wall in this performance space here in Berlin." Well, the Germans went crazy over it. They loved it. They read all sorts of things into it. They thought we were making statements about their society, about blacks and whites in America—we were not. We were making, for us, an abstract dance. It did have some word association in it, but that wasn't even as important as the way we went at it, repeated and sweated right there in front of them so they heard us breathing.

Or another example is a piece we did called *Coffee. Coffee* was something we made one morning in front of the video camera, when we were home and Arnie said, "Why don't I make a video tape?" (The video camera has made tremendous changes in our way of working.) We set it up in the living room and I got up and started talking about the phone call I'd gotten that day. A monologue ensued, with repetition built into it, because that's the way I compose —I find strong images and they become signposts. Any good artist must have a skeleton, and that skeleton is repetition and counterpoint. So the statement "How's your cup of coffee," "the park bench," "her," "her dress," "the missiles,"—all those things were strong images I kept drawing on.

We listened to it and Arnie transposed it onto paper. Suddenly it was frozen. What had been improvisation was frozen. Then he learned one part, I learned the other, and one of our dancers learned the third part. We projected a huge screen of coffee beans and bananas, which had references to other things in the dialogue, and wore business suits and stood in three spots of light, reciting the dialogue with Chopin playing, played by Arthur Rubinstein. It was very beautiful. People said, "Oh, it's about nuclear war, it's about the relationship between men and women."

Social Intercourse: Pilgrims Progress premiered at The Space at City Center, New York City, in 1981. For me, this piece was a turning point. It was my first foray into "midtown dance," a midtown veneer, which says a lot about what I was trying to do and how I came equipped. It also indicated what I would be trying to do in the future and perhaps what I am doing now in a more refined way. I wanted to use pop imagery, so I chose three "colored girl" singers—that's the generic term—because that's traditionally what you do when you want a "hot" show. You get three singers who open their mouths and wail from deep within. I wanted them to sing things which were sentimental, like "I Believe," and I juxtaposed it with the most embracive, ironic statement I could make about that quaint, seductive expression of faith.

As the singers sang this beautiful song, the dancers did extremely hard-edged movement—bodyslapping, stomping on the floor. I also had overt images of sexual energy, people lying on each other kissing. There were a number of combinations and two or three times, in the middle of a particular active section, two men would come crashing mouth to mouth, kissing. One critic got upset and said, "You only had to do that once, the shock value was there." But it's beyond shock value, it's reality. This is our life style, it's real, it's an alternative life style; and this community, the company, represents a community which operates under rules which are sexual, racial, and class-stratified.

We also wanted to pull in a broad audience and I think, in terms of a black community, we did that. More people came to see the piece because of its venue. I wanted to make something with a black voice, while I was trying to understand my own voice.

I think of Chagall and his paintings, which are rich with imagery of Judaism, particularly the Russian Jews, and yet it is also about painting as well as more universal things. I set out to do that in this work. I wanted to make something which would exhaust me. I wanted to make a mini-spectacle which had all the trappings of a revue—one song, the song ends, there is a little interchange, the dancers change costumes, another song, and the singers are right there on stage with the microphones and musicians. It was obviously entertainment, but challenging entertainment.

It was the prototype for many things Arnie and I have been trying to do. We want to make works that deeply affect people and yet are cool and distant enough so that they can be observed as a presence, appreciated for themselves and what they represent. This was our somewhat slick, midtown production. We realized that it wasn't as slick as it could be, but were trying to pull it off at that level of the dance world. It was a very ambitious jump, but it was also taking into account everything we'd been doing up to that point and putting it together into an evening.

There were a lot of dancers in *Social Intercourse.* I used about 15 dancers plus a company of 5 or 6, which I had amassed especially for this piece.

The opening section was the "postmodern section." When people came into the space, a guard was there and most of the dancers were moving back and forth in front of the theater door. We had an agreement with the house that we would never block the door, so when the guard said, "Stop," the dancers had to clear so that the people could walk to their seats.

Apparently the guard said, "Stop" in such an intimidating way that people thought, "Oh, my God, once I get in there, I can't get out!" And that immediately made some people angry. They felt what I was doing was representing New York, the modern world, and what I was saying was that we're all trapped. I hadn't even thought of it in that way. I viewed it as a simple task, where the guard stopped the dancers so people could walk through, like a crosswalk, but people

Brahams. Bill T. Jones. Photo: Dee Conway.

read metaphors and symbolism into it, just as in *Blauvelt Mountain.*

In the next section, the structure was that the dancers were told to make a certain pass in a certain manner. They had to go from one side of the performing area to another, a certain number of times, and then change the quality of the way they did it. Then they were instructed to find partners and to continue this activity, stopping and going, at the command of one performer, another guard, until one by one, the couples lay down together and lay there on the floor on top of each other. Then the piece began.

Many of these dancers were completely untrained, which was something I inherited from my early experimentation with dance making. This section was like the classic postmodern statements where anyone could dance, any two people could partner, any movement could follow any other movement. There was another section where these same dancers were used as a chorus for a production number that finished the first act. They came across the stage doing different motifs, and it kept on going, with very high energy, for the sheer spectacle of it.

Many of us took the experimentations of Laura Dean and, maybe to a lesser degree, Lucinda Childs, to heart. This section was, in fact, statements not so much about vocabulary, as about the way in which movement is perceived through time and space, and the way in which the energy level becomes an emotional, visceral response. In my own way, I was making that sort of task dance to see how much can be absorbed. That was the excitement for me. It was very raw, and it wanted to be what it represented, nothing else.

Social Intercourse was a wild dance, designed to be all red and jagged and full of heart. The craft was secondary. The dance was bigger than we were. The dance was exhausting, but that's what it was about—pushing oneself to that limit, dealing with social issues of race, sexuality, and all those things.

How was it a reflection of its culture? It's a complicated issue because it's dealing with the exchange between the artist and the artwork, the artwork and its audience. The work was a commentary on the way I perceived the society I was living in at that time. It was about the way I perceived the relationships between men and women and men and men, as well as the way I perceived the restraints. The kissing of the two men, crashing face against face, was intended, on one level, to break a barrier, to thumb one's nose, and, at the same time, to suggest the new world we're in, where anything is possible. We are living here now, that's what the work said. We have endless energy, and maybe we're a bit unpresentable, a bit raw, but here we are. Now you must deal with us.

Concerning the exchange with the viewer, that would be determined by class, one's own particular background in modern dance and theater, one's race, and, perhaps, sexual preference. All of those things would put the viewer in a certain relationship to that work.

When I was choreographing, I never thought about it, in perhaps those terms, but I know the power in it. It's never that literal, it's like peripheral vision. I know one thing will produce a certain reaction. For example, the three "colored girl" singers were up there because I feel that black women are exploited. People say, "Oh, they're so hot!"—which means they have a natural, uninhibited sensuality, which is what those people who don't have it want. The disco voice of the screaming Donna Summer or of the colored girls makes us think about sex, makes us feel alive, when we are not alive in that way. It's as if they were a symbol of colonialism or imperialism. Now, that's a pretty rarified explanation for something which is that they basically provided the funk and were live singers who sang from a very natural place.

The musicians were two white boys. Combined with the colored girls, it was truly an aesthetic melting pot, and it was a statement about the faith I had in lower Manhattan. It was an integrated cast dealing with the so-called emerging nations of the world (Harlem is an emerging nation) and it was a liberated vision of educated young people coming to power to make a new world which brings all cultures together into one new one. *Social Intercourse* questioned barriers between people. It was quite a responsibility to make dance about social statements, and yet, at the same time, it was full of ironies—like when the colored girl singers sang "I Believe" while it was undercut with a dance about the death of belief.

I can't embrace the black church, or Jesse Jackson, simply because he is a black man who is finally living the dream we were innoculated with at an early age. (I use the word "innoculated" purposely because it's a word to ward off a kind of rot that comes when there is no self-image.) When Jackson was running for president, there he was, but I didn't believe it. So what do I believe? I believe in the work, that if it's conceived and meticulously attended to, cultivated, it can be something that's pure and lifegiving. It can be as good as religion.

June 5, 1984

Choreography by Arnie Zane

Year	Title of Work	Place and Details
1973	*Self-Portrait*	Santa Cruz Theatre 103, Santa Cruz, California. Solo performance.
1974	*Dances for a Third American Century*	Albany, New York. Collaboration with Lois Welk. Performed by 25 dancers.
1975	*Dancing and Video in Binghamton*	Experimental Television Center, Binghamton, New York. Collaboration with Meryl Blackman. Performed by 8 dancers.
1975	*Rhada a Real Dance*	American Dance Asylum, Binghamton, New York. Collaboration with Per Bode. Performed by 10 dancers.
1976	*Movements for Video, Dance and Music*	Experimental Television Center, Binghamton, New York. Performed by 4 dancers.
1976	*Couple #513*	Everson Museum, Syracuse, New York. Collaboration with Lois Welk. Duet performance.
1976	*Transport Dance*	American Dance Asylum, Binghamton, New York. Music by Ross Levinson. Performed by 14 dancers.
1977	*Crux, an Old Dance Constructed Anew*	American Dance Asylum, Binghamton, New York. Performed by 9 dancers.
1977	*Steppin'*	American Dance Asylum, Binghamton, New York. Solo performance.
1980	*Pieman's Portrait*	Warren Street Performance Loft, New York City. Solo performance.
1981	*Cotillion*	The Kitchen, New York City. Music by Ross Levinson. Costumes by Betsey Johnson. Performed by 9 dancers and 4 musicians.
1981	*Garden*	Danspace, St. Mark's Church, New York City. Duet performance with Johanna Boyce.
1981	*Your Hero*	P.S. 122, New York City. Performed by 5 dancers.
1982	*New Hero*	Riverside Dance Festival, New York City. Performed by 4 dancers.
1983	*Rumble in the Jungle*	Riverside Dance Studio, London. Music by Max Roach. Solo performance.
1985	*Peter and the Wolf*	State University of New York, College at Purchase. Performed by 22 dancers.
1985	*Black Room*	Joyce Theater, New York City. Music by Yoshi Wada. Sets and visuals by James Brown. Duet performance for Bill T. Jones and Heywood McGriff, Jr.

Year	Title of Work	Place and Details
1974	*A Dance with Durga Devi*	American Dance Asylum, Binghamton, New York. Solo performance.
1974	*Negroes for Sale*	Collective for Living Cinema, New York City. Visuals by Arnie Zane. Solo performance.
1974	*Entrances*	American Dance Asylum, Binghamton, New York. Performed by 4 dancers.
1975	*Could Be Dance*	American Dance Asylum, Binghamton, New York. Solo performance.
1975	*Across the Street There Is a Highway*	The Farm, San Francisco. Film by Arnie Zane. Performed by 4 dancers.
1975	*Women in Drought*	American Dance Asylum, Binghamton, New York. Duet performance.
1975	*Impersonations*	American Dance Asylum, Binghamton, New York. Solo performance.
1975	*Track Dance*	State University of New York at Binghamton. Performed by 50 dancers.
1975	*Everybody Works/All Beasts Count*	Ensemble performance at American Dance Asylum, Binghamton, New York, for 14 dancers. Solo performance at Clark Center, New York City.
1977	*For You*	Daniel Nagrin Dance Theatre, New York City. Solo performance.
1977	*Stomps*	Daniel Nagrin Dance Theatre, New York City. Solo performance.
1977	*Walk*	Daniel Nagrin Dance Theatre, New York City. Solo performance.
1977	*A Men*	Daniel Nagrin Dance Theatre, New York City. Solo performance.
1977	*In Bed*	Daniel Nagrin Dance Theatre, New York City. Solo performance.
1977	*Asymmetry: Every Which Way*	Roberson Art Center, Sears Harper Theatre, Binghamton, New York. Enacted by 6 performers.
1977	*Da Sweet Streak La Love Land*	Clark Center, New York City. Performed by 6 dancers.
1978	*Progresso*	The Kitchen, New York City. Solo performance.
1978	*By the Water*	American Dance Asylum, Binghamton, New York. Duet performance with Sheryl Sutton.

Year	Title of Work	Place and Details
1979	*Echo*	The Kitchen, New York City. Solo performance.
1979	*Floating the Tongue*	The Kitchen, New York City. Solo performance.
1979	*Addition*	Washington Square Church, New York City. Solo performance.
1979	*Circle in Distance*	Washington Square Church, New York City. Duet performance with Sheryl Sutton.
1980	*Balancing the World*	University of Northern Iowa, Cedar Falls. Performed by 6 dancers.
1980	*Sisyphus*	Kennedy Center, Washington, D.C. Solo performance.
1981	*Social Intercourse: Pilgrims Progress*	American Dance Festival, Stewart Theatre, Raleigh, North Carolina. Performed by 5 dancers and 3 singers.
1981	*Social Intercourse: Pilgrims Progress*	The Space at City Center, New York City. Performed by 18 dancers and 3 singers.
1981	*Break*	Nicolet Island Amphitheatre, Walker Art Center, Minneapolis.
1981	*Io*	Dance Theater Workshop, New York City. Solo performance.
1982	*Three Dances*	Harvard University, Cambridge, Masschusetts. Solo performance.
1982	*Shared Distance*	The Kitchen, New York City. Duet performance with Julie West.
1983	*Fever Swamp*	Santa Monica Civic Auditorium, Santa Monica, California. Performed by 6 dancers.
1983	*Naming Thing*	Just Above Mid-Town Gallery, New York City. Collaboration with Phillip Mallory Jones and David Hammons. Performed by 3 dancers.
1983	*Corporate Whimsey*	Tisch School of the Arts, New York University, New York City. Performed by 12 dancers.
1983	*21*	Recreation Center, Waterloo, Iowa. Collaboration with videographer Tom Bowes. Solo performance with video work.
1983	*21*	Recreation Center, Waterloo, Iowa. Dance solo performance.

Choreography by Bill T. Jones & Arnie Zane

Year	Title of Work	Place and Details
1971	*Pas de Deux*	State University of New York at Binghamton. Senior thesis for Phil Sykas. Duet performance.
1973	*Pas de Deux for Two*	American Dance Asylum, Binghamton, New York. Duet performance.
1979	*Monkey Run Road*	American Dance Asylum, Binghamton, New York. Music by Helen Thorington. Duet performance.
1979	*Blauvelt Mountain*	Dance Theater Workshop, New York City. Music by Helen Thorington. Duet performance.
1980	*Valley Cottage*	Dance Theater Workshop, New York City. Music by Helen Thorington. Duet performance.
1982	*Continuous Replay*	American Dance Asylum, Binghamton, New York. Music by Bryan Rulon. Solo performance.
1982	*Rotary Action*	Vienna Festival, Vienna. Music by Peter Gordon. Duet performance.
1983	*Intuitive Momentum*	Brooklyn Academy of Music, New York City. Music by Max Roach and Connie Crothers. Set by Robert Longo. Costumes by Ronald Kolodzie. Performed by 5 dancers.
1984	*Freedom of Information*	Théâtre de la Ville, Paris. Music by David Cunningham. Set and visuals by Gretchen Bender. Spoken text by Bill T. Jones. Performed by 6 dancers.
1984	*Secret Pastures*	Brooklyn Academy of Music, New York City. Music by Peter Gordon. Sets by Keith Haring. Costumes by Willi Smith. Performed by 12 dancers.

Nancy Meehan

Photo: Peggy Jarrell Kaplan.

NANCY MEEHAN

Nancy Meehan is a University of California at Berkeley graduate and a native of San Francisco, where she performed with the Ann Halprin–Welland Lathrop Dance Company and presented her first dance works. In New York City, she studied with Martha Graham and Erick Hawkins. She joined the Erick Hawkins Dance Company in the early 1960s and, as Hawkins's partner, toured the United States and Europe. In 1970 she left the Hawkins company to establish her own school and dance company. She has been on the faculty of the American Dance Festival for six summers. Her company has had annual New York seasons as well as appearances at the New York Dance Festival at the Delacorte Theater, the American Dance Festival, and at colleges and universities in the United States. She received a Guggenheim Fellowship for choreography in 1976, a Creative Artists Public Service (CAPS) fellowship in 1979, and National Endowment for the Arts choreography fellowships in 1983, 1984, and 1985. An honor in 1981 was the placement of her archives with the Harvard Theatre Collection.

NANCY MEEHAN

Penetrating the Veil

For me, dance is rooted in the eternal. The challenge is to find fresh ways of presenting ageless experiences through new movement and formal structures which are mutually inclusive of the universal and the particular—the extraordinary and the ordinary.

Until recent times, dance in the West has not dealt with these essential areas of content, nor has it been one of the central art forms. Because of prejudices against dance throughout the Middle Ages, it was not allowed to develop and flourish in a way commensurate with the tremendous growth of its sister arts. In other great cultures (Asian, African, Native American), dance was not pushed aside and denied, but was active at the heart of the culture with the other arts. It was not separated from the life of the people but was a crucial part of their connection to nature and to their religious ideals; a dance culture was allowed to develop simultaneously along with all aspects of life. Dance was not considered light entertainment but was a means of participating in the most serious, important, and central aspects of the culture. It was thought capable of embodying mind, being, spirit, and practical matters.

In the West, because of the very deep and centuries-old tradition of the denial of the body, dance was not taken seriously as an art form, or used as a vehicle capable of conveying deep cultural traditions. It was not until the turn of the twentieth century that Isadora Duncan tried to revive dance in its fuller possibilities. She wanted to see dance returned to the position of centrality in the culture, where it could convey content and depth of meaning. She went back to the Greeks for her ideal and to nature as a source for movement.

It was the first time in many centuries that the West began to think of dance as a form that had great potentiality in depth of expression. From this perspective, it can be seen that modern dance is tremendously young compared to other great dance cultures (such as Bharata Natyam in India) which have been developed and enriched over many centuries.

After Duncan's work in the early part of this century, the main emphasis shifted to dramatic, psychological, and narrative dance, followed by a reaction against emotion which developed into formal, abstract dance. In the seventies, a minimalist, conceptualist, task-oriented interest emphasized formal aspects exclusively. I find these recent directions lacking both in aesthetic depth and content. As I see it, the real breakthrough for dance lies in exploring certain new content areas previously neglected in the West. Out of this breakthrough, fresh formal and aesthetic elements will also be generated.

Since 1970 I have been involved in working with such a new area of content for dance. I see, as a source for developing great richness and depth, the use of nature images which are translated through dance movement into states of mind or being.[1] When using such nature images as a base or ground for dances, I am also searching for their reflection in human experience. The dance landscape includes human experience and is a setting for it so that whatever nature imagery or metaphor is used is in relationship to the human being, to the human condition; this landscape itself then becomes part of an implied vaster context. One of the major problems for dance has been the periodic wide fluctuations or swings between highly personal and impersonal approaches. If dance is placed in a vast context and thereby opened up and increased in scale, these two forces, the personal and impersonal, are brought into a more complete balance and coexistence.

In my dances, I am interested in reality but not in so-called realism. I am not literally trying to copy nature or asking the dancers to be anything other than themselves. They are always themselves as they allow the experience to be translated through them.[2] This is crucial to an understanding of my work. If the movement itself is coming from a deep enough source, the dancers, in the process of actually executing the movement, will convey these states of being to the audience. The greatest challenge is to find such generative

---

[1]Nancy Meehan, Program Notes, Program for Nancy Meehan Dance Company, Schimmell Center for the Arts, New York City, November 16, 17, 18, 1979. "In all of these dances a major emphasis has been to present, through the medium of dance and choreography, nature images as metaphors of states of mind and being."

[2]Ibid. "The individual movements are not attempts at literal representation —each movement has a reality of its own but is not meant to be realistic."

movement and then to place it within the choreographic context to evoke this elusive, ineffable state which I call undefinable reality.[3] The bare movement should be able to do this without the use of elaborate sets, props, or costumes. In order to achieve this, I seek to "radicalize" movement in the sense of that word's basic meaning— to go to the root of something.

I would like to emphasize that I also believe the formal elements should never be sacrificed for the content nor the content for the formal elements, but that they must organically relate to each other. When I start working on my dances both things emerge simultaneously. The two are inextricably mixed and the splitting of them is one of the things I consider a problem in much of current dance. An overemphasis on one produces a reaction swingback to the other. One of the big challenges for the contemporary artist is to solve this problem, and it has been one of the main things that has interested me from the beginning of my work as a choreographer.

I grew up in San Francisco and stayed with my grandparents every summer on a ranch in the Mendocino area of California, where there was no running water or electricity. We raised our own animals and grew most of our food. This kind of contact with natural forces and with their concrete physicality has had a tremendous impact on my choreography. The Sierras and the Pacific coast, the North and Southwest, are other important landscapes that have fed me and will continue to do so. For me, nature regenerates, energizes, and clarifies the mind and body. It opens up the context of the arts to a far vaster relationship by placing them in a truer relationship and proportion to the rest of life.

Another influence has been the Orient. I have always been deeply drawn towards it and had the opportunity to live near Kyoto, Japan, for six months in 1969 where I was able to attend the Noh, Bunraku, and Kabuki theaters, to see the great temples, gardens, and countryside. Japanese literature, art, and theater have always been extremely compelling to me because of the genius in being able to evoke such deep and beautiful works with often very simple means.

As a child, I received ballet training in San Francisco, then later studied with Ann Halprin and Welland Lathrop, danced in their company for three years, and presented my first dances in the Bay Area. I came to New York, where I studied and received a scholarship at the Martha Graham school. Soon after, I saw Erick Hawkins's work and found his approach to movement and aesthetic ideas challenging. I began studying with him in 1962, and toured and per-

---

[3]"Undefinable Reality," *Dance Life in New York*, vol. 2, Fall 1975.

Cloud . . . Roots. Nancy Meehan Dance Company. Ellen Marshall, Patty Bryan, Barbara Denhoff, Lynne Feigenbaum, Betsy Van Ummersen, Annie Sailer, Wendy Shifrin. Photo: © Johan Elbers 1986.

formed in his company as his partner throughout the sixties. In 1970 I left the Hawkins company and presented a performance of first dances for my company in 1971.

I felt that there were unexplored areas both in movement and content that fascinated and compelled me. While I have maintained a basic approach of working in movement without strain, emphasizing placement and letting the movement flow out easily, I have been developing movement which is also dynamic, forceful, and has strong attack. What has interested me about this, is solving the problem of finding a movement vocabulary of wide dynamic range without basing it upon the tensions that so often accompany movements made with strong attack.

An aspect of movement important to my work, and related to some of the problems involved in developing a greater dynamic range, lies in the use of weight. The development of this sense in dancers takes a long time to mature because a paradox is involved here—i.e., to sense weight, its tangibleness, its concreteness without actually dropping the weight, while at the same time, remaining sensitive to the amount of lift necessary and appropriate to any given movement. This sense of weight takes a very fine and sophisticated balancing of these two forces and demands constant attention on the dancer's part. Working with this kind of weight sensibility is a vital part of my technique and I think is unique to it. It brings a fullness and substantiality and provides a different kind of base for the dancer. It provides a grounding for dynamic attack that comes from true strength rather than forced and/or held states of tension. It also allows for a different kind of speed that does not sacrifice fullness of movement to the demands of a fast tempo.

I have worked a lot on developing special timings which reinforce the total concept of each dance. In thinking about the entire structure of the dance, I am always conscious of how the timings are relating to all aspects of the dance and to each other. Each dance has a timing score of its own, so to speak.

Another aspect of dance I have been deeply involved with is the use of scale or dimension to emphasize particular choreographic elements—to bring them out or let them recede—to mention only two kinds of results. This aspect is very intimately related to how the stage and choreographic space is perceived. When choreographing, I take into account the total three-dimensional stage area and how movement patterns are affecting the perceptions of this space—whether it extends beyond its own physical limits, or is used rigorously in its own right.

The clear and sharp choreographic eye is the forerunner of the moving camera eye in that it can shift the audience's focus in or out and move it around to meet whatever is the intent of the choreographer. It can create and alter its own space. These aspects, scale and timing, are essential to the aesthetic/formal areas that I feel help create the totality of my dances.

The first piece I choreographed was *Hudson River Seasons* in 1970. I worked on each season in my studio overlooking the Hudson River during the season itself. The body works differently kinesthetically and emotionally during each season, and I tried to find movement that would evoke in the audience some of the essential aspects of the seasons, as they are found both in nature and in the human life cycle.

Spring was the first section. The metronome timing was 80, a very slow tempo, which was a way of suggesting a child's sense of time. In each section there were specific tempi. The fastest tempo was Autumn and Winter was the most erratic. The entire dance was 45 minutes. I was working to achieve a union between the form and the content, to evoke in the audience a state of mind leading to these root experiences. I think of it as penetrating the veil into a ground that is both a universal and individual experience.

The idea of "penetrating the veil" can be related to the concept of certain Eastern gardens which are not only landscapes of natural scenes but landscapes of the mind providing a way into some of its deeper aspects. When I was in Glacier National Park, where I hiked to Ptarmigan Wall, a natural amphitheater, I felt a clarity, a lucidity, and a transparency so alive that I later tried to recapture that state of being when I choreographed *Ptarmigan Wall* in 1977. I was not attempting to copy or literally imitate the landscape; it was the state of mind generated from that experience, ineffable, yet real—and one that I wanted to translate into dance.

Seven Women, choreographed in 1980, is very much related to my first work, in that I returned to a deep thread in my own experience. While it develops many currents from *Hudson River Seasons,* the choreographic use of structure, groupings, movement, and space made it a very different dance. While *Seven Women* uses an extended sense of space, *Hudson River Seasons* is more spare and contained in its overall use of space.

Hudson River Seasons utilizes unison dancing almost exclusively. *Seven Women* has some unison dancing, but it more extensively employs diverse groupings active at the same time. These are not necessarily related to each other in an obvious way, but resonate and vivify one another, building into greater structural rhythms, which in turn develop the depth of content.

Seven Women and *Hudson River Seasons* are both dances of being, where the dancers can experience the absolute immediacy of their own being at each particular second of the performance. The dances are a way of penetrating the veil, eliminating the clutter that gets into the mind and stops one from experiencing deeper aspects of one's own psyche.

It would be misleading to be specific about the imagery in *Seven Women* because the audience could be sidetracked into looking for cues, rather than experiencing the dance freshly as a whole. The dance has three sections. The opening section is quite fast and very

Hudson River Seasons. Nancy Meehan. Photo: © Johan Elbers 1986.

agitated with a lot of movement, broken just at the end by an extremely sharp drop in speed. The second section is very slow and suspended, until the final unison running movements pitch the time perception to a higher, more agitated plateau. The beginning of the third section continues this speed with very quick, dense, complicated patterns, and then drops down to the lowest point in dynamics and timing of the sitting section. The group performs unison arm movements and slow motion sitting shifts which establish an *ostinato* or grounding to the complex, frenetic rhythmic patterns which spring up and then merge back into it.

Next comes the quietest part of *Seven Women,* where the unison arm movements with slow motion traveling-sitting are performed alone, without rhythmic interruptions. This gives the audience and dancers a chance to experience a sense of suspended and

Seven Women. Nancy Meehan Dance Company. Wendy Shifrin, Marilyn Peck, Catherine Mapp, Mara Greenberg, Connie Kreemer, Shizuko Ijuin, Nina Crumm. Photo: © Johan Elbers 1986.

dilated time. It allows them to soak in the movement and to think about nothing except what is being seen and experienced in the present. The fact that the dance is performed in silence also allows for a more direct perception of timing and rhythms. It closes with each dancer falling, which for me, in this piece, is the recognition of vulnerability and mortality. This rite of passage progresses into the fastness of the ending with a quick pickup of timing.

While *Seven Women* could be viewed purely abstractly, it does go beyond that, because of what was in my mind while I was choreographing and developing the movement and structure. What is it that makes the same line, when drawn by one calligrapher or painter, entirely different from that executed by another? It is the state of mind of the artist that gets translated and makes a difference, and the same thing applies to choreography. This is a phenomenon difficult to verbalize, ineffable, and yet it is nonetheless there, permeating any work. One of the functions of art is to express that which is inexpressible in any other form. Art is a means of entrance to areas of the psyche not otherwise available.

For me, dance or art is not a reflection of the times, but penetrates through time to eternal essences and common and universal experiences. The form of art is always changing; this change is affected by the particular period's perception and interpretation of the content.

In my choreography, states of mind are translated into dance through the use of formal and structural elements evoked by nature images; these are translations, a kind of language, for the core of being. The arts have a tremendous power to generate in people, something of inestimable value which they are unable to get in any other way. That is what is wonderful about art. These things *do* get conveyed. *How* is the great mystery.

June 10, 1980

Year	*Title of Work*	*Place and Details*
1970	*Hudson River Seasons*	Education Auditorium, New York University, New York City. Sponsored by the Dance Program Division of Creative Arts in conjunction with its 1970 college symposium. Music by Jeffrey Levine. Costumes by Anthony Candido. Performed by 5 dancers. 42 minutes.
1971	*Whitip*	Education Auditorium, New York University, New York City. Sponsored by the Dance Program Division of Creative Arts in conjunction with its 1971 college symposium. Performed by 6 dancers. 15 minutes.
1972	*Live Dragon*	YMHA, New York City. Music by Richard Moryl. Costumes by Anthony Candido. Performed by 6 dancers. 22 minutes.
1973	*Bones Cascades Scapes*	YMHA, New York City. Music by Eleanor Hovda. Costumes by Anthony Candido. Performed by 6 dancers. 15 minutes.
1974	*Split Rock*	Theater of the Riverside Church, New York City. Music by Jon Deak. Performed by 6 dancers. 18 minutes.
1974	*Yellow Point*	American Dance Festival, New London, Connecticut. Music by Rocco DePietro. Performed by 6 dancers. 15 minutes.
1975	*Grapes and Stones*	Theater of the Riverside Church, New York City. Music by Jon Deak. Performed by 11 dancers. 26 minutes.
1976	*Threading the Wave*	New York University, New York City. Music by Eleanor Hovda. Performed by 6 dancers. 24 minutes.
1977	*Ptarmigan Wall*	New York University, New York City. Music by Gregory Reeve. Performed by 13 dancers. 17 minutes.
1978	*White Wave*	New York University, New York City. Music by Eleanor Hovda. Performed by 6 dancers. 14 minutes.
1979	*How Near*	Schimmel Center, Pace University, New York City. Performed by 6 dancers. 17 minutes.
1979	*One Eye's Higher Than the Other*	Schimmel Center, Pace University, New York City. Music by Gregory Reeve. Performed by 7 dancers. 11 minutes.

Year	Title of Work	Place and Details
1980	*Seven Women*	Schimmel Center, Pace University, New York City. Performed by 7 dancers. 17 minutes.
1982	*Dreams of Leaves*	Education Auditorium, New York University, New York City. Music by Gerald Busby. Costumes by Anthony Candido. Performed by 10 dancers. 20 minutes.
1983	*Swift Garden*	Marymount Manhattan Theater, New York City. Performed by 4 dancers. 11 minutes.
1984	*Cloud . . . Roots*	St. Mark's Church, New York City. Music by Eleanor Hovda. Costumes by Anthony Candido. Performed by 8 dancers. 18 minutes.
1985	*Guest to Star*	St. Mark's Church, New York City. Music by Eleanor Hovda. Costumes by Anthony Candido. Performed by 7 dancers. 18 minutes.

*Hudson River Seasons. Nancy Meehan Dance Company. Patty Bryan,
Wendy Shifrin, Mara Greenberg, Ellen Marshall. Photo: © Johan Elbers
1986.*

Kenneth King

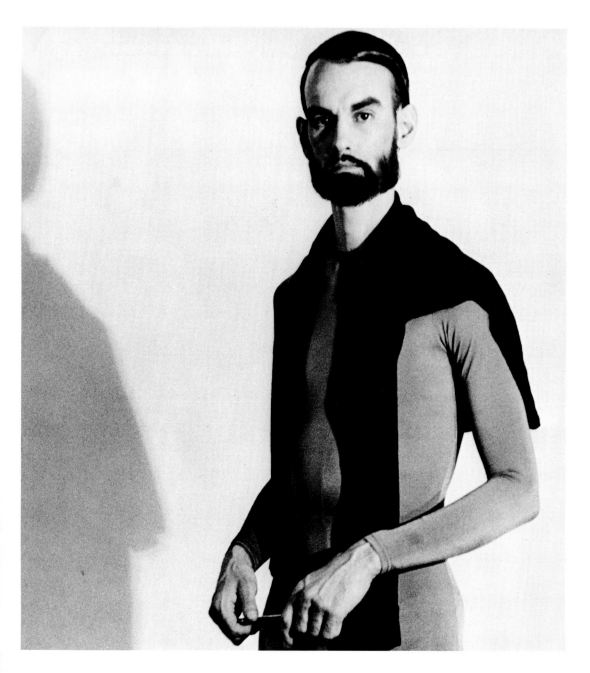

Photo: Peggy Jarrell Kaplan.

KENNETH KING

Kenneth King is a dancer, choreographer, and writer who has been called an inventor and philosopher because of the diversity of his "transmedia" experiments and interdisciplinary explorations that combine dance, voice/texts, music, and technology. King is a graduate of Antioch College.

Since 1964, he has presented dance and performance works at the Judson Memorial Church and Gallery, Brooklyn Academy of Music, the Museum of Modern Art, La Mama E.T.C., The Kitchen, the Cathedral of St. John the Divine, Dance Theater Workshop, Danspace, St. Mark's Church and the Poetry Project, in New York; the Walker Art Center, in Minneapolis; the American Dance Festival, in North Carolina; Expo 67, in Montreal; the Festival d'Automne and the American Center, in Paris; Tanz '84, in Vienna; the International New Dance and Movement Festival, in Utrecht; and the New Dance Festival, in Munich. He has taught, lectured, and mounted dances at many colleges and universities, and has received fellowships and choreography/multimedia grants from the John Simon Guggenheim Memorial Foundation, the National Endowment for the Arts, the New York State Council on the Arts, the Creative Artists Public Service (CAPS) program, the Foundation for Contemporary Performance Arts, and other sources.

King's writings have appeared in *The Young American Writers, The New Art, The New American Cinema, Text-Sound Texts, The Paris Review, Future's Fictions, Film Culture, eddy, Dancemagazine, Ballet Review, Shantih,* and *The Soho News.* His work is discussed at length in Sally Banes's *Terpsichore in Sneakers,* and he is a featured choreographer in Michael Blackwood's film *Making Dances,* produced for European television. He has collaborated with composer/transmedia engineer William-John Tudor since 1976 on over 15 works.

KENNETH KING

Transmedia

One can know self and world, b e i n g and mind, simply by moving the body! Moving the body—dancing—can be synonymous with seeing, thinking, doing—with *action!* There's more to dance than companies, careers, foundations, and corporations. That's all temporary. There's a bigger connection.

Believe it or not, it's possible to move through all of space—(it's a paradox) out of the linear into the relativistic and synchronistic. It's also possible to stop or step out of t-i-m-e-, just by . . . dancing! Dancing is a t r e m e n d o u s motion—movement connects everything across spacetime. Kant was right—space and time are (only) the *conditions* of our experience . . .

I can't wait for the day when the computer is a domesticated application we can have in the home, when dance can have its own *channel,* and poetry, theater, and the other arts their own channels. Can you imagine how computers, cable, satellites will alter and transform our perception (of perception) and the operation of spacetime? Not to mention institutions, cities, governments, and nationalisms as well. Probably it's because of Watergate that we don't have it already. I'd also like to be in a research center (while you're asking) where I could work with my company, space, video, and computer. We need new ways to see and *be* totally. The crisis seems to be about specialization.

You ask about . . . labels and categories. I'm not sure w h a t kind of choreographer I am! Actually, I may be a dancemaker instead— I generate movement possibilities from processes, schemes, and puzzles rather than manipulate bodies in a predetermined form. But— I might be a superrealist too, and, after all, on Fridays a futurist!

Seriously, though, I prefer the word *transmedia* because it's movement that connects and extends whatever we see or know, in our heads, on the page or stage, across a room, or on a screen: even across disciplines. I also like the word k i n e t r i c s as the movement of bodies, ideas, images, lines, words, letters, concepts, tracks, designs, structures, systems, etc., across and through one another. The many texts I've written for my dances can stand and have been published separately. I also incorporate projections, films, and video. *Space City*, a film collaboration with Robyn Brentano and Andrew Horn, was premiered in June 1981 at Lincoln Center's International Dance Film Video Conference. Channels, circuits, and media interfacings let spaces, resources, concepts, and perspectives become interpenetrating and interexchangeable. Movement—following Marshall McLuhan's startlingly insightful lead—extends the signs and signals as well as ambient of the central nervous system, connecting all perceptual processes. There may be only five senses but virtually unexplored an unlimited number of sense "ratios." (Kinaesthetics and Extra Sensory Perception, for example, may be amalgams and combines of these ratios).

Ever since I began making dances in the early sixties, I've *programmed* movement—I like that word—meaning, constantly breaking down, repeating movement with an eye to the variations matrix of possibilities, recombining in any ways steps, changes, rhythms, textures, etc., as well as their density of relay and delay so that any and all elements, components, and permutable options can be called up, assembled, or juxtaposed at any moment, or between and with any dancing body.

As a dancemaker I program structural and organizational options, rather than just set specifically repeatable phrases, so the generation of (im)pulses, and the tracing and tracking of "circuits" in space, activates the firing and fielding of signs and signals which synchronistically become part of the formal performance process. It's asking a lot from dancers, but there's an organization to the dancing body transversing s p a c e that is quicker than the structural logic that the brain can decide, know, or predetermine. It's a kind of *digital*-kinetic semiotics . . .

Just how there are pulses, images, and imageries in the movement stream, sometimes just below the visible surface or dynamic, appearing automatically in the density of high-frequency field formations, or through the warping and deporting of line, time, and contour, intrigues me enormously. Sometimes the imagery only *seems* to be emitted, setting up semblances and (co)correspondences; sometimes it's actual, visceral, mimetic, implied, or disembodied. Dancing brings us to, through, and across, sometimes even beyond, the thresholds of the visible and invisible, the seen and unseen, the contained and uncontained . . .

And one wonders too just what *is* the connection between TV and the kinet(r)ics of perception *and* the dance (and media) explosion. The *programming* of parts, elements, units, modules, and matrices (including texts, voice, music, projections, transparencies, film, and/or video) can stimulate if not create a synchron(icit)y of pulses, pictures, and information relays; behind and through the moving body are other *orders* of projectable imageries. With the computer age there will be dancing words, kinetic grammars, information channels, conceptual continuums, data process services, synchromimetic teletexts, and electric dance mosaics, as there now are concerts and performances.

After six or seven generations, modern dance is still in its initial "volcanic" stage, and necessarily so! I have this expression about the dance explosion—"the f-i-e-l-d is bigger than the form"—meaning that the combined, concatenating activities of all those working in dance today have extended the action and boundaries of the idiom in a kind of joint exchange enterprise—there's now a pool of possibilities, structural and conceptual, extendable parameters, rather than fixed or enforced styles, genres and schools. Postmodernism might be paradoxically an open-ended systemic pluralism . . .

I feel that the art of choreography has reached an intriguing "pass." John Cage has reportedly said he doesn't think there will be composers in the year 2000—the complex aural resonances and synchronistically engineered sound environments will preclude their relevance. (There will be soundengineers and musicmakers.) I've long suspected the same about dance. A dance *can* make itself, even, w i t h o u t a choreographer!

I'm interested in ballet, modern (and postmodern) dance and "natural" movement coming together and f - u - s - i - n - g. One could consider classical alignment and turnout as a kind of technology for locomotion through space, but the tilting, multiple contractions, streamlining of line, pulse, spiral, and the twisting and skewering of line and form by the rotations of the torso—what Merce Cunningham ingeniously discovered—have expanded and changed all priorities. Sometimes I like to try shifting back and forth between "movement" and "dance"—they really can't be separated! I like the idea of a technic rather than technique, because there are larger, organic, holistic connections in the moving body, another *energy resource.* I mean, who or where can one train to move synchronistically?!

I started out as an aspiring actor while in high school and early college and did three years of summer stock, first in 1959 as an apprentice at Adelphi College, where I was fortunate to witness a lecture by Ruth St. Denis! Much of my early work from 1964 to 1975 was theatrical and had dancing and talking characters, and props. Maybe the drama of the moving body was my first connection.

I went to Antioch College, which has a work-study program, so every three or six months I'd trek from Ohio to New York for my jobs. My first was a hospital orderly (1961). Evenings I decided to study dance. I don't know how or why, but I found Syvilla Fort's name in the phone book! She was *fabulous*—a passionate and inspiring teacher who had danced with Katherine Dunham, later teaching and collaborating with many many people, including John Cage. She taught primitive, modern, and basic ballet. And she encouraged me!

In the early sixties I went to a variety of studios like New Dance Group and Ballet Arts and then found Paul Sanasardo, who had the patience and dedication to carefully teach and explain alignment, placement, phrasing, combining ballet and modern, even at the barre. Paul also incorporated what I'd call a kind of adapted "method" or Stanislavsky approach to dance projection, performance, motivation, and focus.

I also went, of course, to the Martha Graham School. It was by then a high drama dance factory with lots of conflicting currents and intrigues. Right after college I took ballet with Mia Slavenska (1965). She didn't talk about electromagnetic circuits or archetypes, but about the *skeleton.* She was both outrageous and endearing, when she wasn't poking or insulting you. She told me I had arms like sausages and was hopeless; it was v e r y inspiring!

While at Antioch, in an early existentialism course we read Nietzsche's *Zarathustra* and that started everything! Isadora Duncan has written that besides *the Bible,* she kept *Zarathustra* on her bedstand throughout her entire life. In 1974 I presented a Nietzsche portrait-play entitled *High Noon,* assembled after carefully researching his writings. Nietzsche has a master key to the dance!

While at Antioch, my most important experience was our much revered "guru" philosophy professor, Keith McGary. He really made things happen! To this day he's really been the biggest influence, meaning, one who l i b e r a t e s.

In his aesthetics class (a turning point) we read Susanne K. Langer. It was a breakthrough. Her writings have been of enormous importance, especially the later *Mind: An Essay on Human Feeling.* During 1975–1976 I presented a Bicentennial dance tribute to her called *Battery,* with 10 dancers at the Cathedral of St. John the Divine. I've met her several times and had the opportunity of visiting and talking with her.

Summer of 1966 I got a scholarship and studied briefly with Merce Cunningham and Carolyn Brown. Merce is the Einstein of modern dance. For more than 15 years I've watched all his work with great excitement and appreciation. He and John Cage are major artistic influences—they're a new juncture point and whole new axis in the experience of movement and sound in spacetime. I consider Merce Cunningham to be our first s p a c e dancer!

There were many other influences—Balanchine, the Judson Dance Theatre, and oh! I'd better mention Charlie Chaplin too—a favorite—he was certainly a first modern dancer, no?—while we're bantering terms!

More recently (1978) Maria Theresa Duncan—the last of the "Isadorables" (at the heroic age of 84)—provided a profound experience in restaging three separate concerts of the heritage of Isadora Duncan. It was so important I had to write a long appreciation essay entitled *Vision Dancing.*

Maybe you're wondering how I've kept my head together . . . New York *is* mania and madness. Ha! OK—I'll confess—only by reading and exploring Krishnamurti, for the past decade. He shows you how to see the *whole* mind—instantly! He's an expressway.

Reading and research are a tremendous and important influence. Here are some mighty thinkers and authors I could not have done without: Nietzsche, Ernst Cassirer, Edmund Husserl, Sigmund Freud, Carl Jung, Wilhelm Reich, Norman O. Brown, Marshall McLuhan, Jacques Ellul, Ludwig Wittgenstein, Gurdjieff-Ouspensky-Nicoll, e. e. cummings, Walt Whitman, John Cage, Marcel Duchamp, Arthur Koestler, Jean-Paul Sartre, Simone de Beauvoir, John Cunningham Lily, Alice Bailey, Nikola Tesla, Virginia Woolf, Gertrude Stein, Susanne Langer, Simone Weil.

I always encourage students to bring something else or o t h e r —an interest, avocation, a study, system, even another art to the dance—to discover a larger organic understanding of the moving body. And in the classroom I insist on being a student too and sharing in the collective kinetic investigation and exchange.

I want dancers to be able to move and generate a dance using their own inner rhythms and body clocks (reaffirming both Isadora and Stanislavsky) and to be able to patternate and problem-solve with an eye to development, design, modulation, exchange—not just present a preset, mechanically manipulated piece. I WANT TO SEE A DANCER'S AWARENESS, INTELLIGENCE, AND SPONTANEITY ALLOWED TO FUNCTION ON STAGE!

There are many formidable challenges to making dances. First and foremost it's the action of dancing that completes my own sense of being. It is a way to bridge the mind-body schizsplits that have fragmented our whole Western field of experience. Dancing is the means to recover the whole being, the primal man—archetypically the way perhaps the shaman is a unitive being before histories' specializations divide him into poet, oracle, priest, medicine man, mystic, medium, magician, etc.

In *The Making of Americans,* certainly the one work that crowns Gertrude Stein a philosopher, there's a big humorous clue in her exclamation at the outset that she wants to have in her all the

Space City. Kenneth King. Photo: Lois Greenfield.

b e i n g of *all* those who have ever lived, are living, or will be living! Now the reason for dancing!—ontological lust!

The challenge of training and discovering one's body—all the ways it can move and the reflexive underlying principles that connect the diversity of its processes and resources. Also, finding new energy thresholds, other senses, and sense ratios by changing the total body *frequency* and engaging multiaxial electromagnetic body field alignments. Dancing into the space age, into and through *s p a c e* . . . finding a bridge between technics and technique, art and science, investigation and discovery, the abstract and the concrete, programs, entertainment, and i n f o r m a t i o n.

Because of the concatenation of diverse styles, techniques, and systems during the last two decades, I sometimes think the only way to cross the new threshold is to work with "open form" and process choreography. Dance is about constant transformation. Even formal choreography can use improvisation, which can, I think, be a kind of meta-science—rigorous, formal, systemic, complexly, and spontaneously revealing of how movement *itself* generates and derives energy, structure, grammar. The most rewarding response to my work by both critics and audiences alike is wondering, and wanting to know what's set and what's not set—it becomes a puzzle for them watching, just as it can be for us d o i n g! Dance can be larger than a choreographer's brain and all linear organizational structures. I always feel the dancers, given the chance, can bring as much new information to a work in progress as any of the choreographer's (pre)suppositions. Movement has its o w n *intentionality;* dance doesn't need a psyche or psychology to motivate it, i.e., it has it's own "MOTORvation" . . .

What's challenging is constantly pushing against one's limits, conceptions, and possibilities. One can never rehearse enough. What's challenging about performing is the o t h e r (larger) projection threshold and the surplus of energy the audience supplies. Marcel Duchamp clarified the modernist intention—the audience provides the energy and attention to *complete* the action of the work. Meaning and stories are now long beside the point because movement as a paranarrative phenomenon expresses and reveals so *many* things! Performing is a tremendously exciting, transforming experience, almost like turning yourself inside out or having a double. Dancing can bring forth the mystic temperament, and I seem to have a large dose of that too! Dancing is always apocalyptic.

The environment is in such DANGER—nukes, chemspills, military, commercial (not to mention political) overkill—we need to rediscover another radiant energy within our bodies. Intelligence doesn't have to be contained by a body or institution, but can inhabit a field or ensemble of dancers. And gesture itself is a secret art—it can reveal, conceal, inform, heal, and transmute conflict and tension; then embrace and celebrate mystery. Einstein: "The most beautiful thing we can experience is the mysterious. It is the source of all true art and science" (*What I Believe*, 1930).

Since the mid-1970s my work has changed in that it involves more and more dance, music, and transmedia exploration, less characters and overt polemics. The information is in the dance; the *doing* is the finding and knowing. Right from my own outset in 1964 my dance changed and developed from working with words, the voice, and with various kinds of texts, the larger sense of language and deep structure to explore. In the information age there emerges a complex digital action to all the parameters of the word—all its rhythmic, intrasyntactical, and *coded* coefficients. Left brain/right brain research has shown that duality *is* physiological, but there are means and programs that can recoordinate polarity and holistically recircuit the brain's separate processes. I've found ways to "synapsulate" both body and rhythm, phrase, sequence, and voice with my "t-e-l-e-g-r-a-p-h-i-c s-o-n-g-s," puns, word games, and tongue twisters that atomize, particalize, and reduce to essential rhythmic bits the modules and matrices of steps, patterns, phonemes, gestures, vocables and activate their complex, *primal* mix.

Another challenge! That the body when heated, toned, and prepared can r e l e a s e itself from (the force of) gravity. Even if only temporarily, for a few moments it's an incredible, even revelatory experience.

I'm a tall, lean, slim person and I like that feeling, the body being light and unimpeded. I like to move full out, very expansively and rapidly. I've devised a lot of arm and spine movements that are all my own, so the body coils, twists, bounds, spins, spirals, gyrates, dips, bounces, curves. . . . The arms scallop spatially and gesturally, revolving around a constantly rotating body axis, revealing intersection zones and interstices. I turn and countertorque, whirl, glide, skim, travel, and dive the vectors. Dancing is more like high-interface action verbs, rather than nouns and subjects. I'm very interested in the *electric* threshold: dance can be like live voltage, or crossing realms. Sometimes the body is flooded and energized by impulses, spasms, jerks, shakes, tremors and responds with quirks and undulations. Sometimes the channel or energy stream makes cresting gestures: the body tracks, paces, swings, pivots, gallops, darts, slashes, skewers, scoops, scampers, vaults, jousts, rotates, balances, and springs into the air. I don't like to jump mechanically, but be *lifted* into the air. Dancing is immensity.

I've worked a lot with speed, fluidity and compression of phrase, step, gesture, rhythm, and activating a rapid-fire pulse. But the most important thing is to find out how one dances for one's self. I can't

Dance Motor. Kenneth King & Dancers. Kenneth King, Carter Frank, Shari Cavin. Photo: © Johan Elbers 1986.

quite teach what I do entirely yet. I try to and like working best by "osmosis" with dancers. The eye is mimetic and dancers should be able to "read" and transfer movement connections instantly. In my company work I try to draw as much on dissimilarities and differences to find or make another sense of continuity and unity. I'm not trying to have people be homogenized doing "my" style. I want dancers to "translate" and problem-solve by isolating and formally recombining the ingredients. I teach specific steps, matrices, and units specifying how to use them in various ways, but let them find and make the connections. My role is generator, conductor, catalyst.

First I give the dancers "space maps"—i.e., grid structures with specific locomotor instructions. During the last few years, starting with my dance *Wor(l)d (T)raid,* it's been grids: horizontal/vertical, diagonal, tilted, rotated, circuited, or diamond-shaped. It's about how very simple basics can visually and rhythmically quickly generate a complex field and fold, and numerous, simultaneous interlocking structures. One can use any battery of movements, though I prefer mixing the basic principles of both modern and ballet. Steps can include tendus and tracking laterally with the legs at 90-degree angles, pivoting the sense of line and structure, then adding lunges, walks, porte de bras, tilts, attitudes, turns, battements, etc. The steps per se are really about "geometry" (i.e., how axis, center, weight, etc., move the body through and across space) and "geography" (or typo-
graphy, mosaic-style), revealing how a discontinuous field of multioptional possibilities and interlocking, intertwining structures breaks through to, or simulates, a kind of kinetic motor or calculus!

Look at this. Would you believe it's all geometry and geography in only three grids!

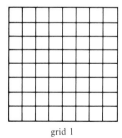
grid 1

grid 2

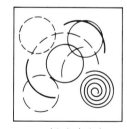
arcs/circles/spirals
rotors (moving arcs)
grid 3

In the random action of assembling parts and steps, dancers develop "radar"—in fact, all technological projection systems have their sources in our central nervous system. And this is not just "my" choreography or "a" dance but also the means anyone could use to explore generative structures, process, composition, geometry, etc. It's what I often teach and work with in workshops and residencies.

To develop and coordinate the rhythmic folding and the overall dynamic I'll give images, for example—for the first grid I'll suggest moving as if traveling, scurrying, darting through a labyrinth, or demarcating precise sets of interlocking puzzles, like Chinese boxes, because space can reveal intersecting layers, integers, rhythms. The circular grids, arcs, and "rotors" (rotating arcs) as well as interpenetrating circles generate contours, vortexes of energy and punctuate line with surprising changes of direction, making for relays, delays, recoils, dynamic change, and detail. As the dancers learn to ply the changes automatically, they find that dancing can happen faster than it seems one *can* think, arrange, plan, predict, coordinate, predetermine. That's the idea! There *is* a tremendous act on and motion within what we call spontaneity and synchronicity that is mysterious because it carries us beyond the limits and parameters of the ways we *think* it possible to move. Isn't that postmodern?!

To develop and coordinate the rhythmic folding and the overall dynamic I'll give images—for example, *Currency* (1980) grew out of the tight formal grid work *(Wor(l)d (T)raid)* and is the most open form work I've generated. Conceptually, the collective motorizing action of the ensemble makes for rotating axial "spools," coiled sprung vectors, pools, and vortexes and a constantly shifting center, multiple foci as the eye "reads" the constantly assembling and disappearing formations and patterns.

Because *Currency* was generated with five dancers (Carter Frank, Shari Cavin, Bryan Hayes, Bill Shepard, and myself), a kind of rapid-fire digital shifting from symmetrical to asymmetrical clusters and configurations made phrasing break through to a kinetic circuitry, threading bodies, lines, and patterns through one another, constantly realigning and recycling itself through space, permuting torque, direction, perspective, foreground, and background and energetically throwing depth of field and dimensionality into relief. I also cited Duchamp's *Nude Descending a Staircase*—the first time we see the fragmented rotation of a post-cubist spine in space; also M. C. Escher and Joseph Cornell are very relevant.

A CAPS grant (thanks again) enabled me to purchase a color video VHS system, to regularly tape and play back rehearsals both in the studio and outdoors in Battery Park. Memory is not just in the brain, but in the visceral and muscle reflexes involving visual and kinetic relays of axis, spine, and scan of the gaze. The spine functions like a revolving antenna. The firing of (im)pulses and signals sets up intertwining, sproketing patterns, ribbons, waves, and threads so that parts, modules, and steps can vigorously be (re)assembled, plied, transformed, permuted, even fragmented from day to day, perfor-

S-C-A-N. Kenneth King & Dancers. Kenneth King, Mary Ann Daniel.
Photo: © Johan Elbers 1986.

mance to performance. The video sound system amplified the caco-
phony of the urban soundscape, simulating a William Tudor score,
with whom I've collaborated since 1976. Later he watched the video
and plotted the time changes, then adapted and composed music for
it.

As McLuhan explained, television is about constantly reassem-
bling clusters and configurations of image, word, picture, information, etc. The dizzying juxtapositions, rapid jump cuts, zero-degree
zooms, and staggered panning shots seem to throw the viewer out
of his body, or one's eyes out of perspective! Rather than paper and
money, the "pulse" may now be the real basic unit of currency in the
transformation of our overloaded modern world.

For me a very active, dense field and stage fabric can be very
satisfying. Besides, computers are going to make for whole new orders and registers of program possibility where word, image, pulse,
design, configurations, and data transparencies with high-density
ratios and motor mimetic transactions will take precedence in re-
defining our perceptual-kinetic and visual currencies. One sees its
intimation in the intense, spellbound fascination youngsters have
riveted to electronic pinball and public computer games, or in business transactions at banks, airlines, and corporations that are beginning to confront the high-process assemblage and digital transformation of high-frequency clustered configurations, feeding and
engaging the total scan and span of our mindfields.

Instead of steps and structures, the layering of post-choreo-
graphed space is really negotiated by *codes*—complex ways we assimilate and process the raw data of steps, phrases, signals, directions,
lines, vectors, matrices, trajectories, directions, changes, etc. Merce
Cunningham made and coined the language and vocabulary and the
Judson experimentation furthered the transformational rules, i.e.,
grammar.

New dance has entered another whole realm, or order of coor-
dination, organization, structuring, energy, intelligence that can
function when bodies move. Inner space and o u t e r space—*why*
separate them! The body *is* contained, but—dancing is *uncontained*
. . . We can move to know ourselves and dance to s e e the wor(l)d.
. . . It's the riddle of being—and goodness! -n-o-t-h-i-n-g-n-e-s-s and
the mystery of universe that keeps dancers making dances, and—
dancers! E - U - R - E - K - A -!

February 19, 1981

Date	*Title of Work*	*Place and Details*
September 25, 1964	*cup/saucer/two dancers/radio*	Washington Square Galleries, New York City. Sound tape by Kenneth King. Performed by Phoebe Neville and Kenneth King.
June 27, 1965	*Spectacular*	Bridge Theater, New York City. Music and sound tape by Kenneth King. Performed by Harry Donovan, Sylvia Jones, Sally Zimmerman, and Kenneth King.
June 27, 1965	*self-portrait* (Dedicated to the Memory of John F. Kennedy)	Bridge Theater, New York City. Sound tape and performance by Kenneth King.
April 5, 1966	*Blow-Out*	Judson Memorial Church, New York City. Sound tape by Kenneth King. Text by René Descartes. Performed by Laura Dean and Kenneth King.
April 5, 1966	*camouflage*	Judson Memorial Church, New York City. Taped excerpts from *In The Labyrinth* by Alain Robbe-Grillet. Text by Kenneth King.
November 10, 1966	*m-o-o-n-b-r-a-i-nwithSuperLecture*	Gate Theater, New York City. Text, props, costumes, and performance by Kenneth King. Film and lighting by Jeff Norwalk.
October 26, 1967	*Print-Out*	Judson Gallery, New York City. Projected dream text, echo tape, and performance by Kenneth King, with Phoebe Neville. Dance film and projections operated by Jeff Norwalk.
October 28, 1967	*Cancellation Performance* (A No-Show Show)	New School for Social Research, New York City. Performed by Alfred North and Kenneth King.

Date	Title of Work	Place and Details
January 4, 1968	*A Show*	Judson Memorial Church, New York City. Honky-tonk player piano recording and music from *Gone with the Wind.* Text and solo performance by Kenneth King.
March 27, 1968	*Farewell Performance*	Judson Memorial Church, New York City. Solo performance and text by Kenneth King.
April 1969	*exTravel(ala)ganza*	Judson Memorial Church, New York City. Text by Kenneth King. Decor by Alan Lloyd. Lighting by Jeff Norwalk. Performed by Kenneth King, Robert Wilson, Elaine Luthy, and Jain Air.
October 24, 1969	*The Phenomenology of Movement*	Loeb Student Center, New York University, New York City. Text by Kenneth King. Performed by Ann Danoff, Kenneth King, Robert Wilson, and Elaine Luthy.
May 15, 1970	*Seercret Cellar* (For Edwin Denby)	Duane Methodist Church, New York City. Music by Melanie. Text by Kenneth King. Performed by Ann Danoff, Kenneth King, with Jeff Norwalk, Elaine Luthy.
December 25, 1970	*Christmas Celebration Events*	597 Broadway, New York City. Music from Handel's *Messiah.* Performed by Kenneth King, Elaine Luthy, and Cindy Lubar.
May 14, 1971	*Inadmissleable Evidentdance* (The CIA Scandal)	Produced with radio station WBAI at Washington Square Church, New York City. Text by Kenneth King. Performed by Elaine Luthy, Kenneth King, and Cindy Lubar. (This work foretold Watergate and the computer/information revolution.)

Date	*Title of Work*	*Place and Details*
June 9, 1972	*Simultimeless Action*	112 Workshop/Gallery, New York City. Collaboration with Elaine Luthy (dance), Pierre Ruiz (composer), and William Stewart (painting exhibition). "The Dancing Jewel" text by Kenneth King. Performance by Kenneth King and Elaine Luthy. "The Void Piece" reading and performance by Kenneth King.
April 2, 1973	*Anyone's Guest Is Nobody's Guess (Introducing Mr. Pontease Tyak)*	Exchange Theater for the Arts, New York City. Text and performance by Kenneth King.
April 2, 1973	*Patrick's Dancing Dances*	Exchange Theater for the Arts, New York City. Music, "Bridge over Troubled Waters," by Simon and Garfunkel. Performed by Mahr Benham, Kenneth King, James Neu, Carolyn Lord, Linn Varney, and Eva Pietkiewicz.
April 2, 1973	*Metagexis (Studies for a Motion Grammar)*	Exchange Theater for the Arts, New York City. Text by Kenneth King. Performed by Mahr Benham, Kyra Lober, and Kenneth King (dancers); Lynn Varney, Carolyn Lord, James Neu, and Eva Pietkiewicz (speakers/characters).
May 23, 1974	*Praxiomatics (The Practice Room)*	597 Broadway, New York City. Texts by Kenneth King. Projected visual design by Michael Martin and Kenneth King. Projectionist: Steve Crawford. Performed by Robyn Brentano, Charles Dennis, Liz Pasquale, Wendy Perron, David Woodberry, and Kenneth King (dancers); Linn Varney and Madeline Slovenz (voice).
May 23, 1974	*The Telaxic Synapsulator*	597 Broadway, New York City. Text by Kenneth King. Danced by Wendy Perron and Kenneth King.

Date	*Title of Work*	*Place and Details*
November 1, 1974	*High Noon* (A Portrait-Play of Friedrich Nietzsche)	Byrd Hoffman Foundation, New York City. Music, Overture to *Tannhäuser,* by Wagner. Selections of Nietzsche's texts compiled and performed by Kenneth King. Set design and lighting by Kenneth King.
November 2, 1974	*Time Capsule*	Byrd Hoffman Foundation, New York City. Text and performance by Kenneth King, with Steve Crawford. Film by Jeff Norwalk. Danced by Arnold Horton.
May 2, 1975	Preview, *Battery, Part I, Mappingg in an Open Field* (A Bicentennial Dance for Susanne K. Langer, Celebrating an American Thinker)	Exchange Theater for the Arts, New York City. Text by Susanne Langer, read by Kenneth King. Danced by Jane Comfort, Charles Dennis, Wendy Perron, and Kenneth King.
August 1, 1975	*Battery, Part II*	Moming Dance and Art Center, Chicago. Text by Kenneth King and Susanne K. Langer. Performed by 14 dancers, including Sally Banes, Carter Frank, Ellen Mazer, Jackie Radis, Jim Self, Eric Traub, and Kenneth King.
November 10, 1975	*The Ultimate Exposé*	Danspace, St. Mark's Church, New York City. Text and projections by Kenneth King. Photography and lighting by Jeff Norwalk. Performed by Kenneth King, with Arnold Horton. A multimedia update of *Inadmissleable Evidentdance* as an ongoing work.

Date	*Title of Work*	*Place and Details*
June 16, 1976	*Battery, Parts I, II, and III*	Synod House, Cathedral of St. John the Divine, New York City. Music by William-John Tudor and Pierre Ruiz. Slides by Zora A. Zash. Lighting by Tom Cayler. Set and production assistance by Alison Yxersa. Danced by Jane Comfort, Karen Levey, Stephanie Woodard, Kenneth King, Robyn Brentano, Steve Crawford, Charles Dennis, Deborah Glaser, Katy Matheson, and Ruth Tepper. Other versions of the work were presented at University of Maryland (1976) and University of Wisconsin (1977).
1976–1977	*RAdeoA.C.tiv(ID)ty* (Dedicated to Pierre and Marie Curie)	Installation I, November 9, 1976. Dance Theater Workshop, New York City. Text by Kenneth King. Lighting by Tina Charney. Performed by Carter Frank, Karen Levey, Jim Self, and Kenneth King (dancers); Tom Cayler and Herndon Ely (speakers). Installation II, December 4, 1977. Danspace, St. Mark's Church, New York City. Texts by Kenneth King. Danced by Jumay Chu, Carter Frank, and Kenneth King. Installation III, December 7, 1977. The Kitchen, New York City. Music by William-John Tudor. Video by Kenneth King; additional video by Dennis Diamond.
March 22, 1977	*Labyrinth*	The Kitchen, New York City. Music by Pierre Ruiz. Danced by Kathy Ray.

Date	*Title of Work*	*Place and Details*
March 16, 1978	*RAdeoA.C.tiv(ID)ty* (Dedicated to Pierre and Marie Curie)	Brooklyn Academy of Music, New York City. Music by William-John Tudor; recorded Tibetan Buddhist rites of the Drukpa Order, Bhutan. Text by Kenneth King; excerpts from *Radioactive Substances* by Marie Curie. Lighting by William Otterson. Photography by Kerry Schuss. Video by Dennis Diamond, Robyn Brentano, and Kenneth King. Costumes and projections by Kenneth King. Production coordinator: Robyn Brentano. Performed by Jumay Chu, Carter Frank, Karen Levey, Kenneth King, Alan Good, Rennie Greenberg, Diane Jacobowitz, Daniel Lambert, Elizabeth Ross, William Shepard, and Megan Walker (dancers); Amy Taubin (voice/actress).
March 16, 1978	*Dance Spell/The Telaxic Synapsulator* (Dedicated to Nikola Tesla)	Brooklyn Academy of Music, New York City. Music by William-John Tudor. Text with projections by Kenneth King. Lighting by William Otterson. Photography and slides by Kerry Schuss. Production coordinator: Robyn Brentano. Telaxic Synapsulator technician: Stephen Crawford. Performed by Carter Frank, Kenneth King, Kathy Ray, Charles Dennis, Diane Jacobowitz, William Shepard, Megan Walker, Daniel Lambert, Rennie Greenberg, Elizabeth Ross (dancers); Amy Taubin (actress).
August 29, 1978	*The Run-on Dance*	Cooper-Hewitt Museum, New York City; presented by the Cultural Council Foundation/CETA Artists Project. Danced by Diane Jacobowitz and Kenneth King.

Date	Title of Work	Place and Details
September 7, 1978	*Pilot 5/Process Collaboration*	Cooper-Hewitt Museum, New York City; presented by the Cultural Council Foundation/CETA Artists Project. Choreocollaborators: Dana Reitz, Kenneth King, Nancy Lewis, David Woodberry.
March 13, 1979	*Wor(l)d (T)raid*	The Kitchen, New York City. Music by William-John Tudor. Film, "Bowling Green," by Robyn Brentano. Lighting by Richard Kerry. Projections by Kerry Schuss. Danced by Carter Frank, Diane Jacobowitz, Kenneth King, Bill Shepard, Nancy Alfaro, Judith Jefferson, and Rena Smolski. Made possible in part by a grant from the National Endowment for the Arts.
March 13, 1979	*Word Raid* (Impossible Tongue Twisters for e. e. cummings)	The Kitchen, New York City. Text by Kenneth King. Performed by Robyn Brentano and Kenneth King.
April 17, 1980	*Stand-Up Comedian*	Merce Cunningham Studio, New York City. Music by William-John Tudor. Lighting by Jeff McRoberts. Performed by Kenneth King.
April 17, 1980	*Space City*	Merce Cunningham Studio, New York City. Music by William-John Tudor. Lighting by Jeff McRoberts. Costume by Ronald Kolodzie. Executed by Robyn Brentano.
April 17, 1980	*Blue Mountain Pass*	Merce Cunningham Studio, New York City. Music by William-John Tudor. Lighting by Jeff McRoberts. Costumes by Bryan Hayes. Danced by Shari Cavin, Diane Jacobowitz, Bryan Hayes, William Shepard, and Kenneth King. Made possible in part by, a grant from the National Endowment for the Arts.

Date	Title of Work	Place and Details
November 10, 1980	*Currency*	YW-YMHA, West Orange, New Jersey. Found sound, Battery Park, New York City. Lighting by Peter Anderson. Danced by Carter Frank, Shari Cavin, William Shepard, Bryan Hayes, and Kenneth King. Video, process work generated, in Battery Park, New York City.
December 8, 1980	*Generator*	Dance Alliance, New Haven, Connecticut. Music and voice by David Moss. Performed by 12 dancers, with Kenneth King.
March 10, 1981	*Dancing Words*	Solo lecture-demonstration performance; University of Minnesota, Minneapolis. Text by Kenneth King.
March 12, 1981	*The Phi Project* (Trilogy of Dances: *Dreamhouse, Currency, Blue Mountain Pass*)	Walker Art Center, Minneapolis. Musical composition, media engineering, project direction and design, graphics, layouts, production, editing, programming, lighting, devices and systems, photography, cinematography, and text for "Densities and Mimetics" by William-John Tudor. For images and visuals: Unit direction, cinematography, design, production, and editing by Donna Clayton. Unit direction, photography, production, and processing by Doug Hansen. Unit direction, photography, production, processing, and special effects by Chris Peregoy. Design/graphics, photography, and production by David Bell. Photography and processing by Jim Funk.

Date	*Title of Work*	*Place and Details*
March 12, 1981	*The Phi Project* (Trilogy of Dances: *Dreamhouse, Currency, Blue Mountain Pass*)	Programming and systems by Roger Donnelly. Photography and special effects by Ed Rowles. Photographic images by Nanette Hatzes. Computer programming and graphics by Richard Johnson. Graphic/designs, production, and processing by Susan Fallowfield. Construction of "Dreamhouse" by Joe Verret. Electronics and construction by Steve Carr. Screens and light bricks by Diane Bisser and Larry Rose. Electrics and lighting by Terry Cobb. Danced by Carter Frank, Shari Cavin, Bryan Hayes, William Shepard, Kenneth King.
June 15, 1981	*Space City*	International Dance Film Video Conference, Lincoln Center, New York City. A film collaboration with film makers Robyn Brentano and Andrew Horn. Music by William-John Tudor. Text and performance by Kenneth King. Scenic design by Richard Brintzenhofe. 32 minutes, b/w and color. Made possible in part by a grant from the National Endowment for the Arts.
October 8, 1981	*Straw Boss*	New Dance Festival, Walker Art Center, Minneapolis. Music by William-John Tudor. Danced by Carter Frank, Jane Comfort, Shari Cavin, Bryan Hayes, and Kenneth King.
July 15, 1981	*Casablanca*	American Dance Festival, Duke University, Durham, North Carolina. Danced by Mary Ann Daniel, Eve Chilton, Melody Eggen, Karen Graubart, Amy Gray, Margaret Hess, Elizabeth Kert, Kenneth King, Ayaz Maile, Jimmy Mori, Stuart Rosenfeld, Philip Wagnitz.

Date	Title of Work	Place and Details
June 8, 1982	*Complete Electric Discharge*	La Mama E.T.C., New York City. Music by William-John Tudor. Lighting by Roberto Guidote. Solo performance by Kenneth King.
June 8, 1982	*S-C-A-N*	La Mama E.T.C., New York City. Text, dedicated to William-John Tudor, by Kenneth King. Performed by Carter Frank, Shari Cavin, Bryan Hayes, Mary Ann Daniel, and Kenneth King (dancers); Pamela Tait, Elizabeth Meyer, Cliff Seidman (speakers).
June 8, 1982	*Dance Motor*	La Mama E.T.C., New York City. Music by William-John Tudor. Lighting by Roberto Guidote. Costumes by Daniel Blauenstein. Danced by Carter Frank, Shari Cavin, Bryan Hayes, Mary Ann Daniel, and Kenneth King. Made possible in part by a grant from the National Endowment for the Arts and the New York State Council on the Arts.
August 18, 1982	*In the Labyrinth*	University Theater, Long Beach Summer School of Dance, California State University. Music by William-John Tudor. Lighting by David Palmer. Costumes by Barbara Cox. Danced by Kenneth King, Tricia Boerger, Karin Jensen, Beth Klarreich, Kala Kollanyi, Christiane Leone, Cynthia Meyers, Emily Schottland, Christine Thorbourn, and Cynthia Vuittonet.

Date	*Title of Work*	*Place and Details*
March 16, 1983	*Scream at Me Tomorrow*	The Kitchen, New York City. Sound and media by William-John Tudor. Text, "Mumble Mumbo Jumble" for Arnold Horton, by Kenneth King. Photography by Christopher Peregoy. Lighting by Jeff McRoberts. Costumes by Daniel Blauenstein. Performed by Shari Cavin, Carter Frank, Mary Ann Daniel, Bryan Hayes, and Kenneth King (dancers); Pamela Tait (actress).
March 16, 1983	*Flextime*	The Kitchen, New York City. Music by William-John Tudor. Video by Tim Purtell. Lighting by Jeff McRoberts. Costumes by Heather Samuels. Danced by Shari Cavin, Carter Frank, Mary Ann Daniel, Bryan Hayes, and Kenneth King. Made possible in part by a grant from the National Endowment for the Arts.
February 23, 1984	*Moose (on the Loose)*	St. Mark's Church, New York City. Music, projected decor, and lighting by William-John Tudor. Text, for Bob Holman, by Kenneth King. Photography by Christopher Peregoy. Costumes by Heather Samuels. Performed by Carter Frank, Shari Cavin, Amy Gray, Bryan Hayes, and Kenneth King (dancers); Pamela Tait (actress). Made possible in part by a grant from the National Endowment for the Arts and the New York State Council on the Arts.

Date	*Title of Work*	*Place and Details*
February 23, 1984	*Strung-Out Newscasters*	St. Mark's Church, New York City. Text by Kenneth King. Costumes by Heather Samuels. Performed by Pamela Tait and Kenneth King.
February 23, 1984	*Complete Electric Discharge II* (for Nikola Tesla)	St. Mark's Church, New York City. Music, projected decor, and lighting by William-John Tudor. Photography by Christopher Peregoy. Costumes by Heather Samuels. Danced by Carter Frank, Shari Cavin, Amy Gray, Bryan Hayes, and Kenneth King.
March 21, 1985	*Planet X* (Repertory Medley Celebrating Kenneth King's Twentieth New York Season)	St. Mark's Church, New York City. Music, media, and lighting by William-John Tudor. Texts by Kenneth King. Photography by Christopher Peregoy. Danced by Carter Frank, Amy Gray, Pamela Tait, Bryan Hayes, Kenneth King, Jim Bonner, Mary Lisa Burns, Elizabeth Caron, Ann Lall, and Ted Marks.

Date	*Title of Work*	*Place and Details*
March 21, 1985	*Critical Path* (for R. Buckminster Fuller)	St. Mark's Church, New York City. Music, media, and lighting by William-John Tudor. Photography by Christopher Peregoy. Costumes by Heather Samuels. Danced by Amy Gray, Bryan Hayes, Kenneth King, Jim Bonner, Mary Lisa Burns, Ann Lall, Elizabeth Caron, and Ted Marks. Made possible in part by grants from Inter-Arts program of the National Endowment for the Arts and the New York State Council on the Arts.

Gus Solomons, Jr.

Photo: Peggy Jarrell Kaplan.

GUS SOLOMONS, JR.

Gus Solomons, Jr., began his dance training with Jan Veen at the Boston Conservatory of Music, while taking his degree in architecture at the Massachusetts Institute of Technology. He subsequently danced in the companies of Pearl Lang, Donald McKayle, Joyce Trisler, Martha Graham, and Merce Cunningham before forming his own company, in 1972. In addition to teaching at universities throughout the United States, Solomons was dean of the Dance School at the California Institute of the Arts, in Valencia, from 1976 to 1978. He has been commissioned to create dances for many companies, including the Alvin Ailey Repertory; Sidewalk Dance Theater in Knoxville, Tennessee; and the Berkshire Ballet, in Pittsfield, Massachusetts. In addition to artistic direction, choreographing, and performing, Solomons has been a frequent arts council panelist for the National Endowment for the Arts and several state councils. He is also writing professionally about dance for the late *Ballet News,* the *Village Voice,* and other publications.

GUS SOLOMONS, JR.

A Nourishing Meal

I consider myself an eclectic choreographer. I feel free to use whatever method I think appropriate to the dance I am making and the purpose for which it is intended. I have made dances for musical shows and revues, for television, and for environmental settings like plazas, gymnasiums, gardens, and galleries, as well as for theater performance. Each different situation presents the challenge of finding dance movement particularly suited for it.

Within the style which is generally called "modern" I also feel free to experiment with various aesthetic approaches: lyric, narrative, minimal, game-rule, serial, et al. The single constant of my aesthetic is motion. All ways of building dances are valid for me at one time or another, and the dances I have choreographed reflect that broad spectrum of methodologies.

My study of modern dance began when I was a student of architecture at Massachusetts Institute of Technology in my home city of Cambridge, Massachusetts. I studied with Jan Veen, a disciple of the Wigman School and the Laban system of dance training. The Laban approach, conceiving the dancer as the center of an imaginary cube of space, was extremely compatible with the architectural discipline.

Shortly after starting with Veen at the Boston Conservatory, I began to study also with Robert Cohan at his Boston studio. There I was introduced to the emotionally oriented Graham technique. My dancing style became a synthesis of these two philosophies: one intellectual, analytic and the other dramatic and emotional.

One of the most important and valuable things I learned from Jan Veen was the ability to grasp movement phrases immediately and reproduce them accurately. That is a skill possessed by too few dancers today, and one that is vital to the needs of choreographers who want to see a quick sketch of their ideas before they decide to develop them. The dancers I train learn very quickly the high priority I place on this ability to translate perception into motion directly.

My chief choreographic concern is the movement, not its connotations, meanings, or symbolism. I try to eliminate from my conscious choreographic process the limitations of the given quantities, and to explore the permutations of the movement energy I am dealing with. I do not dwell on the obvious with considerations of such extraneous matters as "masculine" or "feminine" movement to suit the genders of my dancers. When a man does a movement, it is automatically masculine; when a woman does the same movement, it is feminine. Rather than making some choreographic comment on the fact, I explore the differences in attack, weight, and rhythm given to the motion by different physiques, whatever their genders.

The important factors that shape the choices I make are more like: what are the dancers' skill levels, where will the dance be performed, how long shall the dance be in relation to the time available in which to choreograph it? Nor do I generally predetermine the form the dance will have. The form evolves as a result of the methods I use to devise the movement, the numbers of dancers, the musical accompaniment, etc.

A favorite method of mine for creating dance sections is to devise a process of game-rule system which will automatically produce interesting relationships, and then either select the ones I like best and set them, or refine the rules in such a way that deadlocks or endless repetition will be impossible.

These game-rule inventions grew from my desire to make live performance organically different from film or video performance in which a "perfect performance" could be captured forever. I posed the question: how can I keep the piece and the dancers truly spontaneous without resorting to improvisation? My Virgonian nature cannot quite accept the relinquishing of control that improvisation involves. It is about the only method with which I have not experimented extensively.

I am reputed to have been most greatly influenced by Merce Cunningham, in whose company I danced for three years, and with whom I studied consistently over the course of a decade. When I discovered a system of beliefs and concepts that reinforced my own, answered some of my own creative needs, permitted the controlled freedom I enjoyed, I naturally cleaved to it.

From Merce I gained corroboration for my convictions that dance should be inclusive, not exclusive, of all motion as potential dance material, and that the choreographer's task is to organize his chosen range of infinite possibilities into a structure, which has a logic based on its own kinesthetic identity.

I am influenced by personal and social interactions and by physical environment more than by other artists or by cultural climate. The space around me very much influences the scale of the move-

Gus Solomons, Jr. Photo: Joy K. Aubrey.

ment I create. Dances I make in California are more roomy than those I make in the East; there is more detail, quicker rhythms, closer contact in my New York dances.

My methods for finding movement have changed over the course of my dance-making career. My earliest dances were highly dramatic, since the movement was generated by my emotional response to the music. As I continued to choreograph, I moved gradually away from the use of music, until the period between 1970 and 1975, when I made dances to be performed in silence, or with very sparse word scores that footnoted the movement concepts.

My association with Mio Morales got me reconnected with music again, but in a much more organic way. Mio and I work simultaneously and independently, bouncing off each other's energy and rhythms to shape the motion/sound continuity. We each work with our respective mediums in a similar way, and the collaboration is satisfying.

I am quite sure it is impossible for an artist to analyze his own work with objective accuracy. An artist is an artist if he defines himself as one. Whether his work is any good is judged by the audience who experience it. I make a distinction between art and entertainment with this metaphor: art is a meal; entertainment is only a snack. Each has its rightful place, and each contains elements of the other; but entertainment seeks to delight with secondary nourishment, and art should first nourish, but with delight.

In fact, the critical difference between art and entertainment lies in their respective relationships to reality. Entertainment offers its audience a momentary escape from the problems of reality for the time it is happening. Art, on the other hand, illuminates reality by confronting it, exposing it, and re-examining it to help its audience gain insight into reality and thus deal more effectively with it. The benefits of art outlast the experiencing of it.

To the extent the artist lives in the world and is affected by it, his work cannot help reflecting it. There is no need for me as an artist to be didactic; my solutions to the movement problems I set about finding in my dances are the metaphor for the problems of my real life. My insights as a choreographer are about movement. It is the privilege and duty of the audience members to apply those insights to their own individual experiences and interpret them.

My dances take the viewer along a path of kinesthetic sensations, leading to an unpredetermined conclusion. The relationship of the parts to the whole is sequential, not hierarchical; the movement patterns are built from kinesthetic logic, not intellectual logic. I have been trying to give my dances an overall structure, which organizes the sequence in a way that will be satisfying to the audience, even though it may not be a conventional structure, like those borrowed from music, drama, or opera.

Japanese scroll paintings provide a model of sequence-as-structure. They do not build to some single climax and dénouement, as Western art does; each episode has its own identity, while being related to the whole merely by juxtaposition, not causality. The audience is capable of relating "a" to "b" and deserves the right to do so, each for his or her own reasons, independent of the artist's reasons for making that juxtaposition.

This process of composition is still hard for some critics to accept, even though we all accept similar linear processes in our everyday lives without the slightest question. Every computer-regulated aspect of daily existence reflects this method. Visual arts have broken free of the renaissance mold; why not dance? I conceive dances as temporal/kinetic sculptures, which probe the expressive potential of nonliteral movement, arranged according to the logic of its own kinesthetic content and texture.

Like the buildings of my favorite architect, Eero Saarinen, each of my dances starts from a fresh premise. The problem I set for each new piece is an outgrowth of the previous one, or arises from an appetite stimulated by it.

As audiences become more sophisticated to the medium of dance and learn to accept a wider range of approaches, my dances no longer are considered remote or "intellectual," as they were, especially before my musical collaboration with Mio Morales began. I am eager to reach the audience at a visceral and intellectual level, but I will not capitulate to entertainment at the expense of kinesthetic intent.

My own perception of the stages of my choreographic development is as follows:

At first, my dances fit steps to music, making visual pictures. They were primarily concerned with the superficial look of the movement and the literal idea they were communicating. The form and dynamics were determined by the music.

The next phase was concerned with the way the movement felt to do. The picture was still important, but I became more aware of energy as a factor in devising the movement. The dances still contained literal and dramatic meaning, but I was beginning to discover that my real interest was shifting from the message to the medium.

As motion took precedence, I eliminated musical accompaniment and choreographed in a stream-of-consciousness method, making evening-length dances that flowed continuously from start to finish. The texture and density, the dynamics, the speeds and rhythms were themselves the expressive content.

During this period my work began to puzzle and confound critics and audiences, to some extent. They found the work "aloof" and cold; there were no emotional "hooks" for them to grasp; there was no convenient formal cubbyhole into which they could slip the dances. It was admittedly my period of least accessibility, simply because my focus had shifted from presentation to content.

Now I have returned to music, although I still create the move-

Gus Solomons, Jr. Photo: Guy Cross.

ment in silence. The relevance of the music to the dancing, whether or not it is rhythmically matched, makes the dances accessible without compromising their kinesthetic purity. The music helps trigger for the audience the connotations they need to complete their imagery.

The evolution has gone from how it looks/what it means, to how it feels/where it comes from, to what it is. Classically, architecture has been viewed as "frozen music," and the influence of architecture has been and still is central to my perception of dance. The early dances are architectural in their use of the body as a component of a visual picture. The architectonic aspect has now been translated into kinesthesis. My consideration of the structure of the body dancing is now kinetic instead of static. I see dance as "fluid architecture." Energy and time are elements as important as shape in the conception and the perception.

The dance process represented by the series of *Steps* dances, beginning in 1980, and with the tenth incarnation completed in 1986, is a clear example of the method I have found to crystalize the marriage of structural form and motion content. The structure, which is based on various numerical and geometric progressions, can be fulfilled with movement as simple as walking/running or as complex as the pure-dance movement of *Unplay Dances* (1981) and *Differences of Need: Complements* (1982), two concert dances which embody underlying structures as rigorous as that of *Steps.*

Unplay Dances uses for its dance material a progression of phrases of 4 to 12 beats. *Differences of Need* is a two-part ballet, of which Part I is a minimalist exposition of traffic patterns the progression 3 to 10 and the reverse can create. Part II is a high-energy, full-motion dance, deriving its movement from three extended phrases. The structural outlines of the two parts is identical, although their movement contents could hardly be less similar.

For now, I continue to be fascinated by the possibilities of this composition process. It is compatible with my love of the analytical. It represents a clear, strong organization, which can accommodate great freedom of motion content. Its order appeals to my logical nature.

If there is an overall goal to which I aspire, it must be to make dances that audiences "love," because of their immediacy and kinesthetic impact. I know many of our audiences "appreciate" the dances we do, but that essence that makes them want to shout, that jolts them off their seats, that gives them an instant "rush" still eludes my work. Perhaps the kind of concerns I have choreographically will never lend themselves to that kind of response, but aiming toward that goal still plays a significant part in motivating the next dance.

In taking the inventory of my works and classifying them by the problems each was trying to solve, I found that some fitted into no specific category. These are the dances which have been made simply out of the ongoing process of making dances, because that is what I do. Whenever I ask myself why I make dances, my response is just to table the question and make another dance.

Most of the dances I have made can be classified by the problem-task they were made to solve, or the specific type of experiment that led to their creation.

Gus Solomons, Jr. Photo: Guy Cross.

Dances with word scores

I used the words as accompaniment either for their sound value or their explanation of some aspect of the piece's construction, connotations, or aesthetic premise.

Simply this fondness . . . (1966)	Duet; Gertrude Stein word score.
Notebook (1967)	Solo; theorems about dance form and content by Solomons.
Two Reeler (1968)	Piece for tape recorders, one painting word pictures, the other giving instructions for audience movement in kinesthetic response to an imaginary dance.
Draft Alteration (1969)	Solo lecture/dance with words and verses by Solomons.
Brilll-o (1973)	Live dialogue recorded, altered, and played back by Paul Earls.
Yesterday (1973)	Poems by Ethan Ayer.
Decimal Plum (1973)	Dancers' voices and words by Solomons.
A Shred of Prior Note (1974)	Quartet with words by Solomons.
word/game/time/dance (1974)	Solo lecture/dance; words by Solomons.
Appendix (1974)	Electronically altered verse by Solomons.
Table of Contents (1974)	Word structures by Solomons.
Chapter One (1974)	Trio with live reading of possible interpretations of the movement.
Biograph (1974)	Solo for a woman.
Conversation (1976)	Company dance with rhythmic descriptions of the dance movement used as musical accompaniment.

Dances using game-rule procedures

These dances contain elements of indeterminancy with regard to sequence or choice of movement phrases, which are determined during the performance by the dancers through drawing or dealing cards, numbering floor areas, etc.

we don't know only how much time we have . . . (1969)	Solo using numbered floor patterns to determine lighting and sound cues.
Quad (1970)	Large group piece, using instructions drawn in performance to determine sequence and dance phrase or task.
Par: Tournament (1971)	Flash cards displayed by referee determine competition phrases and order.
THE GUT-STOMP LOTTERY kill (1972)	Dancers draw from piles of cards or deal hands of cards to determine movement phrases and sequences.
Pocketcard Processes I, II (1972)	Cards dealt at beginning of dance determine sequences and tasks.
Meditation (1974)	Solo using card placement to determine phrase and location.
Shuffleplay Process, Audienceplay Process (1974)	Random drawing during piece determines tasks and phrases.

Dances with audience participation

These dances involve the willing members of the audience in active participation with the dancer(s), either in their seats or as volunteers on stage.

Kinesia #5 (for dancer with audience accompaniment) (1967)	Solo with recorded instructions for audience noises to accompany dancer.
Two Reeler (1968)	See "Dances with Word Scores" above.

Audienceplay Process (1974)	Dancers lead audience volunteers in movement tasks.

Dances performed in silence

Title Meet (1971)	Prize fight gong to start sections.
Par: Tournament (1971, 1974)	Athletic competition using dance skills and phrases.
cat. #10/13NSSR-GS jgm (1970)	Music played only when dancer is not dancing.
Steady Work (1975)	Deafening music and noise played during audience seating and intermission to reinforce the silence during the dancing.
Statements of Nameless Root I (Observations) (1975)	Solo.
Ad Hoc Transit (1976)	Company work for eight.

Dances with musical collaboration

The following dances all have musical scores composed specifically for them.

Phreaque (1969)	Score by Pia Gilbert, UCLA.
Crooz' (1972)	Percussion score by Randy Walker.
Beetcan Conserves (1972)	Score by John Herbert MacDowell.
Brilll-o (1973)	Electronic score by Paul Earls.

The following dances all have scores by Mio Morales, the musical director/composer with the company since 1977.

Bone-Jam (1977)
PsychoMotorWorks (1977)

Signals (1978)	Solo.
"Make me no boxes to put me in . . ." (1979)	
Step-Chart (1979)	
NÓZ (1980)	
Nile (1980)	Trio for two men, one woman, all 6′4″ tall or more.
Unplay Dances (1981)	
Differences of Need: Complements (1982)	

Dances made for specific musical selections (after 1970)

These dances were created for particular occasions using the music noted, as opposed to several for which musical compositions were chosen after the choreography was made.

Stoneflesh (1974)	Jimi Hendrix.
Molehill (1974)	Bartok.
Forty (1975)	Made for Alvin Ailey Repertory Workshop Company for Duke Ellington salute.
Acrylic-flake Diagram (1978)	Stravinsky's *Ebony Concerto.*

Theater pieces made with specific dramatic or emotional imagery

Brilll-o (1973)	A soap opera.
Yesterday (1974)	Five solos to poems by Ethan Ayer.
Stoneflesh (1974)	Beefcake with five nearly naked men.
Bone-Jam (1977)	Personal aggression.
"Make me no boxes to put me in . . ." (1979)	Quintet.
NÓZ (1980)	Punk-inspired episodes with songs, sung by dancers.

Dances made for specific environments

These pieces were created for performance in spaces other than theater stages. Some were later adapted for the stage.

CITY/MOTION/SPACE/ GAME (1968)	Solo TV piece shot in various urban locations in Boston; WGBH-TV.
Quad (1970)	Made for large lawn at UCLA, viewed from balcony above.
The Ultimate Pastorale (1971)	With nine sculptured columns by Lou Pruitt.
Patrol (1971), *Decimal Banana* (1973)	Garden of the New School for Social Research, New York City.
Masse (1972)	Sanctuary of Trinity Church, New York City.
4-Day Lobby Event, 5-Day Lobby Event (1972)	Lobby atrium, Massachusetts Institute of Technology, Cambridge, Massachusetts.
3-Day Lobby Event (1972)	Loeb Student Center, New York University, New York City.
Pocketcard Process I, II (1972)	Pedestrian traffic spaces.
Gallery Event #1 (1976)	Main Gallery, California Institute of the Arts, Valencia.
Steps Workshop (1980), *Hits & Runs* (1977)	New York City streets and plazas.

Dances with formalist or serial structures

Boogie (1977)	Built on the geometry of a square.
Steps Workshop, Steps II, III, IIIa, IV (1980–1982)	Geometric patterns and number progressions.
Unplay Dances (1981)	Phrase progression from 4 to 12 beats.

Differences of Need:
Complements (1982)

Progression 3–10, and
structure of solo, duet, trio.

191

A
*Nourishing
Meal*

Structural analysis of *Differences of Need: Complements*

Part I

	Entrances I
A	Sequencing (with phrases)
	Quartet A

Spiral Walking (3 versions)

	(a)	Individually
B	(b)	Couples (one at a time)
	(c)	Couples overlapping

	Quartet B
A′	Counterpoint (2 persons vs. 2 persons)
	Entrances II

Epilog
　　Weaving Progressions

Part II

	Solo—Gus
A	Duet—Ed, David
	Trio—Ed, David, Carl

	Solo—Carl
B	Duet—Ed, Ginny
	Duet—Beverley, David

	Trio—Beverley, David, Sukey
A	Duet—Ginny, Carl
	Solo—Gus

Epilog
　　Double trio, overlapping

May 1982

Date	Title of Work	Place and Details
February 1981	*Unplay Dances*	Riverside Dance Festival, New York City. Music by Mio Morales.
August 1981	*Steps III*	Long Beach Summer Dance Festival, California State University. Popular music.
March 1982	*Steps IIIa*	Riverside Dance Festival, New York City. Popular music.
March 1982	*Differences of Need: Complements*	Riverside Dance Festival, New York City. Music by Mio Morales.
April 1982	*Steps IV*	Marymount Manhattan Theater, New York City. Popular music.
June 1982	*Steps V*	American Dance Festival, Duke University, Durham, North Carolina. Rock music.
November 1982	*Steps VI: Graphic Diminish*	Performing Arts Center, Emanu-El Midtown YM-YWHA, New York City. Music by Mio Morales.

Date	Title of Work	Place and Details
November 1982	*Steps VII: Chatter Traffic*	American University, Washington, D.C. Music by Billy Squier.
March 1983	*Steps VIII:* Pedal-Rock Rebus	University of California at Santa Cruz. Rock music.
April 1983	*Flesh Wine and Sinew to the Bone*	Riverside Dance Festival, New York City. Music by Mio Morales.
July 1983	*Secrets from the Soles of Naked Feet*	Long Beach Summer Dance Festival, California State University. Assorted rock music.
December 1983	*For No Unstated Reasons*	Sidewalk Dance Theater, Knoxville, Tennessee. Music by Tom Dean.
March 1984	*Time-Cycle Unit on Chromium Crystal Desert*	University of California at Santa Cruz. Music by Steed Cowart.
1984	*Bladewalker*	Riverside Dance Festival, New York City. Music by Steed Cowart.

Rosalind Newman

Photo: Peggy Jarrell Kaplan.

ROSALIND NEWMAN

Born and raised in New York City, Rosalind Newman is the second generation of her family to become a dancer and choreographer. She studied at the Martha Graham School and attended the Connecticut College School of Dance for two summers. After graduating with a B.S. in dance from the University of Wisconsin at Madison, she returned to New York and studied with Merce Cunningham, Dan Wagoner, and Viola Farber; in addition, she studied ballet with Maggie Black, Melissa Hayden, Robert Denvers, David Howard, Lawrence Rhodes, and Jocelyn Lorenz.

Newman presented her first work in 1972 at the Merce Cunningham Studio and formed her own company three years later. Since then Rosalind Newman and Dancers has performed in major dance series and festivals in the United States and Europe. Choreographic commissions have included *Juanita* by the University of Wisconsin at Madison and *Untitled White* by the Jacob's Pillow Dance Festival. The narration from the full-evening work *4: Stories* was part of an audio installation for an international exhibition of women artists held in Berlin in 1982. As guest artist, Newman has taught extensively both in the United States and abroad.

Rosalind Newman is the recipient of several awards: a Guggenheim Fellowship, two Creative Artists Public Service (CAPS) fellowships, and two National Endowment for the Arts fellowships. Her company, too, has been supported by the National Endowment for the Arts, the New York State Council on the Arts, and other foundations and corporations. Articles discussing her work have appeared in *Dance Magazine* and several European publications.

ROSALIND NEWMAN

Aliveness in Avant Classical
Garde & Modern Derriere
Post Dance

I've never been able to place myself in a category; it makes me very
nervous and edgy. Call me a post-avant garde, minimalist, classical
postmodern dancer-choreographer, or a classical, postmodern,
avant-garde minimalist choreographer, or all of the above, or none
of the above.

My interests and concerns shift in terms of my work, although
to me it seems a logical progression. In one piece I might want to use
music to explore my movements' relations to someone's music, and
in the next I might just want to work in the silence of the movement's
own rhythms.

If I were to label myself, then that would limit what my choices
might be for the next year, or next ten years. My attitude, however,
seems to make certain people uncomfortable, for if they can't put
you in a box, they don't know how to deal with you.

The complexities of human creativity are so varied, changing,
and surprising that it is too limiting to be molded into a label. I feel
like a lot of people are busy devising vocabularies (i.e. salable words)
about their work or what is going on in dance. I'm not interested in
devising these vocabularies about the work—I'm too busy trying to
do it.

I'm a big studier and I studied with everybody at one time or
another, and did a lot of different kinds of technique. Everything
influenced me, not just one dance teacher, but everything in life has
made me be the person and choreographer who's working the way
I'm working right now. I'm a product of the sixties generation, and
that has been an inevitable influence on my work.

My uncle, Irving Burton, was a dancer with Sophie Maslow and
Bill Bales, and he did his own work. I remember as a child in the early
fifties, we lived in Brooklyn and my uncle had a loft in Manhattan
where Paul Taylor and Dan Wagoner used to rehearse. I remember
as a tiny child, my uncle introduced me to Merce Cunningham and
I was frightened by his bushy eyebrows and thought, "Oh, my God,

197

*Aliveness
in Avant
Classical
Garde &
Modern
Derriere
Post
Dance*

it's the devil!" I feel like I've been around dance since I was really, really small. Even though I wasn't dancing I was influenced by that time in some way—I don't know exactly how, but I know it's there. Just as I was later influenced by studying with Merce Cunningham or dancing with Viola Farber or Mel Wong or any later events.

I used to study with a woman named Marjorie Mazia, who was in the Graham Company and Woody Guthrie's wife. At the end of each class we would make up our own dances, about Halloween or Thanksgiving or spring, and she would remind us that each piece would have to have a beginning, middle, and an end. When someone tells you that when you're 6 years old, it sticks, or you rebel against it and spend your life trying to forget about it. I remember she also used to say, "Dancing has to be about people; you can't be a tree and you can't be a flower or a train, you have to be a person." I see that influence in my work. It has that sense of people and emotion in it, reflecting what a person feels. As a dancer, I tend to color movement with a certain dramatic or emotional quality, and I think it probably came from back then. No matter how much I could try to be an abstract dancer (whatever that is), that quality isn't going to go away.

There's a contrary streak in me. I have to find things out for myself. If somebody does something one way, I'll try to discover how I can go about it another way. I had studied with Merce and worked with Viola for two and a half years after college and hardly ever had been in a dance where we danced to music. I had been in pieces made in silence where the music was added after the piece had been choreographed. My own work had been like that too until I said, "Wait, who says music and movement have to be separate? What other kinds of relationships can I find between music and movement?" I wanted to find out for myself and even started to study piano to try to better understand it. Maybe all of my pieces choreographed to Bach and Brahms were indirectly influenced by Cunningham, because out of curiosity it challenged me to find what else I could do.

For me the greatest challenge of choreographing is everything, the entire process. It doesn't get any easier. Beginnings have always been difficult for me. Before I begin, I feel sick. Going into the studio to begin again, it feels as if I've never made a piece before and I'm never going to make another one and it's all over and I don't know how I ever made the last one and oh, my God, why am I doing this to myself? It's that sense of vagueness of making something out of nothing when you just don't know what the hell you're doing, or what it is you want.

That initial vagueness and insecurity is important, for that's when I find something I didn't know about—something coming from a deep place. It's also about making myself free, of letting myself be

Cairn. Rosalind Newman. Photo: Nathaniel Tileston.

199

*Aliveness
in Avant
Classical
Garde &
Modern
Derriere
Post
Dance*

free when I'm working and not stopping to edit or censor myself, but allowing for that freedom and energy to come out. Once I get into the middle of the work it's hard, but I'm there and I'm involved in it.

My work has to do with exploring energy, the continuum of being alive. I remember having this energy as a kid, jumping up and down and dancing. It sounds religious, but when you dance it puts you in touch with an energy or life force that's a little bit beyond what you are, beyond what your self is. It's the energy or force field that everybody can feel going on around them all the time. You dance yourself into another sphere. For me choreography is an exploration of what that life force or energy is. I think about movement in terms of using energy and taking it into different directional forces and fields. It has to do with something basic like physics or Einstein or sex or something.

I don't think there's any one message I'm trying to get across to an audience. I have lots of different interests and any piece I make has lots of levels and textures within it, lots of different feelings which create a rich atmosphere. Things in life aren't black or white. You look at something in life and your eye and mind take in a thousand different kinds of information about what it is. In art, people want one message, one simple statement, and yet, every day in their lives they're confronted with things that are multiple and varied and textured. When they walk into a theater, especially to look at dance, people want a simple one-dimensional statement. That's babying people's minds. The mind and the eye are trained by life to look at richness and fullness, so why not have that in art? Why not accept that as a part of what art is? I want to be clear about what I communicate to an audience, yet it isn't one simple statement that I'm making. There are lots of different kinds of things which might even be contradictory—wonderment.

When I first started to choreograph, there was a simplicity in the work. After college the first piece I made in New York City was a duet in 1972, called *Anne and Susan.* I was dancing with Viola Farber at the time and I think when you first begin to choreograph you take things from whom you're working with or who you know. I have been teaching myself about movement like an experimentor in a laboratory, finding out about space and dimensions in space. While the duet was very sparse and simple, my concerns about movement have always remained the same, growing with each subsequent piece in different ways.

In the duet they started out standing side by side, leaning forwards and backwards, forwards and backwards. The sense of weight simply used in that piece is something I still use in terms of my ideas about movement itself—the idea of letting your weight go to see how far it can go. There was also a rotational, circular quality where one person would rotate against the other, and I've explored that in much more complex and varied ways in subsequent pieces, but those interests were there at the start.

Chapter II and Chapter III in 1973, was a duet for Tom Borek and me, and it was also very simple and plain. It was about our relationship and had a dramatic quality underlying it like all of my pieces. *Third Watch*, in 1974, was one of the first pieces where I really started to express what was going on inside of myself. It was done for a group called the New York Dance Collective, to a Catholic mass. It was built on a multilayer trio, three sets of trios, and they kept passing along the movement or information, and, again, it was very much involved with the relationships of people and continuity.

In *Octoberrunners,* 1975, the accompanying sound was running and the piece was very much built on running. That was before running became so popular—I would never do a piece like that now because it's too popular, except I just did.

Topaz in 1976 was a big breakthrough, a step forward for me. It was done to Ravel's Sonata for Violin and Piano and Stravinsky's Violin Sonata. It was an exploration of music and movement, when I really began to study the score and used the forms and devices that Stravinsky and Ravel used within the music, which I tried to translate in terms of movement. It was interesting because as I was in the studio, I began to feel like Stravinsky and Ravel were my mentors or teachers about choreography—they helped me learn about movement.

There's no way to learn about choreography except to teach yourself, to look at other people's work or try to figure out how somebody put something together—to teach yourself how to get to the next place. It was real exciting for me to learn about Stravinsky's sense of humor, to appreciate the little quirkiness. When I got inside the work, it was as if the composers were collaborators at that moment.

In *Topaz* I began to use a more lyric form of movement. I don't know if it was because of the music or because I began to want to learn about moving like that. My natural way of moving, from the time I was a kid, was more staccato, more broken up, more quirky. I wanted to broaden myself to learn about other kinds of ways of moving.

The next piece, *Moorings,* 1976, brought in a whole other element to my work. I co-choreographed it with Tom Borek to Russian and Polish folk music. We went back to some kind of Jungian uncon-

201

Aliveness
in Avant
Classical
Garde &
Modern
Derriere
Post
Dance

scious of what was going on, to our heritage and grandparents. Tom's grandparents were Russian. I got interested in folk dances and folk steps and rhythms and in that piece I began to use those folk forms.

The next piece that followed, which put together the folk stuff with the idea of music and movement, was *Dances Strange and Familiar, Antique and New, Festive and Otherwise,* in 1978. The Bach Cello Sonata No. 5 was the inspiration for the piece. The way Casals played and was able to get so much juice and nuances and subtlety out of the cello—the fact that he could take an instrument that was so bare and minimal and get so much richness and variety out of it really interested me. I said, "Okay, what can I do with the human body, with just arms, legs, head, and feet, moving in time and space, to find those kinds of nuances and richness?" So it had both the elements of working with the music, taken even further to a more sophisticated level, as well as the folk elements and movements —American folk figures and clogging, and also folk forms in terms of spatial patterns, that came out of *Moorings.*

IIIII, the pole dance, in 1977, was a continuation of other kinds of things that were interesting to me. I had done a piece with a parachute in 1975 called *Free Fall* and I began to become interested in equipment and equipment pieces. I was having a lot of trouble choreographing—nothing was coming together until I saw a movie on Channel 13 by Sergei Eisenstein, about the Russian Revolution. There was one scene where he had Russian peasants running through the steppes of Russia with long poles. The raw image of the poles and faces stuck with me and I said, "I'm going to try to do something with poles."

Working with 7-foot poles with rubber tips on the ends was a different technical experience, like putting on pointed shoes for the first time, because it called for such different things than just dancing. At the end of the piece it was as if we just began to realize how to use the poles, so in 1980 I made another piece using three poles, called *Necessary Adventures.* It used the ideas that I had started working with in the five-pole piece and some of the elements were transferred into it. We also began to take the poles and use them as framing devices for movement so that one person would be moving and two others would be using the poles as cats' cradles around the movement. It gave a framing effect. From the idea of poles and framing people I got the idea of making a big frame within the space and framing the space.

Juanita, choreographed in 1980, used a set by Michael Selbach and a sound score by Laurie Anderson. From the pole dances I had been playing with the idea about framing, and the image of the frame within the proscenium began to make it seem like a roof. I saw

*Dances, Strange and Familiar, Antique and New, Festive and Otherwise.
Rosalind Newman. Photo: Lois Greenfield.*

203

*Aliveness
in Avant
Classical
Garde &
Modern
Derriere
Post
Dance*

Benjamin Franklin's transparent house in *Art* magazine and decided I wanted one, a wood frame of a house. Just by luck someone I knew knew Michael Selbach, who is a sculptor who works in making little houses. I showed him the picture and said I wanted that kind of house, free-standing in space. It was just one of those lucky circumstances where a collaboration begins to work—where two minds come together and it's the right set of circumstances and it worked.

The piece was choreographed in four weeks and we didn't get the house until a week and a half into working, so as I was working on the movement, I would think about the house being there and how we could run through it. But when the house came, it was too short and too small for the dancers to run through, so we had to open it up into three separate modules. Originally it had been built as one house set up in one way, but because we couldn't run through it, it became more abstract. In opening it up, it began to also open up the possibilities of the shapes within the space. At one moment the house could look like a house and by turning the house slightly, it could look like a church or a tent, or different parts could become different things.

I found the sound score on a record I had actually bought to hear somebody else's music. Laurie Anderson was on the collection and her spoken words had a sense or vitality and energy that struck me. So much of modern music is academic or within the repetitive school, but her music really excited me. I didn't know her but I called her and asked if I could use it.

One of the things that scared me was that there were words in the sound score so the implication was literal. She talked about loneliness, and it was a very New York kind of piece about telephone answering machines, alienation, and art ideas. While working on the piece, I related very much to her energy and time sphere. I was curious about what I would do with the combination of words and movement, and it was interesting to me, for I had never used a set and a sound score with words and all of those things came together and it somehow worked.

For the movement in *Juanita* I wanted to work in a more simple and freer form and style, to go away from all of those choreographic devices into something that felt simpler and easier. There's a lot of unison movement which is fairly simple in terms of spatial patterns. The piece previous to *Juanita* was *Cairn*, which took me a year to make. The two pieces are like direct opposites. In *Cairn* I had been working in silence to see how much emotional juice I could get out of movement without music within the space. It was a very bare piece, very plain, with nothing in the space. In *Juanita* I began to want to make a more lush landscape in space. In

Juanita. Rosalind Newman & Dancers. Victoria Marks, Donald Mouton, Tere O'Conner. Photo: Dee Conway.

life when you walk around you see things—you don't see somebody moving in an empty space, you see them moving with a whole little landscape behind them—a window and a table, bananas and a tea kettle, and you hear sounds and words. Motion exists within that sphere of sound and visual context, and I began to want to bring that into my work.

I see *Juanita* as a logical extension of all my past work, though many people have thought it a great departure. It is more dramatic, with scenes and an element of being like a play, and it's not at all abstract because there are songs and music. But it seems like a culmination and an extension of all the previous work that I've been doing in terms of structure and the objects, and in terms of working with and against music, and that dramatic element that I think has been

205

*Aliveness
in Avant
Classical
Garde &
Modern
Derriere
Post
Dance*

somewhere within all of the work, all of the time. I think *Juanita* just went on to explore that in more depth.

In general I think art is a reflection of our culture. It has to be because it's made by somebody and art is a reflection of the intellect, of the mind behind the work. A dance can't be separate from the cultural and economic systems that we're in. I'm a New York choreographer who exists within the granting system and within a loft situation and the kinds of dances I make have to do with what's going on in the economic world. The number of dancers I have, the way we can work, the kinds of grants that we can get in order to work —although we would work even if we didn't get them—those things all affect what makes a piece. The fact that we live in this loft situation down here in New York City affects what kinds of pieces I'm going to do when I walk into the studio. Because of what the studio looks like and the kinds of things I see outside right before I walk into that elevator to go to choreograph—all those things get interpreted into the piece.

I'm the product of a period of modern dance or dance, or postmodern or avant-garde, or whatever you call it, that seemed to be saying, "You oughta just dance." Even though I don't think it's so pat and simple, that went through me, that "I'm just dancing." And yet, you cannot get away from the fact of your own humanness, and when I go into the studio to make those steps, I'm dealing with my arms, legs, and torso which are connected and part of my vulnerability, my backlog of feelings and thoughts and memories of the world, of other people, of night, day, food, money, sex.

Aliveness is what I deal with.

November 1, 1980

Year	Title of Work	Place and Details
1972	*Anne and Susan*	Merce Cunningham Studio, New York City. Improvised saxophone by Michael Moss. Performed by Anne Koren and Susan Matheke. 7 minutes.
1973	*Chapter II and Chapter III*	Washington Square Church, New York City. Natural outdoor sounds. Performed by Tom Borek and Rosalind Newman. 8 and 10 minutes.
1974	*Orange Pieces*	Tears Studio, New York City. Music from *Faust.* Performed by Kate Johnson, Stormy Mullis, Rosalind Newman, and others.
1974	*Third Watch*	New York University School of the Arts, New York City. Latin mass. Commissioned and performed by the New York University School of the Arts Dance Collective, by 9 dancers. 20 minutes.
1974	*Flakes*	Metropolitan YM-YWHA of New Jersey in West Orange. Music by Steve Drews. Performed by Rosalind Newman. 9 minutes.
1975	*Free Fall*	Merce Cunningham Studio, New York City. Improvised harp. Performed by Livia Blankman, Kate Johnson, Renee Wadleigh, and Debra Wanner. 15 minutes.
1975	*Octoberrunners*	Dance Uptown, Barnard College, New York City. Performed by Livia Blankman, Tom Borek, Donald Byrd, Clarice Marshall, and Rosalind Newman. 17 minutes.
1976	*Topaz*	New York University School of the Arts, New York City. Music by Ravel and Stravinsky. Performed by Livia Blankman, Kate Johnson, Clarice Marshall, and Rosalind Newman.
1976	*Moorings*	Metropolitan YM-YWHA of New Jersey in West Orange. Collaboration with Tom Borek. Russian, Polish, and Middle Eastern folk music. Performed by Tom Borek and Rosalind Newman. 21 minutes.

Year	Title of Work	Place and Details
1977	*New Berlin Dances*	New Berlin Arts Forum, New Berlin, New York. Music by Brahms. Costumes by Judith Shea. Performed by Clarice Marshall and Mark Taylor. 12 minutes.
1977	*IIIII*	Eden's Expressway, New York City. Performed by Tom Borek, Kate Johnson, Clarice Marshall, Rosalind Newman, and Mark Taylor.
1978	*Dances, Strange and Familiar, Antique and New, Festive and Otherwise*	St. Clement's Theater, New York City. Music by J. S. Bach. Performed by Christina Backstrom, Ellen Bogart, Tom Borek, Clarice Marshall, Judith Moss, Rosalind Newman, Nancey Rosensweig, and Mark Taylor.
1978	*Spindle*	Cooper-Hewitt Museum, Outdoor Garden, New York City. Performed by 9 dancers. 16 minutes.
1978	*A Night at the Glen Island Casino*	Dance Umbrella, Entermedia Theater, New York City. Music by Claude Thornhill. Costumes by Denise Mitchell. Performed by Christina Backstrom, Ellen Bogart, Rosalind Newman, Nancey Rosensweig, and Mark Taylor. 18 minutes.
1979	*Cairn*	14th Street YM-YWHA, New York City. Music by Charlemagne Palestine. Performed by Christina Backstrom, Ellen Bogart, Kristin Eliasberg, Rick Merrill, Rosalind Newman, Nancey Rosensweig, and Mark Taylor. 45 minutes.
1980	*Juanita*	University of Wisconsin at Madison; commissioned by the university. Music by Laurie Anderson. Set by Michael Selbach. Performed by Ellen Bogart, Kenneth De Lap, Kristin Eliasberg, Kate Johnson, John McLaughlin, Rick Merrill, Rosalind Newman, and Nancey Rosensweig. 19 minutes.
1980	*RopeWorks*	St. Clement's Theater, New York City. Music by Meredith Monk. Performed by Ellen Bogart, Kenneth De Lap, Kristin Eliasberg, Kate Johnson, and Rick Merrill. 15 minutes.

Year	Title of Work	Place and Details
1980	*Necessary Adventures*	London Dance Umbrella, England. Music by J. S. Bach. Performed by Judith Moss, Ellen Bogart, and Rosalind Newman. 20 minutes.
1981	*Solo*	Japan Society, New York City. Music by Conlon Nancarrow. Performed by Jocelyn Lorenz. 8 minutes.
1981	*Ssandd*	Art on the Beach, Battery Park City Landfill, New York City. Performed by 12 dancers. 35 minutes.
1983	*4: Stories, Parts I, II, and III*	Dance Theater Workshop, New York City. Music by Margaret De Wys, Tom Marioni, and Aqsak Maboul. Costumes by Gabriel Berry. Full-evening version. Performed by Kristin Eliasberg, Victoria Marks, Clarice Marshall, Donald Mouton, Rosalind Newman, Tere O'Connor, Emily Pease, and Keith Sabado. 60 minutes.
1984	*Maps: In a Green Place*	Joyce Theater, New York City. African music of Gabon. Costumes by Miriam Ellner. Performed by Kevin Coker, Kristin Eliasberg, Paul Engler, Karin Hague, Victoria Marks, Clarice Marshall, Kate Mitchell, Emily Pease, and Keith Sabado, 14 minutes.
1984	*Modern Dance*	Joyce Theater, New York City. Music composed and performed by Gerry Hemingway. Costumes by Norma Kamali. Danced by Kevin Coker, Kristin Eliasberg, Paul Engler, Victoria Marks, Clarice Marshall, Rosalind Newman, Emily Pease, and Keith Sabado. 23 minutes.
1984	*Untitled White*	Commissioned and performed by the Jacob's Pillow Dance Festival, Lee, Massachusetts. Music by Fred Frith. Costumes by Charles Schoonmaker. Performed by 9 dancers. 16 minutes.
1985	*Free Speech*	Laban Centre, London. Commissioned and performed by the Welsh Repertory Dance Company; 6 dancers. Music by Skeleton Crew—Fred Frith and Tom Cora. Costumes by Pamela Moore. 22 minutes.

Year	Title of Work	Place and Details
1985	*Mirror Lake*	Lake Placid Center for the Arts, New York. Music by Antonio Vivaldi. Visual background design by Pamela Moore in collaboration with Rosalind Newman. Costume design by Charles Schoonmaker. Performed by Rosalind Newman, Kristin Eliasberg, Emily Pease, Daniel Peters, Nancey Rosensweig, Bryan Fisher, Clarice Marshall, and Sylvain Lafortune. 11 minutes.
1985	*Heartbeat*	Lake Placid Center for the Arts, New York. Music by Buddy Holly. Costumes by Clarice Marshall. Performed by Rosalind Newman, Kristin Eliasberg, Emily Pease, Daniel Peters, Nancey Rosensweig, Bryan Fisher, Clarice Marshall, Sylvain Lafortune, and Keith Sabado. 23 minutes.

Molissa Fenley

Photo: Peggy Jarrell Kaplan.

MOLISSA FENLEY

Molissa Fenley was born in Las Vegas, Nevada, and moved with her family to Nigeria, West Africa in 1960. Her last two years in high school were spent in Spain, where she became acquainted with flamenco dancing. The school from which she received her B.A. degree in dance in 1975—Mills College, in Oakland, California—stressed the Martha Graham–Doris Humphrey technique; in fact, Martha Graham has had the greatest impact on Fenley's development as a choreographer.

After graduating from college, Fenley came to New York City, where she studied with Kelly Holt and worked with Carol Conway's school and dance company for a year. In 1977 she created a performance ensemble and, in the next two years, self-produced her first works at independent dance studios. Since then she has performed at The Kitchen, the Holland Festival, the American Dance Festival, the Dance Theater Workshop, the Next Wave Festival at the Brooklyn Academy of Music, and in a number of other places both in the United States and overseas.

Fenley's works have an athletic quality that stems from her participation in running and weight lifting in college and her continuing commitment to physical training. In her dances she has explored, as well, the distinctive patterns of Balinese and other non-Western forms of movement.

Molissa Fenley has been the recipient of a Beards Fund fellowship, National Endowment for the Arts choreographer's fellowships, and a Jerome Foundation grant.

MOLISSA FENLEY

Cultural Architecture

Growing up, some of us are artists and some of us aren't. Some of us are interested in understanding the world and describing our sensibility through art, while others accept this world. I think I'm artistic, and I found that dance was my medium. I do a lot of drawings as well, but I communicate best of all through dance. For me, being both a performer and an audience member watching other performers, there is an immediacy that doesn't happen through a drawing or my writing. I choreograph so that I can perform; it's a need, and it's also extreme pleasure. For me the performance experience is quite unbelievable. I'm very devoted to it.

I am interested in the psychology of architecture on the stage. By architecture, I mean the way the stage is utilized to describe metaphors. Spatial metaphors, to me, are the most important aspect of a choreographic work. I'm captivated by the idea of sculpting movement on bodies and making the stage an immediate graphic metaphor for our lives.

Since I don't work in a narrative vein, the architecture, psychology, and meaning has to come through the way people are spatially oriented towards each other on stage. There is a psychological reaction when people are seen in a circle, versus when they are seen on the diagonal. It is subliminal and archetypal.

Space is agitated in a different way if you're moving slow than if you're moving fast. I like the idea of moving very fast because perceptual changes can take place in the mind's eye. Afterimage effects, the aura effect from the lighting hitting the body, and the body moving like lightning through the light, to me suggest metaphors that are animalistic and primitive, yet tied into a structurally contemporary understanding. Through these imagistic metaphors, strong memories transmitted from kinesthesia to the brain can be tapped in people's minds as they are watching. I'm trying to touch the collective memory of spatial understanding and abstract form.

I'm interested in the Jungian idea that we possess symbols, both Western and non-Western, and that there's a very deep reason for why we do what we do and why one culture had decided on one set of symbols and another culture on others. Underneath it all, before the borders of who decided what symbols were important, is something very universal. I'm trying to discover what that is.

I think there are incredible experiences available to us at our fingertips, but our minds are so blocked from the world and from reality, we don't experience half of what there is. I want to know what I'm missing. I've had glimpses of these moments through performing, researching, or making the work.

I'm trying to communicate our culture's repressed view of movement and lack of understanding of that movement. We as a culture don't understand our bodies. We're now obsessed with health and fitness, but we still don't understand our bodies. Today the most dance people do is social dance, and that's all sexually oriented. There's very little communication between the body and the mind. I'm trying to shed light on that particular issue. If you listen to what the body is doing, there will be meanings, nonlinear, but the mind doesn't have to tell the body what to do, it can be the other way around, intuitive and childlike. This can lead to rediscovering those memories and that incredible sense of being a full human being. It's very ephemeral, but it is an important aspect our culture is lacking. I want people to understand dance phrases as sensual, visceral, and meaningful experiences.

To me, choreography and dance are about getting away from mundane events into time-travel. It's like watching an imagistic art film that develops without a story. You're given the elements and point of view, and yet, you are not given any real reason for it. If you're an open-minded person, then the idea is to take this and time-travel with it. What you get out of the experience is, of course, pleasure from watching it, but underneath all that, one hopes that what you get out of it has more to do with yourself than it has to do with the actual film experience. Perceiving the image, the concept, or the meaning elicits a moment of realization. It isn't factual, nor linear. The movements speak for themselves and tap images, both cultural and inherited. They tap the amazing bank of collective memories through people's lives.

As a choreographer, my interest is to suggest these elements, to work with them structurally, to work with them in layers, to be very devoted to the idea of live performance, and to be very committed to the concept that dance is enough on its own. I'm interested in an egoless dance where the body is a medium for dance which takes over the body and its spirit. It's fabulous when a dance is not about the self, but is focused on the purity within the elements themselves and their interaction. Dance is enough on its own. Incredible sets or a context placed onto it are unnecessary, because if it's dance done in its purest form, it's going to reveal something.

My work is very controversial. When people first see it, they are immediately struck by the vitality and the energy because it is very high-energy, athletic-type work. People wonder how we can do it for so long, and they think it's a marathon. And some people say it's aerobic dance. There are people who see it for what it is and enjoy it, but some people say, "Okay, we watched them jump and leap for over an hour." Other people even go so far as to say that I do the same step over and over, which is just preposterous. It's because they can't see it, it's going by so quickly and they have so much antagonism towards it.

A bizarre thing about dance is that when most people come to see it, they only see it once. They're looking at something I've devised for six months. I have a deep understanding of it and a meaning that I want to get across, but at the end of the evening, everyone is saying, "Energy, energy, energy." And I say, "Okay energy, but so what?" "Did you see anything underneath?" Because, to me, the energy is the most obvious aspect of it, it is really just the very beginning.

I have gotten a lot of criticism that my dances are too energetic and if I'm interested in forming metaphors, I have to slow down, because people just can't think that fast, the images are coming at them like strobe lights. And I say, "Tough, quicken up," because I think that the images come because of the speed, in the fleeting qualities and in the staging.

I don't use a standard dramatic sense, but, on the other hand, the dance phrases I choose can be very dramatic in and of themselves. They're not just cool, calculated dancing through space. The movement quality is inherently emotional: the way the head is used and the hands. As soon as hands are used it's immediately very meaningful for people. And then there's drama of how people are placed on stage. So I think, in essence, it is a dramatic form, a nonlinear drama. It's not about someone going through angst or having something particular happen to them. It's noneventful drama, perhaps nonevent-specific, and yet the movements are very touching and visceral. Consequently, they produce the resonance intrinsic in drama.

I was born in Las Vegas, Nevada, and moved with my family to Nigeria, West Africa in 1960. When I was 16 I entered Mills College. Right at the beginning I learned technique as well as choreography. I think that's a main difference between myself and a lot of other dancers. Usually dancers work with another company for a while and then, having been in a choreographic situation, they start choreographing themselves.

At Mills College there was basically a Martha Graham–Doris Humphrey school of dance technique taught. I went through the anthropological basis of dance, learning the gigue, the sarabande, allemande, and primitivism, and learned the Louis Horst method of choreography. When I left Mills after graduation, I came to New York City. I had studied quite extensively with Kelly Holt, who was from the Hawkins company. I'd worked with him a couple of summers at Santa Cruz workshops. Technically, he was very important for my dance training.

I took some classes at the Cunningham studio. I can appreciate Merce Cunningham's work, but I'm not particularly attracted to it or necessarily stimulated by it. I don't have a strong feel for the Cunningham aesthetic, because the movement vocabulary doesn't appeal to my senses. Even though, in essence, he's dealing with abstraction and many of the same things I am, his frame of mind has a much different orientation. I don't think he is necessarily interested in Jungian psychology, although I could certainly be wrong about that.

When I came to New York I did go to the Hawkins studio, but I couldn't stand the way they approached the movement. The movement is very beautiful, but the way they dealt with it was boring. When a dancer first comes to New York, you have to pay your dues. I was floundering, and even though I knew I wanted to do my own work, it was enticing to feel the security of belonging to an established group. I went to Carol Conway's school and was actually in her company for over a year. I like the Hawkins teaching method very much and I think Carol is a very fine teacher.

Choreographically, the person I've learned the most from is Martha Graham. She is my hero. I've been reading about her life, and knowing what she has been through, I am very appreciative of her lifetime career. Her work is intensely sound and moving to me. I don't think that that is necessarily true about her work right now [in 1984], although her *Rite of Spring* was just as powerful as some of her earlier works. As any great artist, she moves in and out of masterpieces to lesser works, but as an artist overall, I'm after the same lifelong career—a lifetime of ups and downs and masterpieces and not so masterpieces.

I go to a lot of dance concerts because I enjoy watching how other choreographers stage dance and construct spatial orientations. I've learned a lot from Martha Graham about that. In fact, I've learned a lot from watching many different choreographers. The list would have to be endless, because I go to so many concerts. I'm not looking for rhythmic variations or content; I have my own particular rhythms and my own particular movement vocabulary. What I find interesting is how people stage the architecture of dancers.

I consciously try to see as many dance concerts as possible, as well as have a first-hand knowledge of the visual arts, music, theater, and film. I go to be stimulated and because I feel it is important to know what everybody else is doing. Whether viewed in the affirmative or the negative, I want to know what they're doing.

When I decided to cut off roots and start doing my own choreography, it became very clear that I should also start doing my own training. To continue practicing other people's movement would have been antithetical to making my own movement, so I took classes here and there and very gently honed myself. As a dancer, there's a neuroticism one gets into that requires taking class every day, or big trouble will arise. To alleviate myself from that neuroticism took some time.

Definitely a major influence is my physical attraction to very athletic work. Before college I'd been a runner. In college I'd done running and weight lifting. Finally, when I was not in classes anymore, I started getting much more serious about my weight training and endurance running. Of course, I know how to keep myself in dance condition, and I do pliés and brushes every day on my own. I don't believe I need to be in class to get that.

I've used Nautilus weights for years. That began because I was interested in having the upper body be very different from other dance, to define the contours of the sculpted body rather than have the normal ethereal type of body which seems to be in vogue for so much dance. Much of the training has come from the choreographic needs. If you want to be able to make an hour-long piece where you stay on stage the whole time and do a lot of activity, then you have to be in shape aerobically.

The choreography also comes from the training. Specifically, my dance vocabulary deals with the upper body in a very different sense than most dance. In most dance the upper body is an extension of the back, or it's used to perform quirky non sequitors like the Viola Farber people or the Dan Wagoner types who scratch their heads or all of a sudden do a gesture, out of context, which means something to our culture. I don't do that.

I don't like gesture which pulls you into the real world again, because that is a reality we already know. To me the whole dance is about getting outside of the self and time-traveling. To all of a sudden see something in lay terms, to me shatters the magic, confuses, and makes it difficult to rekindle the experience. I try to use universal gestures within dance phrases rather than to separate them, because I think the metaphor comes easier, is perhaps more philosophically deep, when it's done as a dance rather than when it's stopped and positioned.

The ceremonies and rituals I saw when I lived in West Africa were a major influence on my work. Though I never studied dance there, my use of rhythm, ritual, and nonstop dance is perhaps derived from there. I also lived in Spain during the last two years of high school and saw a lot of flamenco dance. The arm movements, the carriage of the upper body, and the hauteur and extreme pride of the upper back is very beautiful and also influential.

A lot of my upper body movements are taken from Balinese and Indian dance. I've studied pictures, done a lot of reading, and seen a number of exhibitions at the Asia Society and other places. I think the fact that I've never studied the dance is important because the essence rather than the actual steps are conveyed. I'm very aware of how arms read, what they mean, the orientalia of the way I use my hands. Some people think I've studied t'ai chi for years; I haven't, but I'm aware that there is an exoticism of a different culture.

I'm after the essence of world dancing rather than secular. For that reason, I'd like to be called an experimental choreographer, because if you tell someone you are a modern choreographer, then you already have that linkage of coming out of a very distinct heritage. I like to think of myself more as having come out of the world, with an American mind and an American body.

I like the term "experimental" because it's open-ended. The term "avant-garde" just bores people to death because they remember sitting through John Cage evenings. The term "new dance" is nice, but, of course, that goes back to the Doris Humphrey ideas. To me, "experimentalist" suggests that I've been working with dance, experimenting with different possibilities during full-evening works. The linkage between them all is the dance movement itself, and there has been a distinct progression of my devising a movement style and a personal movement vocabulary.

It's all so confusing. I'm definitely not a minimalist. I think I'm an academician because I really know my dance history and can appreciate it and utilize it and go with the craft of choreography. I wouldn't say I'm a postmodern choreographer because that means something very specific: from the Yvonne Rainer, David Gordon lineage. To me, postmodern dance means working with natural movement, having tasks and depicting their solutions during the evening or completion of the work. It does not necessarily involve the body speaking to the mind, but the mind telling the body what to do. Nor does it necessarily include the use of music. It seems to be more of a theatrical, performance experience rather than a dance experience.

I am not concerned with those ideas. But if Lucinda Childs and Laura Dean are put into the grouping of postmodern, I feel I have something to do with them. Although they have certainly done their pedestrian pieces, they work more with architecture using dance movement, not walking.

I like their use of structure and I understand their compulsion. Obsession is a very important aspect of making anything. It's the obsessive people who really come up with something new. Martha Graham is certainly obsessive. With Childs and Dean, the obsession to repeat is very graphic, and yet it's always modularly changing. To me, that has more to do with modern dance than with postmodern dance, because it's taking elements of dance and working on them as givens. It is about musical elements, rhythm and movement of the body rather than task-oriented work or problem solving where the mind decides the movement and puts it onto the body.

The biggest difference in terminology to me is the analytical versus intuitive process of the way the dance phrases are made. For me, the body tells the mind what to do with the dance phrase, and then the mind decides to set it choreographically. Although, I must admit, there are times when I need a phrase of 5,5,3, 5,5,3, and then I devise it. But when I'm making up the dance phrases, it's really done through flinging the head and arms and then trying to remember what I did. That's the hardest part!

When I first started performing my work, in 1978, the movement in the arms was devised from Egyptian and Abyssinian friezes, moving from positions and the body would carry them around. Until 1982, the lower body basically transported the upper body through space. Now after more years developing, the lower body has a much wider use: Whereas before it was a lot of hops and skips with the arms on top of it, moving through space very fast, now there are more leg extensions and other things. The pieces have also gotten more and more structurally convoluted and sophisticated as I've gone along, but spatial paths taken by the dancers have always been important.

Also, my work has always had a very rhythmic base. The first work started with the rhythm coming solely from the dance. We wore ankle bells and played maracas and all the music came from the movement itself. It had a ritualistic sense. The first piece in New York was called *Planets.* It did have the orbiting of the planets and then each planet would have a solo. In a sense, it was much more narrative then. It was still imagistic, but the solo movements were taken from readings about mythologies of Venus. There were ten dancers with a lot of ensemble work in unison.

Then the next few pieces after that were more and more honed down to smaller groups. I did a couple of duets, trios, and quartets, and then started dealing more with music and working with understanding the movement of the upper body and how to get it into actual dance so that it wasn't so positional.

In 1980 I did a piece called *Energizer,* which was a breakthrough in that I used much more repetitive music. That's when everything started getting speeded up and the idea came about the afterimagery of space and the concepts of perception.

I don't think I've diverged once from what I've set out to do. In dealing with the elements of structure, rhythm, spatial design, speed, and movement vocabulary, there's been a very distinct progression which has become more sophisticated and developed with each dance. Though *Planets* had a dramatic understanding to it, it wasn't linear. Since then the narrative has gotten less and less, yet the elements are more developed and stronger. Now there's no need

Energizer. Molissa Fenley & Dancers. Photo: Paula Court.

for the narrative to give a reasoning for what should follow what; the elements suggest it. I am trying to make a strong visual, physical, and cognitive statement combining elements of music, dance, costume, and sometimes decor.

There's nothing factual, nothing linear, and the movements speak for themselves, but it's not that dry, movement for movement sake; it's dance. I won't even say movement, because movement, to me, is a postmodern term. It's dance purely of the moment which looks spontaneous. It looks improvised, and yet it's all been rehearsed and completely set. Nor is there improvisation in the dance process of making it. I have everything completely choreographed and know exactly what's going to happen when.

For me the greatest challenges of choreographing are all self-induced. It is to devise an overall form, an ideology for each new piece, to find the psychology of what I want to do. I'm very good at finding the "micro," the actual dance phrases, and I'm good at setting that onto the dancers. It's the question of the "macro," the ideology of what I want to do which is difficult. Another challenge is to find people I want to collaborate with for the next piece and then to decide on the format—is it going to be continuous or in four parts, or the first half versus the second half? In an evening-length work I like to have things with a beginning, which eventually culminate, and then in the end, reestablish the dance themes. It's probably a subliminal Horst influence that I like the culmination of A, B, A choreography.

I've had a concerto-type format in the last few pieces and it's a form that has made a lot of sense and I like, so I'll probably do it for a while. It tends to give the evening context. It has an opening half that might have two or three pieces, separated by a 30-second blackout. The whole first half is basically nonstop. Then there's an intermission and the second half opens with a slower piece—slower in my terms. And then there's a break in which costumes usually change, followed by a finale.

Trying to work within an abstract form, a format is needed, some kind of clues. I hate it when I go into an art gallery and something is called "untitled." I might have my own metaphor of what I think the work is, but I still like that clue of the artist's own poetic image. It's still a milestone, even if I don't understand what the artist means.

My titles sometimes come even before the piece is made, as a map of how to coordinate the whole evening. They are another way of suggesting or giving clues of what it is supposed to mean, and they are usually very poetic, like *Gentle Desire* or *Peripheral Vision*.

In 1982 I choreographed *Eureka*. "Eureka" usually means a moment of illumination, but to some people it means Eureka, Cali-

Eureka. Molissa Fenley. Photo: Chris Ha.

fornia. So the titles can be open-ended. To me, *Eureka* was meant to be a state of mind, moments of the mind awakening to the body. There were three parts. *Willpower* suggested powers of the will over elements and over the mind, and how the will and the mind are always in counteraction against each other—perhaps, more specifically, the will against cultural habits as blockages to our experience. The second piece was called *Second Sight.* It was the concept of seeing into the future and seeing through movement understandings through deep, intense, physical experience. Then the last part was called *Racial Memory,* the Jungian concept of memory tapping.

I have a bank of movements or phrases to which I go back and rework. I still do movement from *Planets* because I like having a continuation so the movement gets transformed, transmuted, makes sense to me, and gives me a sense of cohesion. It doesn't repeat itself; I do it on a different leg, or change it so that no one would ever know it's the same material. By fiddling and going back, I feel I'm making my personal movement vocabulary. Of course, I bring totally new material too, so it's both.

Another evolution of my work is the interest I have at this point, in working with other artists. I have commissioned scores for the last three or four pieces, where the music was made specifically for the dance. In each case, I've worked with someone I think has been in the forefront of their particular idiom, and who has voiced an interest in doing something for dance. They have understood that it's very different than writing a composition for their own ends.

I like the idea of working with people who don't have any idea of what the theater should do or be, and I've been interested in dealing with a lot of different worlds, like the fashion world. The body can look very beautiful when it's draped in an artistic way, when it's not draped in a costume way. I get a lot of criticism about being trendy, but I view it as the dance world being unwilling to realize what is at our fingertips, to utilize fashion and make the stage a contemporary place, to be involved in a new idiom.

Hemispheres premiered in November 1983 at the Brooklyn Academy of Music's Next Wave Festival. The ideology that went along with it was the concept of the two hemispheres of the brain, the left versus the right, the analytical versus the intuitive, and the idea of the world hemispheres of the north, south, east, and west, of all different cultures coming together and the fusion of it all.

Hemispheres opened with *Before Borders,* which was meant to describe before the borders of cultural heritage, before the borders of what is considered proper, what is considered normal, before the borders of style, and before there were too many fences placed on the mind and body. The second part was called *Telepathy,* which was an idea that there could be telepathic communication. Then the next piece was *Eidetic Body,* the idea of the body as image for archetypal symbols. The last part was called *Projection,* meaning the projection into the future, projection of a map, projection of geographical fences between peoples. To me these titles were clues or suggestions so people would look for more than just energy in the dancing.

I think *Hemispheres* was my most successful piece because I was more in command of my elements (speed, structure, rhythm, spatial design, dance phrases, etc.) and it grew to its most sophisticated and developed sense. Anthony Davis did the music and he worked polymetrically so it made perfect sense for me to work polymetrically, although the interest for me was not to work in the same polymetrics as he. We would have a downbeat together, about every 40 beats, but not the same counting system.

I worked with the music; I didn't work with the score itself, because I didn't want to know what he was doing. I don't like mimicking or the question of what is primary and what is secondary. In our culture, the music is usually first, and then the dance follows the music. My idea was to have a very strong coexistence so that the dance and music paralleled each other. I would listen to the music on tape and write down what I thought he was doing, using my own dancer's counts. Or I would ask him how many beats he was in 4-4 time, and he would say, "Forty-eight." Then I would devise a phrase so we would have a downbeat together. There were only myself and two dancers, but there was a lot of rhythmic variation and counterpoint. Mathematically I was fascinated by it and I think it has drastically changed what I will do with my next piece.

The music was performed live at the Brooklyn Academy by ten musicians with a conductor. It was a mixture of jazz, classical, contemporary, and gamelan. Performed live it was very fascinating and exhilarating, but also extremely expensive. At other performances the music has been on tape.

The costumes were designed by Rei Kawakubo from her Comme des Garcons collection. They weren't specifically made for the piece; they were off the rack, but Rei Kawakubo selected them for me. They were well tailored and a meaningful, distinctive concept of the world in 1984—great dance costumes.

The decor was by Francesco Clemente, and it was prints that were held in one's hands while watching the dance so that there was a sense of touch involved in the theatrical experience rather than a backdrop or something on stage.

The iconography of Francesco Clemente was particularly bizarre. It dealt with dismembered bodies. Yet there were some that were very simple, like a small, very beautiful snail. The quality of the

Hemispheres. Molissa Fenley. Photo: Chris Ha.

way they were made, the ink, was very beautiful. Whether or not the prints had anything to do with the piece wasn't the issue—something was happening in Francesco Clemente's frontal lobes and he was going with it, so I thought it was all a great part of *Hemispheres*.

For me, the prints caused introspection, it put people into the right frame of mind to watch the dance. It also brought in the outside world with images of death, and images of things that weren't described on stage, yet were happening hemispherically all the time. It contrasted with the optimistic American viewpoint of Anthony Davis and myself and it furthered the whole concept of what the *Hemispheres* experience should be. Some critics thought the prints were the stupidest thing in the whole world, but they worked for Francesco Clemente, and they worked for me, and that's really all that matters.

It furthered my life to deal with someone like Francesco. The whole idea of *Hemispheres* broadened my mind, so for me it was all very worthwhile. All I can do as an artist is to give suggestions. There's a sense of a nonliteral phenomenon to my work. Luckily, people do come away from watching it having had a meaningful experience. Some people just enjoy the energy, and that's fine too.

I think there's a lot to be gained from understanding that my dances are in their own class, in their own form. I'm not a ballet dancer, so I'm not interested in getting classical lines. I use a lot of lifting of shoulders and isometric pressure in the arms. For a person who's had a lot of ballet, it's difficult, because their mind says, "No, that's not right." To them, it's tension; to me, it's attention. It's a different form. When people come to look for classical line and criticize it in ballet terms, they shouldn't, because it's not there, that's not what it's about. I have a very raw, very personal way of dancing, and when I train every day by running and lifting weights, I'm going to look very different from someone who is in ballet class.

I don't know whether my work is a reflection of our culture. I don't think I consciously hold up a mirror to it. Perhaps on a subliminal level and a conscious level I take in what we as a culture are up to, because I'm a modern person and live in the modern world. I have to be affected by it, but I don't think I'm reflecting it in the work so much as perhaps giving my concept of it, my understanding.

I consider myself an apolitical person, and yet, because of the fact that I'm a young woman who dances only with other women, some people consider that a political statement. People will read into anything. What is usually the case, is that when people read in politicisms, they usually do not understand the artistry, so they see the superficiality of the fact that we're all women dancers, with short hair, who wear contemporary clothes.

I've traveled extensively and it is surprising how the barriers between cultures are getting less and less. There are very archetypal things from each culture that have a lot to do with the world at large. Though there is a cultural fusion to be seen, the reason why I use

Baliisms or Indianisms in my dancing, is not because I want to show fusion, so much as it is because I find it interesting, captivating. It goes both ways: an artist wants to continue on his or her own road versus the fact that he or she is affected by the modern world. Those things which are meaningful to the artist are used, and those which aren't are discarded.

There is a very literal fusion of cultures making a world which is more universal than one with traditional cultures existing as separate entities. And yet I'm speaking about a contemporary urban truth, because while in Japanese suburbia, the average person may be Americanized by wearing Western clothes and listening to Michael Jackson, there is still a very definite cultural tradition and decorum between people. Maybe it's that the big cities feel the fusion, but in small towns they are merely aware of it. The urban mind is becoming very universal, whether in Tokyo, Rome, Paris, or New York. It's an urban understanding and that's what I'm dealing with.

June 13, 1984

The music for *Planets, The Willies, The Cats, Video Clones, Red Art Screen,* and *Mix* consists of percussion instruments played by the dancers. The music for *Energizer, Peripheral Vision, Gentle Desire, Praxis, Between Heartbeats, Eureka,* and *Hemispheres* consists of original scores commissioned by Molissa Fenley for Molissa Fenley and Dancers.

Year	*Title of Work*	*Place and Details*
1977–1978	*Planets*	Merce Cunningham Studio, New York City. Music and costumes by Molissa Fenley. Performed by 10 dancers. 1 hour.
1978	*The Willies*	Dance Theater Workshop, New York City. Music and costumes by Molissa Fenley. Performed by 2 dancers. 10 minutes.
1978	*The Cats*	Merce Cunningham Studio, New York City. Music and costumes by Molissa Fenley. Performed by 3 dancers. 12 minutes.
1979	*Video Clones*	School of Visual Arts, New York City. Collaboration with visual artist Keith Haring. Music and costumes by Molissa Fenley. Performed by 2 dancers. 1 hour.
1979	*Red Art Screen*	School of Visual Arts, New York City. Music and costumes by Molissa Fenley. Performed by 2 dancers. 1 hour.
1979	*Mix*	The Kitchen, New York City. Music by Molissa Fenley. Performed by 4 dancers. Costumes by Carmen. 1 hour.
1980	*Boca Raton*	Grey Art Gallery, New York City. Music, a special extended dance mix of Talking Heads, by Paul Alexander. Costumes by Perry Ellis collections. Decor by Steven Keister. Performed by 2 dancers. 12 minutes.
1980	*Energizer*	Dance Theater Workshop, New York City. Music by Mark Freedman, based on an original idea by Molissa Fenley. Costumes by Yonson Pak and Ariel. Performed by 4 dancers. 45 minutes.
1981	*Peripheral Vision*	Washington, D.C. Music by Mark Freedman. Costume by Yonson Pak. Solo performance. 4 minutes.
1981	*Gentle Desire*	American Dance Festival, Durham, North Carolina. Music by Mark Freedman. Costumes by Yonson Pak. Performed by 3 dancers. 15 minutes.
1980–1981	*Praxis*	CAPC, Bordeaux, France. Music by Mark Freedman. Costumes by Yonson Pak and Emanuel Zoo. Performed by 3 dancers. 90 minutes.
1980–1981	*Between Heartbeats*	Institute of Contemporary Art, London. Solo version of *Praxis.*

Year	Title of Work	Place and Details
1982	*Eureka*	Dance Theater Workshop, New York City. Music by Peter Gordon. Costumes by Yonson Pak. Solo performance. 45 minutes.
1983	*Hemispheres*	Brooklyn Academy of Music, New York City. Music by Anthony Davis, with Episteme. Visual element by Francesco Clemente. Costumes by Rei Kawakubo, Comme des Garçons collection. Performed by 3 dancers. 75 minutes.
1985	*Cenotaph*	Jacobs Pillow, Lee, Massachusetts. Music by Jamaaladeen Tacuma. Spoken text by Eric Bogosian. Costumes by Donna Sarina. Lighting by Gary Mintz. Performed by 5 dancers. 20 minutes.
1985	*Esperanto*	Joyce Theater, New York City. Music by Riyuichi Sakamoto. Costumes by Jean Paul Gaultier. Performed by 5 dancers. 75 minutes.

Hemispheres. Molissa Fenley & Dancers. Photo: Chris Ha.

Gail Conrad

Photo: Peggy Jarrell Kaplan.

GAIL CONRAD

Gail Conrad was born in Brooklyn, New York, in 1952. The child of professional ballroom dancers, she learned ballroom as well as tap at a very early age and has since had extensive training in modern, flamenco, ballet, and jazz dance. She began doing her own productions in 1978 and within the next two years formed Gail Conrad/Tap Dance Theater.

Conrad has taught workshops and performed with her company throughout the United States and in Europe. She has also taught, performed with, and/or choreographed for such theater companies as Mabou Mines, the Performance Group, and Richard Foreman's Ontological Hysteric Theater. Conrad did choreography for both the play and the film versions of Joanne Akalaitis's *Dead End Kids* and the Mabou Mines's production of *Pretty Boy.* In 1985 she began working on the film project, "Late Twentieth Century," with BBC director Roger Guertin. She worked on *The Censorship Project* by Valeria Wasilewski and Ruth Maleczech during 1986.

Conrad has received three choreographer's fellowships from the National Endowment for the Arts, a Eugene O'Neill choreographer's fellowship, and a choreographer's grant from the Foundation for Contemporary Performance Arts. In 1983–1984 she was the recipient of a Guggenheim Fellowship.

GAIL CONRAD

Different Strokes

My parents were my earliest dance influence. They were a professional ballroom dance team and also had a dancing school downstairs in our home in New Jersey. Here they both taught ballroom, but my mother also taught tap. When I was about 4 years old, I took a few years of baby ballet, and then, years later, went into New York City to study folk dancing. The person I worked with used a lot of his own choreography, including ballet and modern dance, and it got me interested in studying technique again.

The first person I went to was Merce Cunningham, whose school I studied at for four or five years. At the same time I took ballet with various people: Nanette Charisse, Zena Romett, Finis Jhung, and Peter Saul. Over the years I also studied with Marya Warshaw, Trisha Brown, Viola Farber, Nancy Topf, and Louis-Nikolais, and took jazz with Lee Theodore, Betsy Haug, and Charles Kelly. In 1984 I began studying flamenco, which I've always had a passion about, with Mariquita Flores. I'm not sure how I've retained these individual influences. For example, with modern dance, it's the sensibility that took hold of me—the vocabulary and the lines. I love what Cunningham does imagistically, his clarity of visual image, rhythmic use, and the lines in his technique and choreography. I love his warm-ups and use of the upper back. All of that has affected me.

My most important tap teacher was Charles Cook, "Cookie" of the Copasetics. I studied privately with him for three years, and we'd work out once a week. Cookie provided something very special, especially in his use of tap as a melodic line. His use of African rhythms and his particular syncopation were quite different from what I had known. For me, it was more than just improving footwork; it was thinking with a different accent or language. He was extremely important in this way.

I had never planned to work with tap—I literally fell into it through my acquaintance with certain theater companies. It began when Mabou Mines asked me to give them tap and ballroom classes. At that point, I hadn't studied tap in a long time, so what I did, while reviewing my tap technique, was combine tap with all the forms of movement which I had been studying more recently. I started performing with Richard Foreman and then taught tap to his company. Next, the Performance Group asked me to teach them tap, and also to choreograph a ballroom sequence for a new work they were doing. People began calling, asking for tap classes. At that time in the seventies, there weren't many people teaching tap. It was very slowly beginning to have a resurgence in New York and I found myself one of the few downtown teachers.

Almost everything influences my dances. Certainly Balanchine, Cunningham, Paul Taylor, and tap masters like Cookie, Fred Astaire, Honi Coles, and Jimmy Slide all have made a great impact. I see something on a street and it makes me think of a dance, or I'll see a film—film often influences me. In fact, I see many dances as films in my mind, even before I choreograph. Perhaps this was why I always described one of my dances, entitled *The Racket,* as a film noir. Just as strong, for me, are books. I read a story called "Pale Horse, Pale Rider," by Katherine Anne Porter, and it ended up to be a duet called *Scotch & Soda.*

I've always enjoyed using all kinds of music with my dances. Initially, I used a lot of Latin music because I grew up with it and I knew and loved the dances to those rhythms. Not surprisingly, the first major piece which I did was to all Brazilian music. However, these days, I tend to use a broad range of musical styles. Certain works by Nino Rota, Kurt Weill, Carla Bley, and Luiz Bonfa are among my favorites.

To me, choreography imposes new kinds of stylization and abstraction onto the natural movements of people. It's the creation of these moving pictures which is so exciting to me. It's like traveling and it's the adventures in making or doing the piece which fascinate me. Here the greatest challenge is to physicalize what I visualize. Often before I begin a new dance, there's one initial image, movement, rhythm, or gesture which I see. Usually there's one quality that interests me the most, which for me is the core of the dance, and it is from this takeoff place that I want the audience to see the dance. Sound is very important. Since I use so much tap in my work, often I hear a very specific rhythm as well, or a certain accompanying melodic line.

Another challenge is to be specific enough, to really crystallize that one movement, that one image or rhythm. I usually know when I get it right, and, curiously enough, the dancers also know. It's usually that which is the most organic to them, feels the most natural

The Racket. Gail Conrad/Tap Dance Theater. Gail Conrad, David Parker, Cheryl Wawro Johnson. Photo: © Johan Elbers 1986.

and makes sense. Because I've worked with so many of the same dancers for a long time, I'm interested in choreographing for these dancers—finding out who they are as dancers, who they are as characters, and what their traits and strengths are.

Always the combination of tap with other dancing varies. I adore using tap and love what it can do, but not every dance needs it all the way through. It's not always about how complicated, eccentric, or fast it can be. Some dances are primarily tap. Others have the tap more integrated with other kinds of movement, where the tap is there, but just in certain places. My search has been to use tap in many ways which are, perhaps, not always traditional. However, sometimes I don't want to use any tap at all and realize that I have that choice also.

Then there's the question of how to use music with tap. Traditionally, tap has been performed to very light music—light drums and percussion, a little piano. And tap has always been closely aligned to jazz. I'm trying to experiment with other kinds of music to see if tap can stand out against it. One can tap to any kind of music, but sometimes the music has such a full arrangement that any more sound, even tap, sounds like an unwanted intrusion. Some new music of today would be extremely difficult to use because you wouldn't hear the tap unless the tap were electrified. One of my musician friends had an idea about putting a synthesizer in a tap shoe. He figured it would cost between $1200 and $2000 per toe or heel—I would have to do a solo first.

The company has worn all different kinds of shoes with metal taps on them. I've thought of making taps out of other materials. For example, Bojangles had wooden taps. In my piece *Wave*, the man who played the son in the family wore sneakers for his costume—he remade them with a leather sole with taps on the bottom. It was quite wonderful because it defied the visual image, to look at sneakers and hear the sound.

At this point, I don't think of myself as just a tap choreographer. Basically, I think of myself as a choreographer; among other things I am a tap choreographer. For me, it's all dancing, it's all choreography.

I've been written about as an avant-garde choreographer, but at the moment it has no meaning to me. Words like *avant-garde, postmodern, modern, new wave* have lost their initial significance. Perhaps at one point they did have a very special association, but these days I really have no idea what they mean, so I try to avoid using any of them. It's become too easy to categorize. There are many kinds of work to be found in the tap world of today, and I think that conceptual definitions have not widened enough. For example, whenever postmodern dance is discussed, it never includes tap. It's much more interesting to think in terms of dancing, and then if discussing one person, talk about his or her specific work and style. To me, the work and style are inseparable.

In the past it was difficult for people to consider tap as a serious art form that required a lot of work and training, or to think of it as anything more than something like "Tea for Two," Busby Berkely, *Forty-second Street,* or some cabaret routine. When I first studied at the Cunningham School and told people I was tapping, I would get the sense that they considered it trite or frivolous. Other people had the complete opposite reaction and were delighted, tickled, or fascinated. Now the feeling about it is quite different. More people are studying tap and more respect it as an art form.

Having a dance company was never premeditated. After working with a number of theater companies, I started performing outside in the street with a friend of mine who was a great accordion player. This was in the summer of 1977 and our "street act" was quite unusual. It was the first time I was actually choreographing tap and our musical repertory included such things as "Brazil," "Amarcord," "Take 5," "Honeysuckle Rose," "Mack the Knife," and "Darktown Strutters' Ball"—all played on accordion. I was dancing on a 4-by-8-foot masonite board and we performed all over the West and East Village and later in Little Italy [all in New York City]. It was an adventure and I loved dancing outdoors. I felt free to try anything and started to realize how interested I was in choreographing for tap. I also decided that next I wanted to do something indoors.

In 1978 I had an image for a piece I wanted to do, *Travelers.* I wanted to call it a tap dance epic, use only Brazilian music, and I knew I needed five dancers. Just finding dancers was extremely difficult. One or two people I found had a lot of tap in their backgrounds, but not very much ballet or modern. Another person, one of my students, was a raw beginner in tap but a very good modern dancer. Another was a fascinating theatrical performer, but also a beginner in tap. It was an odd potpourri of strengths and weaknesses in dancing, tapping, and theatricality; I had to tailor the roles for these people.

We did four performances of *Travelers* early in the spring at the Performing Garage and then performed it for three weeks at Theater for the New City. Three or four months later, I had another idea for some more dances. I thought I would call up the same people because they were getting to know my style and knew how to tap. We started working again, and as the time between performances and ideas for pieces became shorter and shorter, I realized the value of a group of people who continually work together. I realized I wanted a company.

When I first started choreographing, the work had a much rawer look. It was an interesting situation because in 1978 there weren't many young trained dancers who had studied tap, unless they had come from out of town, or from one of those little dancing schools where they had simultaneously studied tap, jazz, and ballet. What changed over the years was that more and more people, including trained dancers, have been studying tap seriously, so the level of technique is higher.

As time went on, I was interested in going further with other aspects of dancing besides tap. If I wanted to put something very complicated in tap, I could, and I wouldn't have to make it just for one person. Now I have more choice about what kind of role it is, or what kind of movement; I'm not as limited by the individuals.

As the technical capabilities of the company have become more rounded, its potential has grown. I've had more time to work on what I want to do choreographically. In the beginning, I needed to concentrate mainly on learning how to make long rhythmic phrases, so perhaps not enough attention was given to the upper body, though it was always quite stylized. Now the dancing has gotten fuller and more varied, but it probably doesn't have much to do with what people think about when they envision movement for tap.

I seem to have alternated between smaller dances and large, full evening pieces. The smaller ones are like little nuggets of one quality or element I wanted to work on, and the large pieces resemble a blowup of these ideas. They are often more elaborately produced and based upon a linear series of events—sometimes a story. One genre gives me a rest from the other. And always the proportions change between movement style, tap, and music.

After *Travelers* I did *Dancing in the Streets* in 1979, first outside in Sheridan Square Park, and later as a series of five or six dances in a gym, called *Dancing in the Streets—A Tap Dance at the Gym.* Following that I did *Wave—A Tap Dance/Melodrama,* an hour-and-45-minute piece which was performed at La Mama Annex in 1981. Afterwards, I decided I wanted to work smaller again, and choreographed a series of what I called "tap dance shorts." These new dances were *The Racket, Love Street,* and *Rialto.* They were performed the following year at the Jazz Forum, a jazz club in New York. In 1983 Dance Theater Workshop produced *Mission,* a 40-minute piece which was my version of a sci-fi story. And then, in 1984 I made a few smaller dances. I did a dance called *Waterfront,* a duet called *Scotch & Soda,* and another dance, *Beyond the Bases,* which has to do with three men and their fantasy of baseball.

Wave—A Tap Dance/Melodrama was a major work for me. I started working on it in early 1980 and it was performed at La Mama Annex for one month in July of 1981. What really helped me was to be one of the choreographers chosen in the summer of 1980 for the Eugene O'Neill Choreographers' Conference. My company was in residence for two weeks in New London, Connecticut, and it was the first time I was given almost everything I needed in terms of space, time, materials, and, most important, my dancers, who this time didn't have to disappear to other jobs.

Wave was an adventure story—also what I decided to call a "tap dance/melodrama." The first image I had was of a very stylized giant Japanese wave (which ended up to be a giant cut-out, 18 feet high, with a smaller 13-foot wave behind it) entering a family's living room. Then I thought that I wanted it to be a melodrama with classic character types. There was a mother, a father, a maid, a lodger, a son, and the long-lost daughter who returned home from sea. Perhaps one reason I wanted to use these kinds of characters was that I'd been seeing a lot of Griffith's films. I was very taken by certain special qualities in those old, silent films and wanted to capture their sensibility in dance.

Wave was a comedy, though I didn't deliberately plan it as such. I described it in one sentence as "a typical American family encountering a classic disaster (WAVE enters living room)." Aside from being a comedy, the dance was also a satire.

The piece was in three acts: Part I entitled "In the House," Part II entitled "In the Water—The Suburban Boat People," and Part III, "Three Years Later—On Anniversary of Wave." Franco Colavecchia designed the three-part set and Walter Hackett, Jr., arranged all of the music. I must admit the music was a wild combination, meaning I think I used all the music I'd ever thought of and adored. There was a Balkan folk dance song, a mambo percussion melody for the maid and the lodger scene, the mother's dance was to "Moon of Alabama," and I also used music by Nino Rota and Randy Newman. Perhaps *Wave*'s saving grace (at least its synthesizing principle) came from these very diverse sounds and styles being arranged exactly for the dancing and played live by the same five musicians.

What was fascinating to me was to develop these characters, to find a trait and specific characteristics for each one and then try to develop scenes, almost as if in a play. This was my first attempt at it and I would say that sometimes it worked smoothly and other times it didn't. Some of it was very clear, while in other places there was too much division between the dancing and more obvious theatrical parts.

Part I of *Wave* opened with a scene between the maid and the lodger. As the other family members entered in the next few minutes, the scene took on a quality not unlike that of a surrealistic

*Wave—A Tap Dance/Melodrama. Gail Conrad/Tap Dance Theater.
Muriel Savaro, Gail Conrad, Tony Scopino, Anthony Peters, Steven
Albert, Cheryl Wawro Johnson. Photo: © Johan Elbers 1986.*

Molière farce. Each character had a program subtitle, such as the
lodger's—"three-time divorcé, who prefers other people's homes."
The set in Part I was minimal, but realistic—that of a family living
room. There a number of events took place: the arrival of a messen-
ger with a telegram telling of the daughter's imminent arrival, an
elaborate dinner ritual—repeated twice and constantly interrupted
by family squabbles, the arrival of the "long-lost daughter home from
sea"—and one final scene of chaos culminating in a furniture fight
(set to Tchaikovsky's waltz from *Eugene Onegin*), the family asleep
(recuperating from the fight), and the Wave's arrival. The daughter
was prepared for the Wave (just happening to have six life preservers

in her trunk), and in many ways she foreshadowed its arrival. Part I ended with the family, duly attired with life-saving gear, jumping into the water.

In Part II, "In the Water," seven additional performers (the suburban boat people) had also joined the family. My initial image

Wave—A Tap Dance/Melodrama. Gail Conrad. Photo: © Johan Elbers 1986.

was of long ropes and buoys stretched horizontally across the stage, the upstage ropes being highest from the ground, and getting progressively lower and lower, as with water closest to shore. The dancing also followed this pattern of horizontal crossings, winding slowly downstage. All the characters kept grouping together, losing one another and regrouping as they traveled through the lines of ropes and buoys. In the last image, everyone was washed ashore and the daughter was leaving once again.

In Part III, "Three Years Later—On Anniversary of Wave," the original living room set appeared, but it was up 4 feet on bamboo stilts. A "wave ritual" had replaced the dinner ritual and plastic swimming tubes were served instead of food. Daily life continued, just 4 feet higher. A parody of rituals, the last scene showed the family putting on their swimming tubes and climbing up their furniture on bamboo stilts, as if to show that in the event of another wave, they would be safe. It represented a satire about the impossibility of averting disaster, how we deal with disaster, and how life goes on.

For me, *Wave* was a reflection of the state of our culture, in a few different ways. There's something very American about these melodrama characters who also serve as classic archetypes. The family was personal for me. Not that it was exactly like my own, but, for example, the character of the mother was a lot stronger than that of the father—much more detailed. Perhaps that's because my father died when I was young and I had no image of what fathers were really like. The fact that it was a suburban family probably also reflected the larger part of my childhood.

The sense of how ritual was used was quite personal. I wasn't brought up religiously, but whenever my family did get together, there was a form of social ritual. Some of this was quite absurd, devoid of all original intent and meaning. For example, I have an aunt who, on religious holidays, likes to invite many people over for elaborate dinners. Next to every plate at the table, she has a little name tag and a number, and the prayer books she has also organized with corresponding numbers. In order to make the religious part of the meal as brief as possible, many pages are x'd out completely and in thick black magic marker is written, "Skip this."

What has always fascinated me is how, especially after certain very traumatic incidents, the need to keep ritual prevails. There is a current political idea concerning disaster and what can be done about averting it or how people act to avert it, which, to me, doesn't work except for giving a false sense of security. Backyard nuclear shelters or the rotation of secret missile sites seem completely senseless. But perhaps, sometimes, this false sense of security allows a culture to continue, and continue with its rituals. Even in the midst of a war-torn city, people don't hide forever. They may stay off the streets for many days, but then, one afternoon, stores and movies open up and people walk to the beaches. I guess I've always been concerned with how disaster affects societies. In *Wave,* the emphasis wasn't so much political as it was satirical. And often it was quite comic.

I think that art is absolutely a reflection of its culture. It's always been inseparable—it *is* the culture. Everything I make is influenced by everything I've ever seen or done or studied. I can't pretend that at times I'm not completely like a sponge. That my home background was what it was, that I listen to a certain kind of music on the radio today but was brought up with another kind of music—all of that was influential and can't be ignored. If I was living in a different city instead of downtown on Bleecker Street in New York, I probably would make very different dances.

I care about audiences and want them to be connected to the work. But most important, I try to think about the essence of a dance and what it needs. What interests me is remembering that initial feeling or sound or image which made me want to make the dance. For example, in *Love Street* the first image was that of a man saying goodbye to two women; the second image was of a dark street—lots of running and chasing—the rhythms in the section that I call "Spanish Caravan." Or in *The Racket,* the first image was of a body lying on the ground, something about a gold bag and something about two teams of couples passing the bag. I knew the music should be a combination of a tango and Brazilian samba percussion. I kept hearing this whistle, like a police whistle except that it's also a Brazilian carnival whistle, and then I had the image of certain martial art positions combined with tap. I wanted it to be like a film noir. For *Rialto,* it was Nino Rota's music which I fell in love with, which made me want to do the dance—that, and because I had found these wonderful umbrella hats. . . .

June 6, 1984

Date	Title of Work	Place and Details
June 1975	*Wing and a Prayer*	Performing Garage Theater, New York City. The Performance Group, directed by Ellen LeCompte.
June 1976	*House-Boat Tales*	302 Bowery, New York City. Musical recordings "Jack Was Every Inch a Sailor" (Burl Ives); "The Drunken Sailor" (sung by Cecelie O'Reilly); "Cacak"; and "Haul Away Joe" (Burl Ives). Sound and drums by Beverly Crook. Lighting by Jack Kramer. Danced by Alain Le Razer, Ara Fitzgerald, and Gail Conrad.
April 1977	*Brides*	Film on *Saturday Night Live*, NBC-TV.
September 1978	*Travelers—A Tap Dance/Epic*	Theater for the New City, New York City. Musical arrangements by Seth Tomasini: "Samba #2 (Strictly Percussion)"; "Na Baixa Do Sapateiro, E de Lei" (Baden Powell); "Marginalia" (Maria Bethunia); "Madame Verdurin" (Seth Tomasini); "Chattanooga Choo Choo" (Carmen Miranda recording); "Rhythms from the Northeast" (Batacada); "Third Man Theme Cha-Cha" (Karas). Music performed by Steve Lockwood, Dave Pentecost, Jesus Perez, Jr., Ernest Provencher, Suresh Shottam. Set design by Tim Button. Lighting design by Arwin Bittern. Danced by Anny DeGange, Bob Duncan, Muriel Favaro, Seth Tomasini, and Gail Conrad.
Spring 1978	*Sammy & Cleo*	Henry Street Playhouse, New York City. Directed by Andrea Balis.

Date	*Title of Work*	*Place and Details*
July 1979	*Dancing in the Streets*	Christopher Street Park, at Sheridan Square, New York City. Composed of five dances: *Line Dance; Baden Powell*—music, "Canto de Ossanha" (Baden Powell); *The Race*—music, "Darktown Strutters' Ball" (Sheldon Brooks) and "Bo Diddley" (Bo Diddley); *Rialto*—music, "Amarcord" (Nino Rota); *Los Mariachis*—music, "Los Mariachis" (Charles Mingus) and "Soul Sauce" (Cal Tjader). Music performed by John Hagen, Jesus Perez, Jr., and Ernest Provencher. Danced by Bob Duncan, Muriel Favaro, Diane Johnson, Seth Tomasini, and Gail Conrad.
December 1979	*Dancing in the Streets—A Tap Dance at the Gym*	The Gym, Elisabeth Irwin High School, New York City. Composed of the five dances first performed in *Dancing in the Streets* (at Sheridan Square) plus three additional dances: *Tango*—music, "Besame Mucho" (Consuelo Velazquez); *Midnight Stroll*—music, "Midnight Stroll" (The Revels); *On Broadway*—music, "On Broadway" (B. Mann, C. Weil, J. Lieber, M. Stroller). Music performed by Martin Balk, John Hagen, Jesus Perez, Jr., and Andy Potter. Danced by Bob Duncan, Muriel Favaro, Diane Johnson, Seth Tomasini, and Gail Conrad.
Winter 1979	*Ballad of Brooklyn*	Brooklyn Academy of Music, New York City. Directed by Margot Lewitin.
July 1980	*Tap Dance Excerpts*	Eugene O'Neill Theater. Choreographed *Huba, Huba*.
November 1980	*Dead End Kids*	Film version; also live at the Public Theater, New York City. Produced by Mabou Mines Company. Directed by Joanne Akalaitis.

Date	Title of Work	Place and Details
July 1981	*Wave—A Tap Dance/Melodrama*	La Mama Annex, New York City. Musical direction by Hoong Yee Lee. Musical arrangements by Walter Hackett, Jr.: mambo percussion; "Cacak"; Chopin (Luiz Bonfa); "In the Mood" (Joe Garland and Andy Razaf; Shapiro Bernstein); "Alabama Song" (Kurt Weill); film scores from *La Strada, Les Vitelloni,* and *La Dolce Vita* (Nino Rota); "Take 5" (Dave Brubeck); "Big Noise from Winnetka" (Baudoc-Crosby-Rodin-Haggart); "Lonely at the Top" (Randy Newman); waltz from *Eugene Onegin* (Tchaikovsky); "Pantano" (Lonnie Hewitt). Music performed by John Hagen, Hoong Yee Lee, Andy Potter, Tim Sessions, Nina Tax. Costume design by Naimy Hackett. Set design by Franco Colavecchia. Lighting design by Dennis McHugh. Graphic design by Steven Albert. Danced by Steven Albert, Gail Conrad, Muriel Favaro, Anthony Peters, Tony Scopino, Cheryl Wawro, Stefani Renee Briggs, James Coleman, Niko Corolla, 'Lectra, and Meghan Prior.

Date	Title of Work	Place and Details
April 1982	*Tap Dance Shorts*	Jazz Forum, New York City. Musical arrangements and direction by Walter Hackett, Jr. Composed of three dances: *The Racket*—music, "Tango delle Rose" (Shreier/Bottero) and samba percussion; *Love Street*—music, "Love Street," "Spanish Caravan" (The Doors); *Rialto*, revised version—music, "Amarcord" (excerpts, Nino Rota). Music performed by Michael Blair, Walter Hackett, Jr., John Hagen, Jesus Perez, Jr., and Ernest Provencher. Costume design by Frederick V. Grzyb, assisted by Launcey Saunders Clough. Lighting design by Greg Fauss. Graphic design by Steven Albert. Danced by Gail Conrad, Mary Clare Ditton, David Parker, Tony Scopino, Thomas Sinibaldi, and Cheryl Wawro.
February 1983	*Mission*	Dance Theater Workshop, Bessie Schönberg Theater, New York City. Music written and arranged by Walter Hackett, Jr. Music performed by Michael Blair, Walter Hackett, Jr., John Hagen, Jesus Perez, Jr., Ernest Provencher. Costume design by Nanzi Adzima. Set design by L. B. Dallas. Design and execution of cut-out figures by Lawrence Cappiello. Lighting design by Phil Sandstrom. Danced by Gail Conrad, Mary Clare Ditton, David Parker, Tony Scopino, Thomas Sinibaldi, and Cheryl Wawro.

Date	Title of Work	Place and Details
June 1983	*Waterfront*	Outside on Pier 11, New York City. Music, "Sofisticada," by Luiz Bonfa; additional music by Ernest Provencher. Musical direction and arrangements by Ernest Provencher. Music performed by Frank Ferrucci, John Hagen, Jesus Perez, Jr., Andy Potter, and Ernest Provencher. Costume design by Frederick V. Grzyb. Danced by Gail Conrad, David Parker, Tony Scopino, Thomas Sinibaldi, and Kathryn Tufano.
January 1984	*Scotch & Soda*	Bollème, France. Music: "Step Closer" (Ernest Provencher, recorded at Sound Prism Studios by Ernest Provencher and Frank Ferrucci); "Scotch & Soda" (David Guard, recording by Manhattan Transfer). Costume design by Robin Klingensmith. Lighting design by Tina Charney. Danced by David Parker and Kathryn Tufano.
June 1984	*Pretty Boy*	Performing Garage Theater, New York City. Produced by Mabou Mines Company. Written and directed by Greg Mehrten.

Date	*Title of Work*	*Place and Details*
July 1984	*Beyond the Bases* (A Baseball Fantasy in four parts)	Outdoor theater in Ancona, Italy; revised in 1985 for New York City premiere at Marymount Manhattan Theatre. Music written and arranged by Ernest Provencher. Music performed by Todd Green, John Hagen, Jesus Perez, Jr., Andy Potter, and Ernest Provencher. Sound by Phil Lee (Full House Productions) and Michael Carey (Sound Prism Studios). Costume design by Robin Klingensmith. Props by Susan Block. Lighting design by Tina Charney (1984, Italy) and Mitchell Bogard (1985, New York City). Graphic design by Steven Albert (1985, New York City). Danced by David Parker, Tony Scopino, Thomas Sinibaldi; Heather Cornell, Diane Johnson, and Kathryn Tufano in 1985 revised version in New York City.
January 1985	*Red Skies*	Marymount Manhattan Theatre, New York City. Musical arrangement and direction by Ernest Provencher: "Transformation" (Kevan Staples and Nona Hendryx). Music performed by Bill Cammarota, Rick DePofi, Todd Green, Jesus Perez, Jr., Andy Potter, and Ernest Provencher. Costume design by Robin Klingensmith. Lighting design by Mitchell Bogard. Danced by Gail Conrad, Heather Cornell, Dennis Gingery, David Parker, Tony Scopino, and Kathryn Tufano.

Wave—A Tap Dance/Melodrama. Gail Conrad/Tap Dance Theater.
Anthony Peters, Tony Scopino, Niko Corolla, Cheryl Wawro Johnson,
Stefani Rene Briggs, Meghan Prior, 'Lectra, James Coleman, Muriel
Savaro, Steven Albert, Gail Conrad. Photo: © Johan Elbers 1986.

Meredith Monk

Photo: Bob Shamis.

MEREDITH MONK

Meredith Monk is an internationally acclaimed composer, director, choreographer, singer, and film maker who integrates music, dance, and drama. Her works achieve their particular effect from the striking juxtaposition of movement, sound, and visual elements.

A graduate of Sarah Lawrence College, Monk has created more than 50 music/theater/dance and film works since 1964. In 1968 she founded The House, a company dedicated to an interdisciplinary approach to performance. A decade later she formed the Meredith Monk Vocal Ensemble to perform her unique vocal compositions. Her companies have toured extensively across the United States and overseas.

In celebration of her twentieth anniversary as a creative force in the performing arts, a year-long retrospective was held in 1984–1985. Events included the October premiere of *The Games* (in collaboration with Ping Chong) at the Brooklyn Academy of Music, Monk's debut at Carnegie Hall in February, and a film/video retrospective at the Whitney Museum of American Art in March. In addition, the Vocal Ensemble toured nationally and internationally and the Obie award-winning production of *Quarry* was revived. In August 1985 Monk began work on her first feature length film, *Book of Days.*

Monk has received numerous accolades, including two Guggenheim Fellowships, a Brandeis creative arts award, two Obies, two Villager awards, and six ASCAP awards for musical composition. Her video collaborations with Ping Chong have received prizes from the Corporation for Public Broadcasting and Video Culture Canada; her film *Ellis Island* won prizes at the Atlanta and San Francisco film festivals.

MEREDITH MONK

Mosaic

I work in between the cracks. My work does not fit into any one category but in between the cracks of what are considered categories. That is where I find all of my information, my discovery, where the music, theater, and movement correspond or where they do not correspond; it is always in the in-between places. Just like a visual artist who does painting, lithography, and drawing, I work in a variety of mediums. But all the different aspects of my work are really all part of the same vision. People seem to have more trouble understanding that in a performance artist—it's hard for some people to see how it all fits together.

We are taught to think in categories. For me the joy is in breaking down categories; finding new hybrid forms or discovering the place where things resonate with each other. In ancient times and in many theaters throughout the world, such as Kathakali, Kabuki, or Chinese opera, creative functions were not separated. People sang, danced, played roles. Now we separate things. The challenge for me is to break down that kind of thinking.

I do not think of myself primarily as a choreographer. I think of myself as a composer: of music, of movement, and of images. There are actually three branches of my work: the music concerts, the large multimedia performance pieces, and the films. The concerns of one overlap into another. For example, in a large performance piece, I orchestrate different elements into one form. I am very conscious of the musicality of the images and the rhythm of the whole. When I am presenting my music in a concert format, I am meticulous about the visual aspect—the costumes, the lights, how the piano or organ is placed on the stage, and how we move when we are singing and playing.

Sometimes I begin a piece by writing music, or sometimes I have images or a thematic idea, or possibly the music and images come simultaneously. There is no set formula for each piece, but it would be very rare that I would start a piece with a movement idea. Every time I work on a new piece, I try to find a form, a formal structure that fits the current work and I try to discover a vocabulary of movement that is right for the piece.

This way of working may have developed from Bessie Schönberg while I attended Sarah Lawrence. She was a major influence on my work. She was and is an extraordinary teacher and an inspiring person. She set standards of craft and taught principles, without imposing a particular style that had to be copied mechanically. She taught me to work in terms of my own body, to find an integrity and form correct for what I wanted to do. She had a disciplined eye for a person's capabilities and had a strong demand in terms of craft.

While I was in school I had the idea that there could be a form incorporating music, dance, and theater. I have been working in those three areas throughout my life. I had to figure out how I could make interests that seemed divergent merge into a living, breathing whole.

As a child I first studied Dalcroze eurhythmics with the Rohm sisters at Steinway Hall. They taught an integrated feeling about music and movement. I have retained this and never separated it throughout my working life.

Then I worked with Ernestine Stodelle, a Humphrey–Weidman dancer who taught movement in a rich and vital way. There was technique as well as creative work within one class. I also took ballet for a long time. My first teacher was Olga Tarassova. What I remember the most about ballet classes was the character classes. I always loved folk dancing and had a good feel for it. That quality of movement is still in my work.

When I first started working, I had not figured out how to sing and dance at the same time. The movement played a more significant role. It was more technical in a conventional sense than today's. In terms of the music, the pieces were very simple. I worked on my own voice and the piano, or keyboard, trying to find my own vocabulary: different qualities of the voice, different timbres, ranges, rhythms, and textures. Gradually I became interested in sounds happening at the same time. For the last several years I have been working with three women and three men singers and have been able to play with all the wonderful possibilities of ensemble music— counterpoint, weaving, unison, polyphony, etc.

In 1966 I created *16 Millimeter Earrings,* for which I wrote my first score and did a lot of singing. It was also complex in terms of other elements: films, multiple tapes, and images as the base of movement. With this piece I started realizing that I was interested in integrating elements into poetic forms, containing different layers, levels, or dimensions. I realized that I wanted to work on a mosaic form with multidimensionality.

In working with these different layers of materials I discovered that the way these elements work against each other creates a luminosity, a radiance. It was a real breakthrough piece for me because at that point I understood what my goals would be during my working life. Then I started concentrating on the voice as a vocal instrument and creating vocal music, and that has been a real continuity for me over the years. It has become more and more the major element of the work.

Since I am musically oriented, the *rhythm* of the piece is the primary concern in terms of my work. I am working with time in the same way I am working with space: stretching it, compressing it, twisting it, manipulating it. It is a way of dealing with reality in another manner.

In using imagery I try to compress the material in such a way that I can get as many levels into one image as can be packed into it. I try to make each image as evocative as I can, on as many levels as possible, so that a person can hook into one level or another, or more than one. It is like a mosaic with bits of information which can be put together in different ways so that each person comes away with something individually meaningful.

When I structure the images, I often think in terms of film cuts. *Break,* a solo piece created in 1964, was one of the first pieces where I worked like a film director using cinematic syntax. *Break* dealt with a continuity other than what is usually thought of as choreographic, and I still work like that today.

I never do a piece about a movement theme like circles, for example. I am not interested in movement for its own sake—not that I do not like looking at it or admire and respect that point of view.

My movement has always had a human and gestural aspect to it rather than abstract, geometric shape. I am interested in a very articulated body with a lot of attention to isolation and detail. That influence was from Beverly Schmidt, who was, at the time that I studied with her, a former Nikolais dancer.

Another influence was Judith Dunn, who also taught at Sarah Lawrence. She could change modes of movement quickly and fluidly, and the rhythms of the movement were very intricate. She was both elegant and deliberately awkward. The primal quality that she was exploring affected me very much at the time; it made me start thinking about the beginnings of movement. That prehistoric essential movement quality still interests me. Wit and subtlety have also always been important.

People have said that my sense of movement is not Western. I haven't concentrated on Eastern forms per se, but I do pay a lot of attention to detail and to a nonlinear time sense. I am dealing with figures in space, but the movement of each person is more self-contained than in ballet or modern dance. I rarely use movement in a pure geometric design function, and I'm very interested in posture as a physical basis of character or of psychic characteristics.

The last major thread that has held through the years in my work is a nonproscenium use of space. Even *Break* was performed in a gallery, and I used the corners almost in a cubist sense. I have always worked with an architectural use of space.

What am I trying to get across to an audience? An existential sense of reality. I am trying to create a world with layers of perceptual situations where people see and hear things in a new, fresh way. It is a way of sharpening the senses by creating a world with its own laws. It takes an audience someplace else, while at the same time letting them be right here.

I am working with archetypes to elicit in the audience memories and feelings that are usually covered up by daily living. The greatest challenge to me as a creator is balancing the elements, both in making music as well as in large theater pieces. In music, it is creating forms. The challenge is to balance the movement, music, visual imagery, sound, objects, and light so that everything works together with a certain inevitability and liveliness. It is also having the discipline to cut, to essentialize, so that it all works together as a whole.

I think of theater as a time and place where you can find wonder, stimulation, some magic—where you can be quiet; where you can laugh; where a performance is experiential, not a routine that only confirms what you already know. I try to make work that cleanses the senses and that has a freedom to it that is like a prototype of possibilities.

Quarry: An Opera was a piece presented in 1976 at La Mama Annex. I worked on it for two years. The idea came to me when I was frequently going to Europe and thinking about nationalities and wars —how different nationalities dealt with war. I wondered what the world was like in cataclysm, about the phenomenon of the world in spasm.

It occurred to me that even though people in America, of my generation, never experienced a world war, it has still affected us. It is in our "collective unconscious." So I asked myself how I would create a piece about World War II like the "collective unconscious" version of World War II. It was a gigantic subject and had to be pulled down. I realized that I could not do a definitive statement about

Quarry (The Child at the Window). Meredith Monk. Photo: Nathaniel Tileston.

World War II with complete honesty, because I hadn't lived through it—I was only a baby at the end of the war and I didn't live in Europe. But I could do it through imagination, so I came up with the idea of presenting it through an American child's eyes, as events seen or imagined from afar. The sick child, in a sense, is a metaphor of the diseased world.

I started thinking of *Quarry* as a kind of visual radio play. I began writing music while simultaneously working out ideas. I also did a lot of research in Paris, which was unusual for me. I had to create my own rules for myself as always, and my rule (as much as I love music of the period) was to create my own music. In a piece like this it is easy to use documentary information—films and music of the period—but I was very stubborn about wanting to create my own world even though I was working with a concrete subject.

I used Ping Chong as a dictator, instead of someone who looked like Hitler, because I wanted a more archetypal idea about what a dictator is. That archetype exists in all of us, and I was trying to investigate how it worked.

The child was lying in the center of the floor and was the constant in the piece. As it turned out, I was the child, and, in performance, since I could not see everyone, I actually directed by ear. I could hear by the rhythm when something was or was not working.

Around the child there were four environments, which I thought of as similar to the four corners of the world. I am always fascinated by the existential sense of simultaneity. I love the sense of mystery of seeing things happening at the same time, like peeking in one window and seeing two people in Vienna, in another a woman in an apartment in London, in another three women in St. Louis, Missouri, and in another a Hebrew couple in a tent in the year 3000 B.C. Some people thought the four corners were four rooms in one house. That interpretation is also acceptable and interesting in another way.

Besides the four corners there was a maid, who was the child's friend, and a radio which played music that I taped, of my own singing and piano. The radio was the central metaphor of the piece because it was a period when the radio was the primary informational medium, when a lot of information was aural. An aural medium creates another kind of thinking from what we are used to now in our visual, TV society. There was also a film of a quarry, filmed in Vermont, which I jokingly refer to as the "Dictator's Newsreel."

There were three large choral dance and vocal sections: the Wash, the Rally, and the Requiem. Each had a different function. The Wash was like a procession, a literal film device like a "wipe," where one image is replaced by another horizontally. The Wash wiped out the space for the next section, which had a very different mood.

Quarry was called an opera in three movements: Lullaby, March, Requiem. The Lullaby movement had a soothing warmth to it. Towards the end of it crept in an ominous feeling which started to build. Then the Wash cleaned it out and next came the dictator section, the second movement called March. Then it got very ominous. The Rally was the epiphany of that section.

With the Rally, I was thinking about how powerful media are and how the Germans changed the whole consciousness of a people with theatricality. Their rallies were gigantic and clever spectacles of power. I wondered how difficult it would be to create a similar atmosphere, and started working with only ten people, a rhythmic, guttural sound, and strident, strong, calisthentic movement. The phenomenon of that hypnotizing situation is not hard to create. The result (the fact that it could be done with ten people) was shocking.

*Quarry (Waiting Room). The House. Pablo Vela, Lee Nagrin. Photo: ©
Johan Elbers 1986.*

Essentialized, it has to do with rhythm, sharpness, strength, and
stridency.

In contrast, I thought of the Requiem as a mandala, where
people were streaming patterns similar to a blood vessel, or like
water or a liquid going though a pipe system. The movement was
quite simple, mostly walking, but the vocal music sung by the entire
cast was fairly complex and polyphonic.

The reason I did *Quarry* in the first place was that I was getting
the feeling that those forces of fascism were starting to build again.
I wanted to examine the elements of what those forces were.

I am always thinking in terms of society. If I am working well,
I am in touch with certain currents, but I am a poetic artist, not an
analytical one. So the political element is usually there, but only in
an oblique way.

I purposely create theater pieces with gaps so that the rest can
be filled in by using individual creativity. That is also why I like music

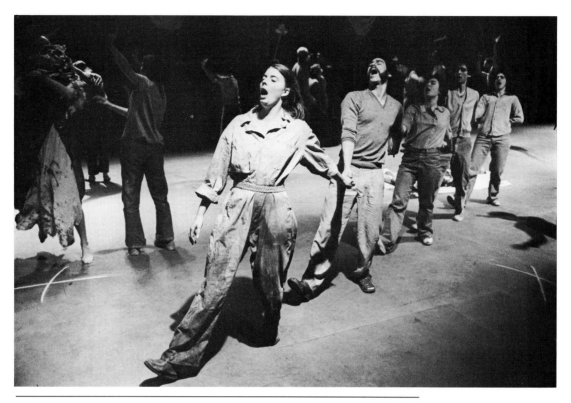

Quarry (Rally). The House. Susan Kampe, Avi Danis, Gail Simon, Eli Pollack, Ellen Goldsmith. Photo: Nathaniel Tileston.

so much—it creates an emotional field in images which are triggered off in each person's head.

My work rearranges mental habits. It cannot be "figured out" while the audience is watching and hearing it. It is created to use the mind in another way, and for me, that is one reason for making art. Art facilitates an experience of another mental set so that you become aware that you are usually thinking in a habitual way and are not as alive as you could be.

Performance Works (Works Performed in Theaters or Proscenium Spaces; Works Designed for Specific Sites; Operas and Musical Theater Pieces)

Date	*Title of Work*	*Place and Details*
January 22, 1964	*Timestop*	Sarah Lawrence College, Bronxville, New York.
April 13, 1964	*Diploid*	Clark Center for the Performing Arts, New York City.
September 28, 1964	*Break*	Washington Square Galleries, New York City. Collaboration with Elizabeth Keen.
April 3, 1965	*Cartoon*	Judson Memorial Church, New York City.
May 1, 1965	*The Beach*	Hardware Poets' Playhouse, New York City. Tape collage by Meredith Monk.
September 10, 1965	*Relache*	Judson Hall, New York City. Collaboration with Dick Higgins.
September 10, 1965	*Blackboard*	Judson Hall, New York City.
September 12, 1965	*Radar*	Judson Hall, New York City.
April 6, 1966	*Portable*	Judson Memorial Church, New York City. Tape collage by Meredith Monk.
December 4, 1966	*Duet with Cat's Scream and Locomotive*	Judson Memorial Church, New York City. Tape collage by Meredith Monk.
December 4, 1966	*16 Millimeter Earrings*	Judson Memorial Church, New York City. Music by Meredith Monk.
May 8, 1967	*Excerpt from a Work in Progress*	Village Theatre, New York City. Tape collage by Meredith Monk.
August 7, 1967	*Blueprint*	Group 212, Woodstock, New York. Music by Meredith Monk.
September 10, 1967	*Overload*	Youth Pavilion, Expo-67, Montreal. Music by Meredith Monk.
January 29, 1968	*Blueprint (3)*	Colby College, Waterville, Maine. Music by Meredith Monk.
April 10, 1968	*Blueprint (4)*	The House, New York City. Music by Meredith Monk.

Date	*Title of Work*	*Place and Details*
May 16, 1968	*Blueprint (5)*	The House, Julius Tobias's Studio, New York City.
November 3, 1968	*Co-op*	Loeb Student Center, New York University, New York City.
February 4, 1969	*Title: Title and Untidal: Movement Period*	Billy Rose Theatre, New York City.
March 10, 1969	*Tour: Dedicated to Dinosaurs*	Smithsonian Institution, Washington, D.C. Music by Meredith Monk.
April 18, 1969	*Tour 2: Barbershop*	Museum of Contemporary Art, Chicago. Music by Meredith Monk.
1969	*Juice: A Theatre Cantata in 3 Installments*	November 7, Solomon R. Guggenheim Museum, New York City; November 29, Minor Latham Playhouse, Barnard College, New York City; December 7, The House, New York City. Music by Meredith Monk.
March 3, 1970	*Tour 5: Glass*	Nazareth College, Rochester, New York. Music by Meredith Monk.
March 10, 1970	*Tour 6: Organ*	Douglas College, New Brunswick, New Jersey. Music by Meredith Monk.
May 1, 1970	*Tour 7: Factory*	State University of New York at Buffalo. Music by Meredith Monk.
July 20, 1970	*Needle-Brain Lloyd and the Systems Kid: A Live Movie*	American Dance Festival, Connecticut College, New London. Music by Meredith Monk.
February 19, 1971	*Tour 8: Castle*	Midwestern colleges. Music by Meredith Monk.
October 18, 1971	*Vessel: An Opera Epic*	The House, Performing Garage, Wooster Parking Lot, New York City. Music by Meredith Monk. Received Obie award for outstanding achievement.
December 12, 1972	*Paris*	The House, New York City. Collaboration with Ping Chong. Music by Meredith Monk.
May 19, 1972	*Education of the Girlchild*	The House, New York City. Music by Meredith Monk. Solo performance.

Date	*Title of Work*	*Place and Details*
June 13, 1973	*Education of the Girlchild*	Common Ground Theatre, New York City. Music by Meredith Monk. Complete performance.
January 25, 1974	*Chacon*	Oberlin College, Oberlin, Ohio. Collaboration with Ping Chong. Music by Meredith Monk.
April 30, 1975	*Anthology and Small Scroll*	St. Mark's Church, New York City. Music by Meredith Monk.
April 2, 1976	*Quarry: An Opera*	La Mama Annex, New York City. Music by Meredith Monk. Received Obie award for outstanding achievement.
June 20, 1976	*Venice/Milan*	Washington Project for the Arts, Washington, D.C. Collaboration with Ping Chong. Music by Meredith Monk.
March 1, 1977	*The Travelogue Series* (Complete)	Roundabout Theatre, New York City. Collaboration with Ping Chong. Music by Meredith Monk.
May 18, 1977	*Tablet (House of Stills)*	Mo Ming, Chicago. Music by Meredith Monk.
June 1, 1978	*The Plateau Series*	St. Mark's Church, New York City. Music by Meredith Monk.
October 15, 1978	*Vessel Suite*	Metamusik Festival, Berlin, West Germany. Music by Meredith Monk.
November 16, 1979	*Recent Ruins: An Opera*	La Mama Annex, New York City. Received Villager award for outstanding production. Music by Meredith Monk.
November 1981	*Specimen Days: A Civil War Opera*	Public Theater, New York City. Costumes and decor by Yoshio Yabara. Music by Meredith Monk.
April 19, 1983	*Turtle Dreams: Cabaret*	Plexus, New York City. Music by Meredith Monk. Received Villager award for outstanding composition.
November 28, 1983	*The Games*	Schaubuhne, West Berlin. Collaboration with Ping Chong. Costumes and set by Yoshio Yabara. Music by Meredith Monk.

Date	*Title of Work*	*Place and Details*
October 9, 1984	*The Games* (American version)	Brooklyn Academy of Music, New York City. Collaboration with Ping Chong. Costumes and set by Yoshio Yabara. Music by Meredith Monk.
February 7, 1985	*Book of Days* (work in progress)	Carnegie Hall, New York City. Costumes by Yoshio Yabara. Music by Meredith Monk.

Music Concerts by Meredith Monk

April 27, 1970	*Raw Recital*	Whitney Museum of American Art, New York City.
January 11, 1973	*Our Lady of Late*	Town Hall, New York City.
April 23, 1974	*Roots*	The House, New York City. Collaboration with Donald Ashwander.
February 15, 1975	Merce Cunningham *Event #118*	Cunningham Studio, New York City.
April 30, 1975	*Anthology*	St. Mark's Church, New York City.
December 2, 1975	Merce Cunningham *Event #148*	Roundabout Theater, New York City.
October 1976	*Trio Concert*	Town Hall, New York City. Premiere of Songs from the Hill.
March 18, 1977	Merce Cunningham *Event #189*	Barnard College Gym, New York City.
March 25, 1978	Merce Cunningham *Event #215*	Roundabout Theater, New York City.
January 1979	*Dolmen Music Concert*	The Kitchen, New York City. Premiere of Dolmen Music.
May 1981	*Music Concert with Film*	The Space at City Center, New York City. Premiere of *Turtle Dreams (Waltz)*.
April 1984	*Duet Concert*	Japan American Theater, Los Angeles. Premiere of City Songs.

Films, Videos, and Recordings

December 4, 1966	*16 Millimeter Earrings* (film)	Judson Memorial Church, New York City.
May 8, 1967	*Children* (film)	Village Theater, New York City.

Date	Title of Work	Place and Details
August 17, 1967	*Candy Bullets and Moon* (record)	Garrick Records, New York City. Music by Meredith Monk.
August 21, 1967	*Mountain* (film)	Goddard College, Plainfield, Vermont.
November 3, 1968	*Ball Bearing* (film)	Loeb Student Center, New York City.
June 1, 1971	*Key: An Album of Invisible Theatre* (record)	Increase Records, Los Angeles. Music by Meredith Monk. Re-released on Lovely Music, Ltd., 1977.
January 16, 1974	*Our Lady of Late* (record)	Minona Records, New York City. Music by Meredith Monk.
August 15, 1975	*Quarry* (film)	Goddard College, Plainfield, Vermont.
April 17, 1977	*Home Movie circa 1910*	550 Broadway, New York City. For *Humboldt's Current* by Ping Chong.
November 16, 1979	*Ellis Island* (film)	La Mama Annex, New York City. 7-minute version.
August 29, 1981	*Dolmen Music* (record)	ECM/Warner Brothers Records and Tapes, Munich, West Germany. Received German critics award for the Best Record of the Year.
December 20, 1981	*Ellis Island* (film)	ZDF, West German Television. 30-minute version. Music by Meredith Monk.
August 1982	*Paris* (video)	KCTA Minneapolis television. Collaboration with Ping Chong.
April 19, 1983	*Mermaid Adventures* (film)	Plexus, New York City.
September 1, 1983	*Turtle Dreams* (record)	ECM/Warner Brothers Records and Tapes, New York City. Music by Meredith Monk.
September 15, 1983	*Turtle Dreams (Waltz)* (video)	WGBH Boston television. Music by Meredith Monk.

Meredith Monk. Photo: Walter Kranl.

SELECTED BIBLIOGRAPHY

Armitage, Merle, ed. *Martha Graham.* Los Angeles: Armitage, 1937.

Aristotle. *Poetics.* Translated by Ingram Bywater. *Politics.* Book 8. Translated by B. Jowett. In *The Basic Works.* Edited by Richard McKeon. New York: Random House, 1941.

Baker, Robb, "Landscapes and Telescopes, A Personal Response to the Choreography of Meredith Monk." *Dance Magazine.* April 1976, pp. 56–69.

Banes, Sally. "Earthly Bodies: Judson Dance Theater." In *Judson Dance Theater: 1962–1966.* Bennington, Vt.: Bennington College, 1981, pp. 14–19.

———. "Lucinda Childs: Making the World Whole." *Performance.* December 1981, pp. 24–25.

———. "Reviews." *Dance Magazine.* April 1982, pp. 95–98, 100.

———. "Reviews." *Dance Magazine.* June 1982, p. 20.

———. *Terpsichore in Sneakers: Post-Modern Dance.* Boston: Houghton Mifflin, 1980.

———. "The Art of Meredith Monk." *Performing Arts Journal,* Vol. III, no. 1 (Spring/Summer 1978): pp. 3–17.

Brown, Jean Morrison, ed. *The Vision of Modern Dance.* Princeton, N.J.: Princeton Book Company, 1979.

Brown, Trisha, and Rainer, Yvonne. "A Conversation About Glacial Decoy." *October* 10 1980, pp. 29–37.

Cage, John. *Silence.* Middletown, Ct.: Wesleyan University Press, 1961.

Carroll, Noël. "Post-Modern Dance and Expression." In *Philosophical Essays on Dance.* Edited by Gordon Fancher and Gerald Myers. New York: Dance Horizons, 1981, pp. 95–104.

Coe, Robert. "A Master of Modern Dance." *New York Times Magazine.* April 5, 1981, sec. 6, pp. 40, 43, 47, 74, 78, 80, 82, 85.

Cohen, Marshall. "Primitivism, Modernism, and Dance Theory." *Ballet Review.* Fall 1981, pp. 41–52.

Cohen, Selma Jeanne, ed. *Dance as a Theatre Art: Source Readings in Dance History.* New York: Harper & Row, 1974.

————. *Doris Humphrey: An Artist First.* Middletown, Conn.: Wesleyan University Press, 1972.

————, ed. *The Modern Dance: Seven Statements of Belief.* Middletown, Conn.: Wesleyan University Press, 1965.

————. *Next Week Swan Lake. Reflections on Dance and Dances.* Middletown, Conn.: Wesleyan University Press, 1982.

————, ed. "Nik, a Documentary." *Dance Perspectives 48,* Winter 1971, pp. 1–56.

Copeland, Roger. "The 'Post-Modern' Choreography of Trisha Brown." *New York Times.* January 4, 1976, sec. 2, p. 1.

————. "Why Women Dominate Modern Dance." *New York Times.* April 18, 1982, sec. 2, pp. 1, 22.

Cunningham, Merce. *Changes: Notes on Choreography.* Edited by Frances Starr. New York: Something Else Press, 1968.

Daniels, Don. "Paul Taylor and the Post-Moderns." *Ballet Review.* Summer 1981, pp. 66–82.

Davies, Douglas. "Post-Everything." *Art in America* 68 (1980):11–13.

Duncan, Isadora. *The Art of the Dance.* New York: Theatre Arts, 1928.

————. *My Life.* New York: Liveright, 1927.

Dunning, Jennifer. "Paul Taylor—Looking Back and Ahead." *New York Times.* April 11, 1982, pp. D-26, 32.

Forti, Simone. *Handbook in Motion.* New York: New York University Press, 1974.

Gautier, Théophile. *The Romantic Ballet as Seen by Théophile Gautier.* Rev. ed. Edited by Cyril W. Beaumont. London: C. W. Beaumont, 1947.

Hardy, Camille. "New Dance in America." *America Arts.* March 1982, pp. 4–7.

Hassan, Ihab. "The Question of Postmodernism." *Performing Arts Journal* 16 (1981):30–44.

Highwater, Jamake. *Dance: Rituals of Experience.* New York: A & W Publishers, 1978.

Howell, John. "Four Choreographers." In *Live 6/7.* Performing Arts Journal, 1982, pp. 66–79.

Humphrey, Doris. *The Art of Making Dances.* Edited by Barbara Pollack. New York: Rinehart, 1959.

Kirby, Michael, ed. "Post-Modern Dance." *Drama Review* 19 (1975): 3–77.

Kirstein, Lincoln. *Dance: A Short History of Classic Theatrical Dancing.* New York: Dance Horizons, 1935.

Kisselgoff, Anna. "Merce Cunningham: The Maverick of Dance." *New York Times Magazine.* March 21, 1982, sec. 6, pp. 22–25, 60, 62, 65, 66, 68.

———. "Notes on Post-Modernism." *New York Times.* October 25, 1981, p. D-16.

———. "Where Are the New Balanchines?" *New York Times.* November 4, 1979, pp. II-1, D-8.

Klosty, James, ed. *Merce Cunningham.* New York Dutton, 1975.

Kostelanetz, Richard. "Metamorphosis in Modern Dance." *Dance Scope* 5 (Fall 1970):6–21.

———. *John Cage.* New York: Praeger, 1970.

Kramer, Hilton. "Today's Avant-Garde Artists Have Lost the Power to Shock." *New York Times.* November 16, 1980, sec. 2, p. 27.

———. "When Modernism Became Orthodoxy." *New York Times.* March 28, 1982, pp. D-1, 32.

Kraus, Richard, and Chapman, Sarah. *History of the Dance in Art and Education.* 2nd ed. Englewood Cliffs, N.J.: Prentice-Hall, 1981.

Leatherman, Leroy. *Martha Graham: Portrait of the Lady as an Artist.* New York: Knopf, 1966.

Lloyd, Margaret. *The Borzoi Book of Modern Dance.* New York: Knopf, 1949.

Louis, Murray. *Inside Dance.* New York: St. Martin's Press, 1980.

Noverre, Jean George. *Letters on Dancing and Ballets* [1760]. Translated by C. W. Beaumont from rev. and enlarged ed. published at St. Petersburg, 1803. London: C. W. Beaumont, 1951.

Owens, Craig. "The Pro-scenic Event." *Art in America.* December 1981, pp. 128–133.

———. *The Laws.* Books 2 and 7. Translated by Trevor J. Saunders. New York: Penguin Books, 1970.

Plato. *The Republic.* Book 3. Translated by Desmond Lee. 2nd ed. New York: Penguin Books, 1974, pp. 129–185.

Rainer, Yvonne, Meredith Monk, and Kenneth King. "R.E.: Croce." *LIVE, Performance Art 4* (1980):18–22.

———. *Work 1961–73.* New York: New York University Press, 1974.

Shelton, Suzanne. *Divine Dancer: A Biography of Ruth St. Denis.* Garden City, N.Y.: Doubleday, 1981.

Siegel, Marcia B. "New Dance in America—An Excess of Success?" *Ballet International,* no. 1 (January 1982):81–85.

———. *The Shapes of Change: Images of American Dance.* Boston: Houghton Mifflin, 1979, pp. 11–67.

Tompkins, Calvin. *The Bride and the Bachelors.* New York: Viking Press, 1968.

Weaver, John. *Essays Towards an History of Dancing.* London: J. Tonson, 1712.

Wigman, Mary. *The Language of Dance.* Translated by Walter Sorrell. Middletown, Conn.: Wesleyan University Press, 1966.